To [illegible]
good to see you
again — give me
a call —
Best — [illegible]

Almost a Mensch

281-681-0564
281 364 3010

Almost a Mensch

A memoir by

David Gottlieb

Designed by Bookdesigns.net. http://www.bookdesigns.net

For information, write:

Halcyon Press, Ltd.
6065 Hillcroft Suite 525
Houston, TX 77081

Printed in the United States of America

BISG BIO000000 BIOGRAPHY & AUTOBIOGRAPHY / General

ISBN 1-931823-01-4

This book is dedicated
to my beloved wife
Brenda

Acknowledgements

My brothers were and continue to be central players in my life.

My wife Brenda more than compensated for my grammatical inadequacies by taking on the role of editor and advisor.

My initial intent in undertaking this memoir was to provide my children and grandchildren with a written account of my childhood, adolescence, and early adulthood.

The motivation to pursue a publisher was the result of encouragement from my wife, Brenda, and my good friends Sidney Berger, Bob and Noni Stearns, and David and Bette Chenault, who provided candor, insight, and suggestions.

"A bissel un a bissel macht a fullen schissel
(A little and a little makes a full plate)."

- an old Yiddish saying

Author's Note

Every Jewish boy has a bar mitzvah, the traditional rite of passage wherein the Jewish male is accepted by the Jewish community as a man. Becoming a man, however, must be differentiated from becoming a *mensch*.

A *mensch* is a state of being to which many may aspire but few attain. There are no formal entrance criteria or ground rules. Being a devout, wealthy, influential, well-educated Jew is not sufficient. A *mensch* is a truly honest, compassionate, generous, warm and loving soul.

To be a man is one thing; to be a *mensch* is yet another.

Foreword

So here I am about to set down in writing a brief account of my early life, about my three brothers (Bob the eldest, Norman, then myself, followed by Harold), our parents (Morris and Sophie), as well as aunts, uncles, and other people I encountered during my formative years.

Suddenly I recall a conversation with my younger brother Harold when we were on a bike ride in Northern California a few years ago.

We were talking about our parents when Harold said, "Who do you think was Ma's favorite?"

Before I could respond, he went on, "It was Bobeleh (my mother's affectionate name for Bob). He came first and for her he was number one!"

"Not true," I replied. "When I was eight I asked Ma, 'Who is your favorite?'

Ma answered, 'How can I have a favorite? Each child is like a finger on my hand. Can one finger be loved more than another?'

Having recently learned that the thumb is in fact the most essential of the fingers, I quickly said, 'Okay, then let me be the thumb.'

Ma thought for a moment, and then in her desire to reach finality in this matter proclaimed, 'You want to be the thumb. So be the thumb!' "

"Bullshit!" yelled Harold. "I was the thumb and you were the pinky!"

Another example: My brother Norman, two years older than me and two years younger than Bob, asked me not long ago if I remembered the time he had to cut the head off a chicken. Before I could respond, he went on with his telling of the story.

The family had gone to visit a farm owned by one of my father's customers. The farmer's wife was going to prepare a chicken dinner and asked her husband to slaughter one of their birds. The farmer in turn asked if any of us would want to do the job.

Here my recollections of the day's events part company with Norman's tale. He maintains that he took the axe and with one mighty blow the deed was done.

There are two factual errors in Norman's story.

First, prior to any discussion as to who would wield the axe, there was an exchange in Yiddish between my parents, which roughly translated went as follows:

Pa: "We cannot eat a chicken unless it is killed in accordance with dietary law. You know, Zipeh (his name for my mother), that it must be done by a *schochet* (a man who has been ordained by a rabbi and approved by the Department of Health to slaughter select animals in accordance with Jewish law and tradition)."

Ma: "Why are you talking crazy? We are here on a *Goysheh* farm in the middle of nowhere and you are talking with me about a *schochet*. Will you be the one who explains to the farmer and his wife that because we are Jews we will not be their guests for dinner? Go ahead, go ahead and tell them."

Pa: "All right, all right! Here is my idea. Bob and Norman are already bar mitzvhed, and so they are already official Jews. Harold and David are not yet bar mitzvhed, so they are not yet real Jews. So one of them should do the job."

Pointing to me, he said, "David. You do it."

It is important to explain that a *schochet* does not use an axe but a very sharp knife to slit the throat of the bird. Once that is done, the animal is allowed to bleed to death. The thought of chopping off the head of any living creature was not compatible with my cultural or personal sense. Still, the decision had been made, and sibling pressures were such that I picked up the axe and did the deed. I did so with feelings of guilt and apprehension—guilt not being the result of any sense that I was violating Jewish law, but that I was about to murder a helpless and innocent victim of both religious and social dictate; apprehension because Norman, out of sight and sound of my parents, insisted on terrifying me.

"You cut it right off. If you don't cut it right off it will chase after you and spill blood on you and that will make it a lifetime curse and you will never forget!"

Still, my own recollection is that the task was done, though I did not take part in the chicken portion of the evening meal. What is fact to me remains fiction to Norman, who to this day insists that he, not I, committed the infamous Michigan chicken axe murder.

Yet my brother Harold has challenged one more incident that I recall with clarity. My story goes as follows: At about the age of eighteen, my brother Bob and several of his buddies pooled their limited funds and purchased a 1938, powder blue La Salle with a reclining back seat.

Harold does concur with all details with the exception that the car was a Nash and not a La Salle. My brother Norman agrees with me that it was in fact a La Salle and not a Nash. Bob, whose opinion would be the definitive word, chooses, in his typical conflict-avoidance style, to claim that we could both be right, but he does not really remember. I insist to Harold that I am correct in all the details.

"Harold, you are too young to remember anything about that car. You were a little *pisher* and would not even know Bob's friends!"

"Oh yeah? There was Don, Kenny and Irving, and they were always hanging around!"

"Wrong! That was much later. I'm talking about the first car. I know I'm right. I spent hours trying to pry off the logo cameo portrait of La Salle from the rear of the car. I used a screwdriver and then tried a hammer!"

"Look, *Putz*! It had to be a Nash. La Salle was a subsidiary of Cadillac that went out of business."

"Wrong again, *boychick*. La Salle was an independent that got bought out by Studebaker."

"Dovid (my Hebrew name), the only thing Studebaker had to do with our family was that Uncle Morrie, our great Uncle Morrie, owned a Studebaker, the one with the little hanging lanterns in the rear."

"Hershel (Yiddish for Harold), you may be the youngest, but you are first to be affected with senility. Great Uncle Morrie had a Buick—the model with the air vent holes on each side."

As was usually the case, nothing was resolved, and so we moved off the original topic onto yet another debate. So it was and so it will always be with us Gottlieb boys—the eldest brother chooses to avoid conflict, the youngest is zealous and determined in his need to stir the familial waters and challenge his elders.

At one time I asked Harold, "How is it that although you are the youngest, that no matter the event or incident, no matter the date of occurrence, you insist that your recollections are always fact?"

His response was 100 percent pure Harold. "You guys have grown senile and, in addition, because I was the one that Ma hated, I made it a point of never forgetting!"

And there may well be some truth in at least one part of his explanation.

So I mention these incidents to demonstrate that while I believe I am remembering events as they really happened, I also grant that some events are presented perhaps as they should or might have occurred. It's the age-old predicament of Roshamon. We were all there. We remember what we remember vividly, and yet we end up with many versions.

Chapter 1

In 1933, I was five years old. Two significant events occurred that year which would play a very important role in my adolescence as well as my earlier adult years. First of all, there was the swearing in of Franklin Delano Roosevelt as President of the United States; second, but of great personal significance to me, Hank Greenberg became a team member of the Detroit Tigers. Hank was the tallest Jew I had ever seen and one of the first Jews ever to play professional baseball. My parents and many other Jews viewed Roosevelt and Greenberg as twin messiahs—the first would lead the Jews into the promised land of prosperity, the second to a land of social and religious acceptance.

These were neither good nor easy times for Detroit or the country. The Great Depression endured, and in Detroit the automobile plants remained closed. Thousands were unemployed, and the federal government had yet to put in place effective policies or programs of assistance.

Anti-Semitism was very much a part of the popular culture, and most especially in Detroit. Each Sunday morning, Father Charles Coughlin of the Shrine of the Little Flower Church would deliver his radio message of hate. Coughlin was neither subtle nor soft-spoken. Jews were the killers of Christ, never to be forgiven or trusted. Jews were the leaders of an international conspiracy dedicated to the destruction of Christianity.

All of us brothers were enrolled in an after school Yiddish school program. Norman and I got out at the same time—6:00 p.m. We took our usual shortcut through an alley when suddenly these three big guys grabbed us.

"Christ killers!" they yelled and tore the pages out of our notebooks and our Tanach (a Yiddish version of the Old Testament). "You kikes are going to die tonight!"

My brother Norman shoved one guy out of the way and yelled at me to run. We took off and headed for the nearest safe sanctuary: a Jewish bakery. As we shut the door behind us, I started to cry. Norman put his arm around my neck and warned me, "Do not say anything to Ma or Pa, or I will break your neck! I will make up something about the books. Just shut up and stop crying!"

Whatever Norman told my parents seemed to work. Then as now, he has a way with words and a most persuasive style.

The summer I turned five, we moved to a two-story, yellow brick house in a working class neighborhood of Detroit. The address was 4051 Elmhurst. It was a mixed neighborhood—one side of the street was Jewish, the other side all non-Jews. Our side had two-story houses constructed of brick, on their side were single homes built of wood. One side had menorahs for Chanukah, the other side had Christmas trees for Christmas.

I shared a single bedroom with my three brothers. Norman and I slept in one bed, and Harold and Bob in the other. The sleeping style for both beds was feet to face. Our parents, Morris and Sophie, had their own bedroom, and Clara, a boarder, occupied the third. It was quite common during those difficult times for families to rent a room in order to have an additional source of income. In the matter of Clara, as I was later to learn, economics was only a partial explanation for sharing our home.

Clara was a young woman in her mid-twenties who worked as a clerk in a suspender-manufacturing factory. She would leave early in the morning and return in the evening. Clara had her own section of our icebox (it would be several years before a refrigerator was to become part of our lives). She would quickly and quietly prepare her dinner before retiring to her room. I don't recall her ever having any callers—men or women. Occasionally, I would see Clara sitting with my mother and conversing in Yiddish.

One day, when I was about ten years old, I was walking by Clara's room and noticed the door was open. Disregarding the many times my mother had told us never to enter her room, my curiosity got the better of me. I wanted to see if I could find anything that might give me a clue to this mysterious person.

The room was barren of any pictures or walls coverings—just a small bed, a bedside table with a lamp, and a chest of drawers. No books or magazines, no radio. I opened her closet, which held nothing but a few simple dresses and a bathrobe. Growing bolder, I quietly slid open the drawer of the bedside table. There were three photos in black and white that I recognized as being from the old country, since they were similar to those my parents brought with them when they came to America from Russia.

As I sat on her bed looking at the pictures, the door opened and Clara entered. We were both surprised. I stood up and handed her the photos and stammered about being sorry, that I was not trying to steal anything, and begged her not to tell my mother. Like my parents, Clara was an immigrant who had only recently come to America. She spoke a combination of English and Yiddish. "*Zu zein ma vel ich sogin gornischt—ergesich nisch* (To your mother I will say nothing—don't worry yourself). *Do vilst visen fum dese bild ich vel derzailen fum zem* (You wish to know about these pictures, then I will tell you)."

She asked me to sit next to her on the bed as she told me about each of the photos, pointing out her mother and father, a younger sister, and two older brothers.

Another photo was of cousins and other family members. All of the pictures had been taken in front of Clara's home, a village not far from Lublin in Poland.

I was old enough to have heard about Hitler, concentration camps, and the efforts of Jews to flee Germany as well as other countries in Europe. I also knew that relatives of my parents had migrated to Palestine in an effort to escape what would eventually be referred to as the Holocaust. But I had never, to that moment, known or met someone who was a victim, a refugee, of that terror.

Clara began to cry as she told me how her parents had bribed Polish officials in order to obtain the necessary travel documents. She described how she was taken by truck and later by train through France and finally by boat to England. Once in England, she was put in the custody of representatives of a Jewish immigrant assistance agency. From England, she made her way to New York and on to Detroit, where she had two cousins whom she had never met.

"From my family, I know nothing," she said, "I do not know if they are alive or dead."

I wanted to comfort her, but more than that I really wanted desperately to be out of that room. I put my hand on hers and mumbled something like, "They're okay. Things will work out and they will also come to America."

Later on that same day, I asked my mother if she would tell me about Clara and how she came to be in our home.

"That is not something you need to know about now," Ma said, "Leave Clara alone and let her be. She has enough to worry about."

"Ma, I don't want to bother her. I just want you to tell me why she is here living with us. How come she came here and not somewhere else?"

"Clara is here because she needed a place to live and her cousin is a friend of Anna Goldberg and that is why she is here. Now no more questions!"

Years later I learned that Clara married and moved to California. None of her family had survived. All had perished in Nazi concentration camps.

* * * * *

My best and only gentile friend was Bob Snow, who lived across the street in a white, single family house.

In contrast, our family rented from the Gorens, who lived upstairs. Unlike us, the Gorens were Orthodox Jews, pious people who maintained a kosher home. Each Saturday morning, as well as on all Jewish holidays, they walked to the local synagogue (Jewish religious law prohibits driving on the Sabbath or holy days). We were neither Orthodox Jews nor affiliated with any synagogue or temple, although I was enrolled for a brief period of time in the United Hebrew School just around the corner from our house.

It soon became apparent to the rabbi as well as my parents that I was neither a Hebrew scholar nor someone who would sit still long enough to master the traditional mandated bar mitzvah requirements. I remember the rabbi saying to me, "So, Dovid, when will you decide if you want to become a Jew or a baseball player?"

"I can be both," I replied. "Look at Hank Greenberg. He is a Jew and a ballplayer."

"True, but before he became a baseball player, he became a Jew by being bar mitzvhed. With you it is the other way around. Either study Torah or do your baseball—both you cannot do here."

My becoming a student in the Yiddish Folk School followed my brief enrollment in Hebrew School. No rabbi teacher, but Chavers (comrades) Berkovich and Comay became my instructors in the Yiddish language, history and culture. Here the classes were smaller and co-educational. Interpretation of historical events was not based upon the Old Testament or any other formal religious teachings.

Rather, we learned about Yiddish authors like Shalom Alechim and poets like Yud Lamed Peretz. We studied Yiddish, not Hebrew. Preparation for my bar mitzvah was centered around a Yiddish translation and interpretation of the Torah and other religious works. I was fascinated with tales of our heroes both past and current, of Judah the Macabee and the fighters of the Warsaw Ghetto. Most intriguing to me was the language of Yiddish, especially the Yiddish folk songs of the Eastern European Jews—the people of the *shtetels*.

One morning Ma gathered the boys together to inform us that our grandfather was coming to live with us. He would be moving into Clara's former room. "You will all have to help Zaydeh," Ma told us, "Remember, he is an older man and has not lived with children for a long time. Zaydeh and Bobeh kept a kosher home and he should not see any *treif* (non-kosher food) in the house. Do not let him see you eat any meat with milk and do not touch his dishes (Jewish religious law calls for at least two sets of dishes and cooking utensils—one to be used exclusively for dairy products the other for meats)."

My Zaydeh was tall and handsome, with the most beautiful head of silver hair I had ever seen. He walked with a royal elegance—head back and shoulders erect. He spoke little English, but he could read and write Russian, Polish, Hebrew, and Yiddish, and when he spoke, it was with great authority and self-assurance. When he was younger, he had studied in Russia to be an engineer. His studies came to an abrupt end following the Russian Revolution, when many Jews were prohibited from attending professional universities.

Every afternoon, my grandfather would lie down in the living room and take a short nap. I had learned that what he most enjoyed when napping was to have his hair combed. I would sit at the end of the couch where his head was on a pillow and very slowly run the comb through his hair. I would repeat that same motion for fifteen or twenty minutes. When at times one of my brothers would ask to do the combing, I would resist and Zaydeh would tell them that this was "*Dovid's arbet* (David's work)." To me, it was not work at all, but a joy.

It soon became apparent that zaydeh knew that ours was not a kosher home and that the boys, at least, were eating salami sandwiches with milk. Still, he would go along with our game and pretend not to notice as we quickly shoved partially eaten sandwiches into kitchen drawers as he entered the kitchen. Zaydeh would pause briefly by the table, then walk around patting us on our heads and saying in his best English, "You are good boys. Go play *bess*ball."

I do not know how many hours my grandfather sat with me and helped with my bar mitzvah preparation. He knew my readings and my speech as well as I did, if not better. When he died in 1943, I stopped attending Yiddish school.

Our landlords, the Gorens, were also aware that ours was not a devout household, which conveniently enabled us to fulfill a vital function for them. The Gottlieb brothers took turns being a "*shabbos goy.*" A literal translation would be "Sabbath gentile," a person who performs duties on the Sabbath which are forbidden to an orthodox Jew. Any activity that could be classified as work falls into the prohibited category. My Saturday tasks included adding coal to the furnace, turning off appliances, and shoveling snow from the sidewalk.

Although we weren't practicing religious Jews, ours was very much a Yiddish home. Yiddish was a second language for the boys, and for my parents it was the language of choice. In the later years, as we learned more of the language and were able to understand comments exchanged between Ma and Pa, they switched to Russian.

My parents were among the many immigrants who came to America in the early twenties. Like most other immigrants, the selection of a place where they would reside was determined in large part by having friends and relatives already settled in the community. These veteran settlers, no matter how short the time since they had left the old country, were the "lansman"—people who were bonded by a common community of origin, those who came from the same village or town of the newly arriving Jewish immigrant. The newcomers were called "greenhorns"—people who were raw and inexperienced when it came to knowledge of the language, culture, and social workings of the new community. The goal of the newcomer was to move as quickly as possible from the status of greenhorn to that of lansman. To be a greenhorn was to be dependent upon others, to be a stranger in your chosen land. To be a lansman meant that you had now mastered or at least adjusted to the demands of a new way of life. It also meant you had the ability to communicate, even if at the most rudimentary level, with those who could not speak either Yiddish or the mother tongue of the country left behind. The lansman knew his or her way around. He knew not only the location of the synagogue, the grocer, and the Jewish agency that provided assistance to new immigrants, but also how to get to these important places, since most immigrants, including us, did not own an automobile.

The first car to which we had some access was a 1938 LaSalle in which my brother Bob was a co-owner along with three of his buddies. For most of our adolescent years we, like our parents, were dependent upon friends, relatives, and public transportation to meet our travel needs. Given all of the hurdles my parents would have to overcome, the lack of a car could be considered a minor inconvenience.

As a child and even later, I would at times be embarrassed by my parents' lack of knowledge and sophistication. My good friend Jerry's parents were born in America. Jerry lived on Leslie, a street of large, single-family, two-story homes. When I would visit him, his mother would prepare snacks, even using placemats and cloth napkins. Jerry's parents were Jews but spoke flawless English. While my father knew the name of only one member of the Detroit Tigers (Hank Greenberg, of course), Jerry's father knew them all—Goslin, Cochrance, Gheringer, and Rogell. Not only that, but Jerry's father actually took us to see the Tigers.

Ma and Pa were not comfortable with the English language; they didn't know what style of dress was appropriate for various social occasions. They knew nothing about the public school system; elementary, middle school, and high school were terms which had no meaning for them. They were removed from the mainstream of American popular culture and did not subscribe to an English language newspaper, though my father was an avid reader of the Daily Forward, a Yiddish newspaper. For years they did not go the movies, nor were either of them aware of the offerings of daytime radio. In the old country both my parents would have been considered educated and even cosmopolitan. Here in America they were truly "greenhorns," very much dependent upon the patience and benevolence of others.

The Jews of my father's generation, especially if they came to America from Eastern Europe, came with very little in the way of occupational skills. Because of the work and educational restrictions placed upon young Jews, only a handful were allowed to attend school beyond the eighth grade level. In most places, Jews were not allowed to own land or buy or rent office or retail business space. My father did manage to find work as an entry-level clerk with a small governmental agency. My mother had part time employment as a sales clerk in a store that sold second hand clothing. English language limitations and few networking opportunities further restricted employment mobility. When my parents came to America, there were few Jews in any of the major manufacturing, transportation, commerce, or banking industries. The Jews of Eastern Europe had been primarily small-scale merchants and service providers—bakers, butchers, barbers, tailors, nurse's aids, clerk, bookkeepers, carpenters, and students of the Torah.

What these greenhorns did have going for them was a thirst for learning, strong commitment to work and family, and an enduring drive to make it in America. Where Jews have been most successful are those fields which mandate advanced study, those where there was little or no established base, and those which had connections with work in the old country. Compared to other ethnic populations, Jews were predominant in professions of retail and commerce, and the arts and entertainment. There is consensus that Jewish immigrants played the major role in the launching and development of the film industry.

Starting with small, family-owned retail businesses, first and second generation Jews built major department store chains. Entertainment and the arts, both institutions with few ethnic or religious restrictions, were obvious havens for creative and talented immigrants.

My father's first job in America came about through the lansman's network. Like the Jews, Polish immigrants also selected those places where they would have lansman, helping organizations, and relatives. A friend of my father's knew the owner of a small, retail clothing store that was seeking a salesperson who could speak Polish, a language, along with Russian and Yiddish, that my father spoke and understood. The shop was located in the city of Hamtramck, a part of the Detroit metropolitan area, but it might as well have been a separate country as it was so removed and isolated from Detroit and contemporary American culture. Hamtramck was as close as you could get to the old and familiar and still be in America.

My father was hired and so began his dual acculturation process, learning the cultures of two very different social systems: Detroit and Hamtramck.

Accommodating the requirements and expectations of a strange new city must have been an immense challenge for both of my immigrant parents. As I recall these earlier years, I have come to recognize and appreciate what a struggle daily life must have been for my father. Year after year, six days a week, long before any of us were even out of bed, Pa would travel by public transportation—45 miles each way—arriving at home late in the evening. It was only on Sundays and official holidays that Pa was at the supper table. Now I understand that his was an almost schizophrenic existence, traveling between two very different places and living two very different lives. I don't think he ever really felt comfortable with either culture.

It was not for a lack of willingness on his part. His attempts, however, at mastering the ways of his New World frequently met with frustration and failure. One such experience came at the urging of his good friend Sol Goldberg. Sol, who had been driving a truck for several years, persuaded my father that if he ever expected to be a real "Yankee," he would have to drive a car. Pa found every possible reason to resist that idea. Public transportation was good, he told Sol, and he knew all of the drivers. Why should he bother to buy a car when he already had door-to-door, uniformed service?

Mr. Goldberg finally got to my father by pointing out two factors: First, my father was the only one of his friends that did not have a car; and second, Pa's family had to rely on others for our regular Sunday park outings. It was not the validity of the first observation that got to Pa since he could not care less about how he might be compared to his peers. It was the argument about being dependent upon others that finally did the trick.

Ma was not at all pleased when Pa announced to all that he was going to buy a car. She had little confidence in his technical skills and even less in his sense of direction. A compromise was reached when it was decided that the purchase of an auto would be deferred until Pa exhibited that he did indeed have the required driving skills. Pa received the most basic, comprehensive, and swiftest of driving instructions from his mentor, Mr. Goldberg. So confident was Mr. Goldberg that he also arranged for my father to have temporary use of a practice vehicle.

Early the next morning, with my brother Bob at his side, Pa set off on his first and, as it turned out, final driving experience. According to Bob, Pa had just turned the corner into the next street when he hit a parked car. Bob, who was then about nine years old, jumped out of the car in order to check the damage. Pa continued to sit in the car with no signs of fear or concern as he handed Bob a note he had written to put on the windshield of the other car.

The brief note, written in Yiddish, contained only two words: "*Inshulding, Moishe* (Sorry, Morris)." No last name, no phone number, no attempt at explanation, and certainly no reference to insurance.

Pa quickly rejected Bob's suggestion that they drive directly home, having made the observation that the accident was not his fault but rather the fault of the person who had done such a poor job of parking. And so he continued on his way. The second parked car Pa hit was less than fifteen feet from the first victim. The same routine was followed, with Bob doing the windshield-note caper and Pa eager to move on. Pa's total driving time had been less than fifteen minutes and had taken him no further than two city blocks. The damage assessment was a total of four parked cars as well as the borrowed vehicle.

Upon their return, Pa declared there were more important things to spend money on than a car. Thus far we had managed without one and would continue to do so until one of the boys was able to buy a car of his own. True to his word, he never bought a car, and Bob was the first of us to own a car in partnership with a few of his buddies.

* * * * *

In Hamtramck, Pa experienced anti-Semitism. Many times he would angrily tell us of an encounter with a customer that went like this: "You Jews, you sell us shit and want more money!" or, "I would shake hands with you, but if I did you would keep one finger for yourself," or, "You think we are dumb Pollocks, but we know how to deal with Jews."

When it came to dealing with anti-Semitic comments from Poles, Pa was a veteran. He grew up and worked in Poland in a community where Jews were constantly being baited by their non-Jewish neighbors. When he was a child, he was told that he could not participate in a school science project because he was a Jew. Several years later he was beaten by three other students for his failure to move off the path where they were walking. When he was not allowed to graduate from secondary school, my grandparents had to bribe an official so Pa could take a qualifying exam for an entry-level civil service position. After he passed the test, a second bribe was paid so that he could be hired.

As a young man, Pa was defiant and would quickly respond both verbally and physically to any insult directed at him, his parents, or any other Jew. Gradually, he learned that such actions on his part only led to further abuse and retaliation, so eventually he backed away from reactions of anger and adopted a style of indifference and avoidance.

Later, during his civil service career, Pa discovered that he was more productive than his peers were, and they dealt with him in a more tolerant manner when he offered assistance. As he had been dependent for his livelihood on the goodwill of anti-Semitic Poles in Poland, so would be the case with some Poles in America. He could not afford to alienate his peers and supervisors in Poland, and he could not afford to lose his customers in America. Whereas in Poland Pa gave his attackers his skill and intelligence, in America he gave them modest presents for their children and special discounts on sheets and pillowcases.

Pa's absence from our daily lives only added to his feelings of being an outsider. I do not think he was really ever comfortable with neighbors or friends. It was not until the closing years of his life that Pa felt secure enough to venture beyond the familiar, and then only at the insistence of Ma.

Rose Zalmanov was a dear friend of my mother. Her husband, Jack, was a factory worker. They lived next door to us, upstairs in a two-story house. Jack was a heavy-set man whose leisure interests were confined to playing Pinochle and fishing. Like my father, Jack and Sol (the husband of my mother's other close friend) were men who were dominated by their wives. Certainly the women called the shots in matters of the education and discipline of children, household management and attendance at social functions, namely weddings, funerals, bar mitzvahs, and meetings of the Arbiter Ring or Workman's Circle, a Yiddish social and cultural organization

Downstairs from the Zalmanovs lived the Friedsons and their very attractive teen daughter Carol, yet another source of disagreement for my brothers Harold and Norman. Norman maintains that Carol was a "knockout," with Harold, of course, taking the contrary position. A recent exchange between my brothers brought the following information:

Harold: "She was a dog! No matter how kind you want to be, you can do no better than to say she was gross—*mias* (ugly)."

Norman: "A very lovely young lady. I did spend some time with her and can assure you that if hard data is what you seek, I am a far better judge than Harold."

Upstairs on our left was the Katz family with three sons: Boris the eldest, Harry the youngest, and Jacob the middle son. The Katz boys were huge; both Boris and Jacob later played football for Wayne University. Harry was my classmate and protector. He was not the brightest guy in our class and he often wore the hand-me-down clothes of his older brothers. Other kids would make fun of Harry, but never in his presence.

Almost every morning before the school bell rang, a bunch of us would gather in the playground to play stickball. Once, it was my turn to be the umpire and I called a kid named Richard out when he tried to steal a base. He came after me and threw one punch that landed right on my nose, knocking me to the ground. He then jumped on top of me and yelled, "Gottlieb, you are a prick! A kike prick!" And with that he hit me again.

Suddenly, Harry appeared and with little effort lifted Richard well off the ground. As Harry lifted Richard even higher, he began to spin around faster and faster in ever widening circles. We were all certain that Harry was going to let him loose and see how far he could throw him.

Richard was screaming and pleading with Harry to stop and put him down. Harry stopped but kept him raised well above his own head saying, "David, what do you want me to do with him?"

"I want him to say he is sorry for what he called me and that if he ever does it again you will finish him off!" I replied.

With that, Harry set Richard down on the ground and said, "You heard him. Tell him you're sorry, and remember next time you will go down head first."

Richard did as he was told and quickly fled the field.

Harry and I both attended the Winterhalter Elementary School—named for Admiral Augustus Winterhalter. No one ever explained who this admiral was or what he did to have the school named for him. Harry and I shared a desk in the fourth and fifth grades. We were separated by Ms. Doyle, our sixth grade homeroom teacher, because we were "a constant disturbance to others."

Winterhalter was a brick, two-story building with dimly lit halls and endless rows of green lockers. Displayed on the walls were the works of the "masters," as explained by Mrs. Williamson, the school's art teacher: Gainsborough's Boy in Blue, the Mona Lisa, and of course, Washington Crossing the Delaware.

School, we were told, was a serious enterprise, and nothing in the ambience suggested otherwise. I liked most of the teachers, especially Mrs. Green, who taught natural science. Though she was tough, Ms. Doyle was fair, as was her sister, Mrs. Williamson. While Green, Doyle, and Williamson looked very much like teachers—matronly with little makeup and heavy dark shoes—Ms. Seewick, the fourth grade teacher, was different in many ways.

To begin with, she wore brightly colored, low-cut dresses with high heel shoes, nylon stockings, and lots of makeup. Ms. Seewick would assign us a reading, then sit at her desk, rearranging her hair or reapplying lipstick or powder and constantly rubbing her hands with a cream that smelled of lilacs. The only sound you could hear was her hands, covered with cream, sliding back and forth, round and round.

One day Ms. Seewick asked the class if there was anyone who passed Arden's Drug Store on the way to school. Several hands went up; I not only raised my hand but quickly stood up.

"Thank you all. David, would you please come to my desk?"

All eyes were upon me as I approached her desk and Ms. Seewick in a whisper asked, "Would you please be a dear and on your way to school tomorrow stop at Arden's and buy me a jar of Pacquins Hand Cream?"

I readily agreed, pocketed the two dollars she gave me, and went back to my desk. Harry was most curious about why Ms. Seewick was giving me money. I shared with him what Ms. Seewick had requested of me.

My conversation with Ms. Seewick generated interest among some of the girls in my class. Leona Schwartz was tall, heavy, and dark. Her singular accomplishment, which had given her schoolwide notoriety, was an ability to appear as if she was turning her left eyeball completely around. Gail Greenberg achieved school fame by being sent home for wearing a brightly colored, sleeveless sun suit cut too short. Gail, like Leona, was tall and heavy, but unlike Leona, she was very light skinned, with a bosom more adult than pre-adolescent.

Patsy King, on the other hand, was perfect: a blonde with a great complexion and very attractive in her plaid skirts and cashmere sweaters.

My first serious encounter with Leona, Gail, and Patsy came in the fourth grade when Ms. Goodnell, our gym teacher, announced that social dancing would be a regular weekly activity. We were all surprised by this announcement, especially coming from Ms. Goodnell, who exhibited no feminine attributes whatsoever. She was well muscled, wore sweatpants and heavy T-shirts—no makeup. She had a deep, almost baritone voice and a vocabulary not heard before at Winterhalter Elementary School: "Get those big rear ends moving! Everyone sweats and no BS about getting excuses from the nurse!"

Knocking us over with a medicine ball appeared to give her special pleasure. Any crying because of pain, either real or imagined, was met with insult. "You kids are spoiled and you are out of shape. My job is to knock the fat off and turn you into little Marines!"

At our first social dancing session, Ms. Goodnell ordered all the fourth, fifth, and sixth grade boys to line up alongside one gym wall. Girls were required to line up along the opposite wall. "At the count of three," said Ms. Goodnell, "each of you boys will walk over and invite a girl to dance. I want every girl and every boy to have a partner."

At the count of three, no one moved. Ms. Goodnell did not disguise her anger with us: "When I say each boy will choose a girl, that's exactly what I mean! Do it and do it now!" To encourage migration, she grabbed two boys and dragged them toward the girl's line. Slowly and reluctantly we followed.

The problem for the boys in my fourth grade class was that none of the girls, especially those in fifth and sixth grade, wanted to be seen dancing with a "little kid."

Though I did not consider myself a "little kid," I had not yet reached that stage of development where I felt comfortable in either asking or dancing. Knowing that I was bound to be rejected only added to my apprehension.

Ms. Goodnell continued to push and intimidate and slowly partners were selected. It was clear which of the girls would be among those selected and those rejected. Patsy King was the target of a dozen fifth and sixth grade boys. Leona and Gail were among the girls who Ms. Goodnell arbitrarily coupled with the remaining boys. As I approached a sixth grade girl, she made every effort to avoid eye contact with me, as if she were trying to sink into the wall. This was an exercise where, boy or girl, you quickly and painfully found where you stood in peer assessment by acceptance and rejection.

Ms. Goodnell pushed me toward the one remaining girl and said, "Now you ask her to dance and be quick!" The music began and we followed instructions offered by Ms. Goodnell: "No part of your bodies should be touching each other! Keep at least a two-foot distance between you. No fast dancing. We will begin with the waltz."

The fifty-minute school hour seemed endless. I wanted to say something to my partner, but was concentrating on the steps. My partner, on the other hand, was not only a constant talker but made it clear that she would lead and I would follow. "Whatever your name is, get closer and stop looking at your feet; just follow me. What is it with you? You heard Ms. Goodnell say it's a waltz, nothing fancy, like a box. Just keep doing a box."

Finally, the bell rang and there was a wild rush from the gym. I noticed that my ex-partner, whose name I later learned was Sandra, was talking with Gail and Leona. One of the girls pointed toward me and then the three of them began to laugh. Sandra did an imitation of me, head down, stepping on my own feet as well as hers. I felt my face turn red as I became the focus of everyone in the room. I quickly left the gym and ran into the boy's restroom.

It was with dread that I entered the gym for our second week of social dancing. This time the rules were changed and the girls were instructed to choose a partner. I now knew what it felt like to want to disappear.

Then a most amazing thing happened to me. Patsy—Patsy King, the most popular girl at Winterhalter Elementary School—approached me, touched my arm, and asked if I would be her partner. It was as if some miracle had occurred and I quickly went from "little kid" to confident teen. "Yes," I answered, "I would be happy to be your partner."

As we began to dance, I had visions of a Fred Astaire-Ginger Rodgers movie where all eyes were on us as we gracefully glided about the gym. The longer we danced, the more confident I became in my social as well as dance skills. I took Patsy by the hand and raising both of our hands spun her gently around in a circle. Patsy laughed and encouraged me by complimenting my innovative dance routines. We danced together until Ms. Goodnell blew her whistle, the signal for the change of partners. We dropped our hands and Patsy said she hoped we could dance together next week.

My dancing with Patsy had immediate status enhancement payoffs. Before I could return to my place at the wall reserved for those not selected, four different girls, including Gail and Leona, approached me. I accepted Gail's invitation and told Leona that she could be my next partner.

The motivation for my actions were, in part at least, a feeling of sympathy for two social outcasts, having until that very day considered myself to be at the bottom of Winterhalter's social hierarchy. A second reason was my belief that now that I had arrived, I could risk brief mingles with the lower class. I had, in record time, become a snob.

My first dance with Gail went as I feared it might. Gail was without any sense of rhythm or direction—totally dependent upon me for every part of the dance exercise.

"OK, Gail, put your left arm here and the right arm there. Move back a little and try to relax," I explained. How quickly I had gone from clumsy novice to dance master, freely giving instruction and teaching by example. "Just watch and you can see how easy it is. Just keep making boxes."

Our dancing was hardly an example of coordination between two people, but rather my steering and pushing and her resisting every step of the way. Two dances later, the whistle was blown once again and Leona grabbed me. "OK, Twinkle Toes," she said, "show me your stuff and don't try to be cute!" As Gail was passive and reluctant, Leona was assertive and eager to take control. Leona determined all changes in direction or pace, and any resistance was met with scorn. "Gottlieb, you are a class 'A' schmuck! You may be big time with that skinny *schiksa* (gentile girl), but in my book you are double zilch!"

I finally had enough and broke out of her arms and said, "That's it Leona. I was trying to be nice and that's why I picked you for a dance."

Her response was fast and furious: "I know that, you asshole, and that's why I hate you!"

It was not long after that incident that I was to learn exactly what Leona meant and how she felt. But for the moment nothing else seemed to matter. I had a crush on Patsy, and would soon have her in my arms once again.

In our arts and crafts class, we were making nametags using the tiny pasta letters from Campbell's Alphabet Soup. We were to select the desired letters, allow them to dry, and then glue them onto a piece of balsam wood. A thin coat of shellac was applied and a safety pin glued to the back. I carefully went through this entire process and the result was my public declaration of affection: a balsam wood pin that read, "PATSY and DAVID."

After school that day, I waited for Patsy, and as she approached I quickly thrust my gift into her hands before awkwardly bolting around the corner.

The next day, I anxiously awaited her arrival in school, eager to see if she would be wearing "our" pin—a sure sign that she felt as I did. She arrived. I looked and looked again—no pin.

During our natural science class, on the way to my seat, I discreetly placed a folded note on her desk. The message read, "Did you like the pin?" It was a long wait until lunchtime, the next opportunity when I would see Patsy. Walking across the lunchroom, she returned my pin and said, "My church does not allow us to wear any decorations other than a cross." And with that she moved on to sit with a group of her girlfriends.

I did not know how to interpret her statement. Would she have worn the pin if her church did not have any decoration prohibition? Would her church also prohibit her from being in love with someone of a different faith? My only available option was to wait until our next dance session and seek clarification at that time.

The dance day came and I hurried across the floor to Patsy. "Will you please dance with me?" I asked.

Patsy looked right into my eyes and said, "I danced with you because in church we were told to try to find kids who were not Christians and help them to find truth in Jesus Christ our Lord. If you will come to the youth Bible class, we could become friends and then maybe we could dance." She handed me a small card depicting the Crucifixion, printed with "Jesus died for your sins" in small letters, together with a small booklet outlining the necessary steps for salvation.

I was hurt, confused, and felt guilty about holding a card with a picture of Jesus as well as words praising his name. I felt I was committing a sin against my God and my people. At the same time, I was not certain as to what would happen to me if I threw away the card and by doing so offend Patsy's God. I finally took the coward's way out and placed the troublesome card anonymously on Ms. Seewick's desk.

Dismissal by Patsy King was all I needed to begin quickly rebuilding bridges with Harry, Leona and Gail, a trio of Jewish kids with backgrounds more like my own. Leona was the least sympathetic when I shared the results of my brief encounter with fame and Patsy King. She was quick to remind me that now I was the one looking for sympathy. "Gottlieb, the reason I am going to be your friend again is because I feel so sorry for you. Poor Gottlieb, his little heart is broken. Dumped by a *schiksa*!"

That was the final reference Leona ever made about the Patsy encounter.

By the time we entered the sixth and final grade of elementary school, the four of us had become close friends, confiding and trusting one another. Between the fourth grade and the sixth grade there was a marked difference in what non-school topics would hold our interests—primarily comments about peers and teachers or about sex and changes in our physical development. Both Gail and Leona had grown taller and were no longer dumpy looking. A new world was opened to Harry and me when the girls shared with us information about differences between B and C bra cups. They were equally eager to learn from us what changes were taking place with us – namely, physiological changes.

Gail and Leona had not only outpaced us boys in physical growth but also in overcoming any hesitancy whatsoever in discussing any topic that came to mind. Even though I had two older brothers, the sharing of personal or intimate knowledge among us was limited. Going to my parents was out of the question: first because I would be filled with shame, and second because I did not believe it was a topic with which they had any real experience to share with me. It was quite some time before I connected the fact of their having children with the actual act of sexual intercourse.

My own sexual awareness and knowledge was quite limited—mostly jokes and stories shared among peers or my brother Norm, and an occasional encounter with a "dirty" comic book. I was getting to the age where I was starting to take an interest in girls, but had not reached any real level of self-confidence or self-assurance.

In addition to the weekly dance program, Ms. Goodnell and the school nurse offered a three-hour series entitled "Healthy Body and Healthy Mind." This program was available only to graduating sixth graders in an attempt to introduce us to the topic of sex without ever having to use the word. Chairs were placed on each side of a large portable chalkboard in the middle of the gym. Boys were seated on one side and girls on the other. The idea was to prevent us from making eye contact with any member of the opposite sex or from being able to identify who was asking a question. The only area not blocked from view was our feet.

Ms. Goodnell and the nurse took their positions at the border that separated the genders. The nurse began by making the point that males and females were different in their physiology, emotions, and social development. She went on to explain why it is important as we enter our teens to understand how the hormones in our bodies could overwhelm our emotional balance and cause serious personal consequences. Because few of us really understood what she was talking about, her comments were followed by spontaneous outbursts of giggling and chatter.

At this point Ms. Goodnell intervened and said, "OK, knock it off! You know darn well what she is trying to tell you. A boy and girl together can get in serious trouble if you lose control of yourself. One of you girls might think that a little smooch is okay and that ends it, but you are wrong!"

Our school nurse was obviously surprised at Ms. Goodnell's no-nonsense-let's-get-to the-point talk. She quickly sought to take over and move the discussion along in her own style. But it was too late. Ms. Goodnell's comments were the instant stimulus for a barrage of questions.

"If you don't do any French kissing, will you be able to stop in time?"

"Is it okay to kiss if you really love each other?"

"What will happen if you kiss a lot, what happens next?"

The majority of questions being asked were not the result of any desire for knowledge or clarification. Most of us, while we were not terribly sophisticated, were aware how one action could lead to another. After all, we were sixth graders, and we had indulged in games like "spin the bottle" and "post office." My brother Norman had even selectively shared with me certain of his adventures.

No, we were deliberately trying to embarrass the nurse. We knew that nothing we asked would faze Ms. Goodnell. Both boys and girls were also eager to try to identify which student of the other gender was asking which question.

"That's it!" yelled Ms. Goodnell, slamming her hand against the chalkboard. "No more smart ass questions from anybody!"

Since we as a class had spent many hours with Ms. Goodnell, we were neither shocked nor surprised at her outburst. Not so with our school nurse. She was visibly shaken by the combination of our questions and Ms. Goodnell's use of profanity. Tears came to her eyes and in a trembling voice she informed us that in all her years of being a school nurse, she had never encountered a ruder group of youngsters. Then, turning to Ms. Goodnell, she added, "Nor an educational professional so lacking in proper manners!"

So ended our first and last class in "Healthy Body and Healthy Mind."

Chapter 2

In 1939, as I approached my thirteenth birthday, my life became consumed with preparations for my bar mitzvah, baseball, and delivering the weekend morning newspaper, the Detroit Free Press. The newspaper headlines were a constant reminder that Adolph Hitler, Chancellor of Germany, had already unleashed the forces that would lead to the Holocaust.

In Yiddish school, Chaver Berkovitch shared with us the most recent news about what was happening with the Jews in Germany. From him we learned how our own United States government did not take Nazi rhetoric or behavior seriously. Hitler's pathological hatred of the Jews, whom he was convinced would threaten the racial purity of the German Aryan, was not viewed with alarm or concern, but explained simply as localized political propaganda. Rather than taking any direct diplomatic or military action, our government's response was one of appeasement. The Munich Agreement of 1938, wherein Britain joined Hitler in the dismemberment of Czechoslovakia, was yet another example of a lack of willingness and courage to confront the Nazi terror and intimidation.

It was not until late 1938, when the Nazis mounted pogrom against Jews all over Germany—the *Kristellnacht*, the "night of glass" when the businesses and offices of German Jews were shattered by the Nazis—that some in Europe and American finally sat up and took notice.

Chaver Berkovitch, who had family in Germany and Poland, was bitter and anxious—anxious because he had no doubts whatsoever that this was just the beginning of a massive campaign of anti-Semitism, bitter because President Roosevelt was not responding to the pleas of the American Jewish community asking our government to intervene on behalf of the Jews of Germany. Berkovitch spoke to us in Yiddish, saying that what we were witnessing was the same thing that happened to the Jews throughout history. From the earliest times, Jews had been forced to leave one country after another in search safe haven. Most recently in Russia, the Revolution had brought about similar pogroms against the Jews. It was this rampant anti-Semitism in Russia that was the catalyst for the mass migration of Jews to America. America promised to be the land of milk and honey not only for the Jews, but for all immigrants. America would never allow tyrants anywhere in the world to harm innocent people no matter their religion or color.

But now Berkovitch was no longer so certain as he had been. He saw no proof whatsoever that FDR, a good friend of the Jews, would do anything to stop Hitler.

Early in the morning of September 1, 1939, the manager of my newspaper route called me at home. He said that I needed to be on the corner of Elmhurst and Holmur at 7:00 a.m. to pick up papers for a special headline edition. As I walked through the streets of my neighborhood shouting, "Extra, extra, read all about it! Germany invades Poland!" it took less than thirty minutes to sell out all of my papers, except one that I kept for my parents.

At home, my parents had already heard the news and my father was on the phone talking with my Uncle Hyman. My father was very upset and speaking first in Yiddish, then Polish, and then back to Yiddish, "Somebody must do something or they will all be killed! The Nazis will drive them from their homes and God knows what will happen!" Two of my father's cousins who recognized the growing danger for Jews in Poland had joined a Zionist organization and migrated to Palestine. Two other cousins and an uncle and an aunt had left Minsk and relocated in Warsaw. Our last contact with our Polish relatives had been in late August of 1939.

Over the next few weeks, there were many phone calls and attempts to obtain information about family members, but no reliable information about the status of kin seemed to be available. The lansman organizations did their best to provide hope and comfort, bringing together people who shared a common pain and uncertainty.

The most reliable and comprehensible news sources were three Yiddish newspapers and the "Yiddish Hour"—a weekly radio program. A day did not go by that my father did not read all three newspapers. The "Yiddish Hour" program shifted its previous focus from general community news and Yiddish folk music to reporting on the condition of Jews in Poland. My father called the station and gave the names of his relatives and their addresses in Warsaw.

Several days later, the German *Luftwaffe* began the bombing of Warsaw and soon after that the German army entered the city. In November of 1939, we learned that two of the cousins had made it to Palestine. There was never any further word about what happened to my father's aunt and uncle.

In Yiddish School, we learned about a small group of Jews who had gathered in the Warsaw ghetto and resisted the German occupation; most were young and ill equipped to battle the Germans. The resistance was short lived and ended with the death of every Jewish fighter. We asked Chaver Berkovitch what we could do to help. His answer was, "Never forget and never forgive.

* * * * *

Even with a war raging in Europe and the constant reminders about the plight of Jews in Europe, there was baseball. More specifically, there was Hank Greenberg. Hank's hitting was really turning the Tigers into a pennant contender.

For me, even before Hank arrived on the scene, baseball was the activity of choice. Stickball in the schoolyard before school, baseball as part of our gym activity, and weekend pick up games were the regular routine. I was a good ballplayer and the only one of my brothers who showed any interest in the sport. The combination of Jewish pride in Hank and my own determination brought me unexpected status with my parents, aunts and uncles, and friends of my parents. Prior to Hank, baseball—or for that matter any other athletic activity—was not considered to be either a desirable or prestigious pursuit for any Jewish boy. Education and scholastic pursuit were held in the highest esteem. For Jewish parents, Hank Greenberg was the first acceptable sports role model.

My most enthusiastic supporters in my pursuit of baseball fame were both named Morrie: Great Uncle Morrie, my mother's uncle; and Uncle Morrie, my mother's brother. Great Uncle Morrie knew little about baseball, but his children, especially his daughter Rose, were members of the Hank Greenberg fan club.

When Great Uncle Morrie asked what he could do to help me with my baseball, Rose quickly suggested a glove. Rose's response baffled Great Uncle Morrie and he asked for clarification, "Why does he need a glove? Do they play in the snow?" Rose explained how the ball was small and very hard and how it is thrown really fast so you need to protect your hands. This exchange was conducted in Yiddish with the occasional use of English when Rose could not come up with the Yiddish translation, for example, of first base, shortstop, and left field. Eventually Rose was able to communicate that each of the players on the defending team wore a glove, and the shape of the glove varied depending on the position played. Rose added that she thought the best thing my Great Uncle could do was to take me to a store and let me select a glove.

One day after school, Great Uncle Morrie and I drove to a neighborhood hardware store in search of a baseball glove. We found a counter with baseball gloves, and I did my best to explain which gloves were used by the catcher, which by the first baseman, which by outfielders and which were used by infielders. My less than expansive Yiddish vocabulary and my Great Uncle's limited English, as well as the topic we were discussing, did not lead to rapid comprehension. It was the kind of dialogue that would in later years be used by comedians Abbot and Costello and Bob Newhart.

At the time I saw nothing comical, but felt only frustration as I tried again and again to answer his many questions. As Great Uncle Morrie tried on the various gloves, the manager of the store approached and asked if he could help. I explained that my uncle wanted to buy me a baseball glove, and that since I was a pitcher I wanted an infielder's glove. I added that my uncle knew nothing about baseball and would not be satisfied until he was assured that I was indeed getting the appropriate glove.

It was as if a great dark cloud had been lifted. The manager addressed my great uncle in beautiful and fluent Yiddish, requesting that he be allowed to show my uncle just how the game of baseball was played. From under the counter he withdrew a large board covered with a colorful diagram of a baseball field. Laying the board on the counter he placed small molded figures of each of the defensive ball players. As he explained he pointed to the four bases—home, first, second, and third, followed by the outfield and infield positions, then the pitcher's mound and the location of the catcher. Next came the batter, placed in the appropriate position, ready to face the pitcher. The store manager went into detail about strikes and balls, outs, double plays, and so on. I was amazed as my great uncle seemed mesmerized and hung on every word while watching every movement of the model players. Soon other customers gathered around and added comments of their own.

We were there for more than an hour, and I reminded my great uncle about the original purpose of our visit. With his baseball education completed, he turned to the business of selecting my very first baseball glove. Because I was not playing first base, it was not a glove with a Hank Greenberg signature. It was, however, an infielder's glove signed by the great Tiger short stop Billy Rogell. On the way home I thanked my great uncle and suggested that rather than using the word "glove," he use the word the ballplayers use, "mitt."

When we arrived home Great Uncle Morrie took center stage as the authority on the great game of baseball. He held my prized glove and explained, "It's not called a glove by Hank Greenberg. It's a mitt." He went on and on sharing with my parents all that he had learned about three strikes and four balls and how a player, if he is not careful, "can get caught stealing." Neither my mother nor father shared his enthusiasm. They were, however, pleased that with my new possession I would no longer be pestering them for a baseball mitt.

It was 1940, and Hank and I were enjoying a good season. In fact, mine was progressing so well that I was invited to join a newly established softball league, the Junior Intelligence Bureau, or JIB.

JIB was the idea of the Mayor of Detroit and the police commissioner. The idea was to keep young boys off the streets during the summer by inviting them to play neighborhood league ball. Boys between the ages of twelve and sixteen were encouraged to go to their local police station precinct and sign up. At no cost, the League would provide uniforms, bats and balls, as well as a policeman who would serve as coach/manager for each team.

This was a citywide program and, not surprisingly, attracted thousands of guys. I called together five of my buddies—Harry, Irwin, Bob, Larry and Sidney—and we walked over to the Petoskey police station. We were asked for proof of age and address, and were assigned to a 15-man roster with other kids who lived in our area. We met our new coach/manager, Officer Mackey. Officer Mackey said it was okay for us to call him "Mac." We were measured for baseball trousers, t-shirts, and hats. Our team would be called the Rockets and our uniform colors were blue and white. Our first team meeting was on Saturday at 10:00 a.m. at the Winterhalter School playground.

Before reaching the sidewalk, we were slapping each other on the back, not believing the good fortune that had befallen us. Irwin, who was a solid .400 hitter, said he had played ball with a couple of the other guys on our team and they were pretty good players. Sidney, who was always the last to be chosen in our pre-school games, expressed concern that he might not make the team. I reminded him of what Mac had said, "How good a player you are is important, but most important is being a team player, eager to work hard." Mac said that every team member would have an opportunity to play in each game.

Harry was more subdued and said nothing until we came to his house. The whole thing smelled bad to him. "They give us all of this stuff free and they're gonna drive us over to play at other fields, and they're gonna give the winners trophies—all free. I tell ya, there is something not kosher here."

Being enthusiastic and upbeat was never Harry's way. He was always hesitant and usually suspicious.

We said our goodbyes and I ran into the house to share my good news. My mother made only one observation: "More baseball! It's not enough already?" Norman, who had no interest in baseball, said nothing. Bob said something like "sounds like a good idea," and Harold, the youngest, added that they are always doing things for older guys but never for kids his age.

When my father arrived home, I shared my news with him. Not unlike Harry, my father had his doubts about the entire enterprise. He commented in Yiddish, "First, the police are all *goniffs* (crooks), and the mayor is the biggest crook of all of them—the chief *goniff*. Second, they have found a new way of making money, only this time they will steal from kids and not from grown ups."

"*Zei shtil* (Be quiet)," said my mother, "Why do you have to spoil things for the boy?"

"Better he should learn when he is young," answered my father.

All through the summer we played different teams around the city. Whenever we won a game, Mac would buy each of us a bottle of "Sweet Sixteen"- a 16-ounce bottle of highly sugared soda. If a player hit a homerun, Mac popped for hotdogs. We were having a great season and were doing really well—so well, in fact that we had made it to the semi-final playoffs.

The playoff game was not to be held at a local school playground, but rather at Northwestern High School's multiple field athletic complex. This was the place where the City of Detroit High School championship games were played—big time fields with baselines and real bases, a pitcher's mound, and bleachers. We'd hit the big time.

The setup was indeed impressive, but the crowds of people who actually came to watch the game puzzled me. Though the stands were far from being full, there were certainly more in attendance than any of our previous games. At home games we had no more than five or six followers, and these were mostly kid brothers and sisters. The only loyal adult fan was Moishe. Moishe was an older gentleman who made his living selling ice cream from a pushcart. He would travel up and down the streets of our neighborhood, ringing a bell connected to the one of the handles of the cart with a thick red rubber band. Moishe would say nothing to anyone, just push his cart, ring his bell, and sell his Eskimo Bars for a nickel. He would come to our games and stand silently by his cart and watch.

There were never any other adults and never any parents. In the late thirties, Detroit was primarily a blue-collar city with factory workers, many of them first generation Americans. There were no suburbs to speak of and no Little League. Fathers worked long hours, including Saturdays. Labor unions had yet to effectively organize the automobile companies. Very few parents had the time, energy, or motivation to become involved with our after school activities, so I was impressed with grown men in the stands watching us warm up for the big game.

Our turn came and we took to the field for warm up practice. All fifteen members of the Rockets were present in clean uniform. Mac hit us infield liners and long fly balls to the outfield. We had all mastered the mimicking of our professional baseball heroes—chewing gum rather than tobacco, constantly spitting, moving dirt around the pitchers mound and digging in at the batters box. I wore my cap at the same angle that Hank wore his, and I had a Hank Greenberg signature wrist sweatband.

Mac had instructed us that constant chatter, even if not flattering to our opponents, was an effective psychological tool. Our left fielder, Bob, kept repeating the same phrase—"Your mother wears combat boots"—over and over. Harry, the catcher, had something unpleasant to say to every opposing batter. Of course, the other team gave as good as they got, and at times it was necessary for our coaches to call a truce before things got too far out of hand.

As our opponents, the much-feared Owls, took the field, Mac called us together for a brief meeting. From previous pre-game team gatherings, we pretty much knew what the form and content of his message would be. This time, however, there were some surprises. "Guys, this game is the biggest game you have ever played as a Rocket," Mac said. "A win here could take us to the finals and then the championship. On this one, we put it all on the line. When the chips are down, that's when we find out who are the men and who are the pussies. Are you guys going to be men or pussies?"

Obviously, we all knew the correct response, and so we answered that we were men.

"Louder! I want them to hear you all the way over to Woodward Avenue. Are you men or pussies?"

Again we responded, this time in a unified roar, "Men! Men! Men!"

Mac seemed at last satisfied that we preferred to be men rather than pussies. "Guys," he said, "we need to do whatever we must in order to win this big one. Take a look at those Owls. Take a really good look. They are bigger and faster than us. The black guy over there is way over the age limit, and the shortstop plays semi-pro ball. They got ringers, and if we're going to whip their asses, we need our own ringers."

We all knew that ringers were not regular team members but outsiders who were brought in for the sole purpose of winning the game. On occasion they were even paid for their services.

Mac called over three guys who had been standing close by and observing our meeting. We had not seen any of them prior to this moment. No doubt about it, they were genuine ringers. Whereas among our group Harry was the only team member who had shaved, these guys had 4 o'clock shadows, and it was still before noon. They were big and well muscled, and had to be at least in their late teens.

Mac said that we would need to loan our new team members t-shirts and hats. He called out the names of three of our players, Irwin, Sam, and Mark, who were considered the weakest players, though each had participated in every practice and attended every game. Mark and Sam quickly removed their shirts and hats and handed them to Mac. Irwin hesitated and then said to Mac, "No, I'm not going do it."

Mac replied in a sympathetic tone, "I know how you feel Irwin, but remember this is for the good of the team. You do want your team to win, don't you?"

We were all stunned by Irwin's act of defiance since he was usually soft spoken and the most cooperative guy on our team. "Yes sir, I do want our team to win, but these guys are not even members of our team. I am a team member and I should get to play."

It was apparent that Mac was losing patience with Irwin and was about to give him the full force of his intimidating style. At that point Harry spoke up and said that he agreed with Irwin. Mac, disregarding Harry's comment, made one more attempt at persuading Irwin to go along. Finally Harry declared, "Fuck it! I am out of here and you can take this hat and shove it up your asshole."

Mac knew as well as we that without Harry, chances of a victory over the Owls would be impossible, even with the ringers.

"OK, OK! If that's the way you punks want it, that's the way it will be, but you guys are dead meat and the Owls will kick your butts!" If that were not sufficient, he added that this would be our last ball game with the JIB.

It turned out Mac was right about two things: we would get our butts kicked, and it would be our last game in the JIB.

After the game we delivered a less than enthusiastic cheer for the victorious Owls. Mac said nothing more, but turned around and walked off the field. The rest of us stayed awhile, talking and reflecting upon our sorrowful performance. Irwin, of course, felt particularly bad, since he felt that he was the catalyst for our rebellion and defeat. But quite soon the mood changed as we began to acknowledge the virtues of our action. We had, after all, defied Mac and stayed together as a team. We had played by the rules and not broken the team bond. Within a short period of time, the mood swing was complete. We no longer felt like sorrowful losers but proud winners.

Several months later, the Detroit Times, in a front page story, noted that the State of Michigan's Office of the Attorney General had begun an investigation of allegations of a citywide gambling syndicate that was placing wagers on a youth athletic program funded by the state. Mac was indeed correct when he had said that we would never play another ball game with the JIB. The investigation ended with the indictment of both the offices of the mayor and the police commissioner for using the JIB as the avenue for a citywide gambling operation.

My father, of course, felt vindicated, and kept repeating, "*Goniffs, goniffs*! They are all *goniffs*!"

* * * * *

In 1940, I was twelve years old and graduated from Winterhalter Elementary School. Earlier that year we had moved from our house on Elmhurst to a two-story reddish brick house at 11739 Broadstreet. The move represented a first step up in my parents' pursuit of the American Dream. The house on Broadstreet was in a neighborhood called Russell Woods (why the Woods I never learned, since there were few trees and the area could hardly be classified as a suburb). There were, however, many single-family homes, including ours, which was much larger with more rooms than the place on Elmhurst.

In 1940, Pa took the courageous step of leaving his job as a sales clerk and opening his own retail operation in Hamtramck. The sign above the entrance read "Morris's Friendly Store." My father was counting on the continued loyalty of the many people who had been his customers at his former place of employment. He placed ads in the local newspaper and ran short announcements on the radio during the daily "Polish Hour" program. "Malia Morris" (Shorty Morris) was the central theme of these ads. Everyone in Hamtramck seemed to know "Malia Morris."

Pa had achieved a certain level of celebrity in Hamtramck in large part because of his charitable efforts in helping poor families and making contributions to local church schools. Pa also seemed to have astute ability in knowing which political candidates to favor and cultivate. The symbols of his accomplishments were openly displayed in his new shop. On a shelf of honor were a firefighter's hat with his name and the title "Honorary Chief," an official sheriff's badge, as well as one from the office of the coroner, plus a photo of Pa with members of the Hamtramck City Council and the mayor.

Next door to Morris's Friendly Store was a dimly lit tavern with a long bar and a small, dingy kitchen which could have only been approved by the Department of Health through some source of influential intervention. That source, it seems, was none other than my Pa, "Malia Morris." Whenever any of we boys worked in the store, Pa would tell us to take our meals at the tavern next door. "Go in and tell Wozie you are Morris's kids and he will take care of you," he'd say.

So at twelve years of age I thought life was pretty sweet when I could sit at a bar, sip a short beer, and enjoy a fat, greasy hamburger.

Pa also seemed to know most of the bus drivers who did the Caniff, Elmhurst, and Broadstreet route. After I had put in my Saturday hours at the store, Pa would accompany me across the street to the bus stop. When the bus stopped Pa would say something to the driver and I was welcomed aboard. A few blocks from my Broadstreet destination the driver would shout out, "Morris Junior! This is your stop!"

The DSR was my primary mode of transportation not only to Pa's store but also to my new school. Durfee was located within a complex of public schools: Roosevelt Elementary, Durfee, and Central High School. All three schools were located on La Salle, which fell between Dexter Avenue and Twelfth Street, an area that contained the largest Jewish population in Detroit. Central High School cancelled classes on the three holiest of the Jewish holidays.

School was about three miles from my home. Norman was at that time a senior at Durfee and rode the same bus, but he preferred that I sit in another part of the bus while he sat with his buddies. This was the typical Gottlieb brother pattern, with each of us subjecting the immediate younger brother to a form of exile. Bob did to Norm what Norm did to me, which I in turn did to Harold.

Everything about Durfee was bigger than Winterhalter. The classrooms were larger, as were the gym, the auditorium and the lunchroom. The kids also seemed to be bigger, especially those in the seventh and eighth grades. The grade status pecking order was more severe than that of Winterhalter with no mixing of the classes.

At age twelve I was, as my mother would say, "*gezunt.*" Though the direct translation was "healthy," Ma used "*gezunt*" whenever I complained that kids called me fat. "Not fat," she would say, "but *gezunt.* You are a growing boy."

My physical appearance only added to the discomfort I felt with my peers, especially girls. Unlike Norm, who was slim, smooth and confident, I was bulky, unsophisticated and socially reluctant. Norm moved about the school in style. He had lots of friends and girls adored him. There were many times late in the evening when the phone would ring and we all knew it was some girl calling Norm. Norm would race to the phone in order to get there before Pa. On those occasions when Pa grabbed the phone first, we would witness his typical greeting: "Who's there? Why are you calling in the middle of the night?" Silence at the other end of the line was, for my father, confirmation that some female was calling for Norman. "*Kurvah* (Whore)! You calling a boy, that's bad enough, but in the middle of the night! That's a *shondah* and *charpah* (a tragic and unforgivable sin)!" With that, Pa would slam down the phone and threaten to have the wires cut. Still, despite Pa's cursing and threats, the calls persisted, as did my envy and admiration.

It was at Fresh Air Camp that my envy of my brother Norman turned from jealousy into rage.

As kids, we all spent a portion of our summer vacation at Fresh Air Camp, a camp operated by the Jewish Welfare Board of Detroit, and located in Brighton, Michigan, about sixty miles from the city. To us it could have been several hundred miles away, since at that time Brighton was an undeveloped rural area. The mission of the Fresh Air Camp was to provide a wholesome, fun outdoor experience for Jewish kids from families with low to moderate incomes.

As in school, here in camp Norman was the fair-haired boy. He was popular with the counselors and the other campers. Although I was the better baseball player and swimmer, Norman possessed the superior social and leadership skills. He was a great schmoozer, charmer, and had a fine sense of humor. In physical appearance he resembled the current popular idol, Frank Sinatra. Many of the girls had crushes on him and every day there were anonymous notes of affection left at his cabin.

There was a girl named Lollie whom I really liked. She was short with dark, black hair, and wonderful white teeth. During evening programs I would move quickly to take the vacant seat next to her. I offered her my desserts and volunteered to be her swimming buddy.

It was the final week of our two-week stay at camp, and I felt I was making significant progress when I asked Lollie if I could walk her back to the dorm following the evening program. She said that would be fine, and we agreed to meet at the exit of the recreation hall.

I was there waiting eagerly when Norman appeared holding hands with Lollie and another girl. As they approached, laughing and talking, I faded away into the night, hurt and angry.

The next day it rained, so all activities were indoors. Our counselor suggested boxing matches between the boys from Cabin A and our group from Cabin B. We were provided with large, cushioned boxing gloves, and the counselors tried to match boys of the same height and weight.

I told my counselor that I wanted to fight my brother Norman. "Not a good idea," he said, "He is older, taller, and he's your brother." I said I didn't care and that Norman was the one I chose. Norman was also reluctant until several of his camp buddies began teasing andsuggesting that he was afraid of his kid brother. We put on the gloves and the first round began.

It was apparent that Norman was doing his best not to strike a direct blow. On the other hand, I was throwing punches as quick as I could in all directions. Norman managed to avoid my windmill-style punches. At the end of round one, Norman walked over to my corner and suggested that we end the fight.

"What's the matter? Afraid to fight your kid brother?" I yelled loud enough for all to hear. He turned and the bell rang for the second round.

Norman was no longer playing the defensive game. He moved quickly and aggressively, landing blows on my arms and directing punches to my stomach. I tried grabbing and holding on to him before the counselor would break us apart and Norman would come after me again. Finally, a blow got me square on the jaw. Immediately, tears came to my eyes, and I turned and went back to my corner. The fight was over.

The counselor said that good sportsmanship called for us to shake hands. I got up and walked to the center of the makeshift ring, and as Norman extended his hand, I punched him in the nose.

The immediate silence that followed was suddenly broken by a bombardment of nasty comments directed at me by the other campers. I was denounced as a poor sport, chicken-shit baby, and all around schmuck. To protect me from any further abuse, my counselor hustled me off to his staff quarters where I was reprimanded and told not to leave until dinnertime. I knew full well that what I had done was wrong and that Norman as well as the others would never forgive me or let me forget.

A little before dinner, the counselor returned with my brother. Norman came over to where I was sitting, put his arm around me, and said that he was sorry about what had happened. I said nothing at all as he led me from the room and we walked to the dining room. I was reluctant to go in, but Norm assured me that everything would be okay. We sat next to each other, and from that moment on neither Norman nor anyone else made any mention of the incident.

Whereas I was a good student and a good citizen at Winterhalter, I seemed to go off the deep end at Durfee. Within a very short period of time I found myself in the office of the school counselor, Colonel Dudley (retired United States Army).

Having been warned on numerous occasions that my behavior was disturbing the class, I paid no attention and continued with my antics as the class wise guy. During a quiet study period, Ms. Markin finally ran out of patience. She came to my desk and said that I should stand and come with her to the office. I responded that I would not go and she could not force me to go.

Her reaction, and that of my classmates, was one of disbelief and shock. No one in our class had ever spoken to a teacher in that tone or manner. Ms. Markin ordered me to gather my things and leave the room immediately. I grabbed my books and without another word walked toward the door. Ms. Markin was following close behind me. When I got to the door I leaned forward, hit the glass part of the door, shattering it with my books, and yelled, "My face, my face! You pushed me into the glass!"

Ms. Markin was startled and frightened. She quickly put her arm on my shoulder, began to apologize, and volunteered to take me to the nurse's office. I covered my face with my hands and did a great fake of sobbing. Ms. Markin hovered about me saying she was sorry, she did not mean to hurt me. She said she would go the restroom and get a damp towel to apply to my head.

As soon as she left, I lifted my head laughing. As I boasted how I had fooled her, she returned with the towel and quietly observed my performance. Without a word, she turned, walked away, and in a few moments returned with a male teacher who accompanied me to Colonel Dudley's office.

As I sat in his outer office and scanned through an old edition of the National Geographic, I could see Colonel Dudley in his office talking to another student. The door finally opened and out came Colonel Dudley with one very despondent boy. As he accompanied the student to the hall, Colonel Dudley reminded the boy that he wanted not one but both parents in his office the next morning. Colonel Dudley then returned to his office without any word or sign of acknowledgement

An hour passed and I was becoming increasingly bored as well as apprehensive. When the bell rang announcing the final class hour, Colonel Dudley called me into his office. With his large hands and steel gray eyes he was a most imposing and intimidating figure. "Well, Mr. Gottlieb," he said, "You are not off to a good start here at Durfee."

I started to say something about being sorry, that I had learned my lesson and would change my ways. But before I could complete a sentence Colonel Dudley interrupted and made it clear that I was not to speak until spoken to, and to address him as "sir." He commented that he had plenty of experiences with wise guys like me in the army as well as at Durfee; he knew all the stories and excuses and would not be conned by any smart-ass rookie. "If I see you here again, you are through. Is that clear, Mr. Gottlieb?"

"Yes, sir!" I answered, and was dismissed.

Whenever a Durfee student was sent to the office of a grade counselor, we were given a pink card that described our offense. Over the course of the next several weeks, I was given six pink cards to share with Colonel Dudley. The most serious, which led to a third visit to Durfee by my mother, was for leaving school between classes. This infraction was exacerbated by the fact that my exit was made through a window in my homeroom. My motivation for this hasty and unusual departure was my desire to buy a Good Humor ice cream from a vendor parked nearby.

Requesting my mother to visit the school on my behalf was always difficult for her as well as me. She did not drive and was therefore dependent upon public transportation or a ride from either Mrs. Goldberg or Mrs. Zalmanov. Rather than share with others her humiliation at having to come to my school because of my unacceptable behavior, she would travel by bus. For me, the pain came in having to sit and watch my mother cry as she was informed of my misdeeds, and later at home when she would cry even more and ask, "Why are you doing this to me?" The laying on of guilt would be accompanied by comments such as, "From Bob and Norman I never had such problems. Never bad word from the school. What is the matter with you?" followed again by, "Why are you doing this to me?"

It was difficult for my mother to share her problems with me or with my father. She reasoned that Pa already had enough on his mind, so why add another burden? On those rare occasions when Pa was informed of such incidents, he would become angry and shout, "Are you trying to kill Ma, to give her a heart attack?"

On this most recent call by Colonel Dudley, Ma was determined that this would be her final visit. We both sat waiting for the Colonel, who as usual kept us waiting well beyond the appointed time set for the meeting. When he finally invited us in, he made an effort at being funny by suggesting that since my mother was such a frequent visitor she might consider enrolling at Durfee. Ma did not respond except to ask what was it this time.

Colonel Dudley took from his desk drawer a stack of the pink cards and began to shuffle them as if he were preparing to deal a poker hand. "Each of these," he said to my mother, "represents an occasion when your son broke school rules, caused a disturbance, talked back to a teacher, or left school without permission."

This time Ma's response surprised both Colonel Dudley and me.

"Well," she said, "we have a saying—it comes from our holy book—that if a student fails, look to the teacher."

She went on to suggest that perhaps if the school did a better job of teaching, bright boys like her son would not have the time to cause problems. Ma was transforming me from bad guy to victim, and Colonel Dudley was irritated and baffled. He noted that my teachers had been very patient with me despite my repeated offenses and that all Durfee teachers were dedicated to their students. "We do our part and request only that students do their part."

Ma was not placated and persisted with her argument that it was a pity that teachers in the school were so busy sending children to the office that they did not have time to teach. Colonel Dudley had enough and responded that he had come to a point where he agreed with my mother. My mother smiled and winked at me, convinced that she had persuaded Colonel Dudley to recognize the shortcomings of his argument.

He continued, "Since we and you see that there is not a proper fit between our school and your wishes for David, it makes sense that he leave Durfee and attend a school better suited to accommodate his special talents."

Obviously this was not the message my mother sought or desired, but the case was closed. Colonel Dudley stood up and wished us both the very best and herded us out of the office.

At the principal's office, we were informed that two options were available to me: seek transfer to another school or be expelled. If I took the transfer route there would be no record of my poor behavior or suspension. If not, the paper trail of pink slips and expulsion would follow me wherever I went in the Detroit Public School System. We took the transfer route and began a serious look at alternatives.

In reality the options were limited, since there was only one other intermediate school located within our school district, and that was Tappan.

Tappan was at the opposite end of the scale from Durfee in two ways: first, it was geographically to the east while Durfee was to the west; and second, while Durfee had an almost all-Jewish enrollment, Tappan was virtually all gentiles.

While I knew from day one that adjustment to Tappan would not be easy, I had no idea of how difficult things could become. Despite my discipline problems, Durfee had been an accepting place where I had many friends. Tappan, on the other hand, was a cold and unwelcoming school. Determining my ethnicity and religion were the only topics that other students seemed to find of interest. My failure to respond directly to such inquiries was interpreted as acknowledgement of my being different than my school peers. The next question was usually more direct: "Are you a Jew?" The inquiries were usually followed by name calling, knocking my books from my desk, and poorly written, crude notes such as, "Hebes not wanted at Tappan!" or, "Go back to Jew-rusalem!"

Meanwhile, I was doing my very best, with some measure of success, at being a rule abiding and eager student. I am certain that Colonel Dudley would have been most surprised at my transformation from bum to scholar. My teachers were impressed with my class participation as well as my courteous behavior.

My performance, however, gained me no points with fellow students, and seemed to add fuel to the fire of their hostility. The subtle verbal comments turned to harsh epithets and anti-Semitic remarks that I had not heard before. The disguised shoves turned into flagrant knocks and punches. To avoid what I considered to be the most potentially dangerous of places, the lunchroom, I brought my lunch from home and ate in my homeroom. I did my best to time my bathroom visits so that I would not be caught there between classes. The boy's locker room was the setting for most of the verbal and physical abuse. I made efforts to avoid changing clothes when other guys were close by, since that would be the occasion for getting a close look at my circumcised penis. It was also the occasion for ridicule and attempts at humor. "What do you do with the piece you cut off? Eat it because it's kosher? If I had a prick as small as yours, I sure as hell wouldn't cut any of it off!"

It was in situations such as these that I never really knew how to react, since a smart-ass response would only exacerbate the situation. To remain silent, on the other hand, seemed only to encourage those who were standing on the sidelines enjoying the show. To go to a school authority and report these incidents would be considered a violation of the "no squealing" code, and would be met with quick and brutal retaliation.

Sometime in my fourth week at Tappan, I was grabbed by three guys as I arrived at the school entrance. "Its kike-bashing time! A new Jew holiday!" said one of my attackers as he knocked my books to the ground and began punching my head and body. A male teacher who had been standing nearby came running over and pulled me away. He asked what was going on and why we were fighting.

"We were just kidding around. No one got hurt," said the biggest of the three. The teacher then turned to me for my explanation. Not wanting to be a rat, I said, "Yeah, he's right. No harm done, fooling around." I doubt if the teacher believed me, but seeing little more that he could do he turned and walked away.

The notion that if I played the loyal good guy, it would somehow change my status from social pariah to buddy no doubt came from the many James Cagney "tough guy" movies I had seen. Among the Bowery Boys of the East River, not being a "dirty rat" was rewarded with forgiveness and acceptance.

However, at Tappan, life differed dramatically from art. The leader of the trio made clear that nothing was to be forgiven. "Next time we will get to finish the job. What you got today you will get everyday until you get your Hebe ass out of Tappan."

I did not share this episode with either my parents or my brothers but knew that I would never return to Tappan. Each day during the entire following week, I left the house giving every indication that I was planning on going to school. I spent much of time riding buses or walking around the city. On the fifth day of my absence, a school counselor called my mother to inquire as to my whereabouts.

When I returned home my mother was very upset and demanded an explanation. Before I could respond she began to cry, and in a trembling voice expressed her anger and frustration, "Why can't you be like your brothers? Why do you keep doing things that you know will make Pa and me sick? Do you want to be a bum? How many more schools do you think you can be thrown from?"

I felt I had no alternative but to tell Ma the truth. I shared with her some, but not all, of the harassment, abuse, pushing, and the incident with the three students. I told her that all of this was happening because I was a Jew in an all-*goyish* school.

Ma's reaction was one of disbelief. She was not so naïve as to think that anti-Semitism was non-existent in America; what amazed and shocked her was that such behavior could take place in an American school. "When you told the teachers, what did they do?" she asked.

I explained why I had chosen to say nothing and that doing otherwise would have only made matters worse. Ma was now furious with me. "What do you mean, you told no one? How can they help you if you say nothing? This is America and a boy who is hurt only because he is a Jew can ask for help. I will talk with Uncle Morrie and he will tell the school about what happened to you."

I pleaded with my mother not to get my Uncle Morrie, a lawyer, involved. No matter what an.ybody said, I wasn't going back.

Fortunately, Ma spoke with Uncle Morrie, who had an interesting solution that would allow me to enroll in an intermediate school outside of our district. By reporting my place of residence as the address of my mother's sister Mindel, I could attend Hutchins Intermediate, which bordered both Jewish and gentile neighborhoods. The school was some ten miles from my home and would require my leaving at 6:30 a.m. and not returning until 5:30 in the afternoon. The arrangements were made, and one week later I enrolled at my third middle school.

* * * * *

Hutchins was different from Durfee and certainly Tappan. Hutchins students were mainly from blue collar, working class families, and it seemed to me evenly divided between Jews and non-Jews, with a small number of black students. The Jewish population was confined to a smaller geographical area than Durfee, where the population was more dispersed. Hutchins was surrounded by a Jewish ghetto where there were numerous kosher butcher shops, bakeries, delicatessens, and synagogues—a modern version of the Russian *shtetel.* The major commercial artery defining this area of Detroit was Twelfth Street.

When the first Jewish immigrants came to Detroit, they settled primarily on the east side of the city near avenues such as Hastings and Gratiot. As was the case in many other urban areas, the Jewish community was highly mobile; relocations were not unusual. For the Jews of Detroit, the move was westward from Hastings to Twelfth Street, then to Dexter Avenue, next to Livernois, and eventually to suburbs miles and miles distant from the neighborhoods of early immigrants.

Twelfth Street was proof that Jews were not a monolith and not necessarily cut of a common cloth. The area was rich in diversity in both political and religious ideologies. The demographics included people of all ages, occupations, and educational levels, and greenhorns as well as those who were born in America.

For me, there were two historical landmarks that best defined my generation of Jews born in America from those young Jews who arrived with their immigrant parents. Both of these places were restaurants located on Twelfth Street. The older of the two was the Cream of Michigan on the corner of Pingree and Twelfth. The other was Boesky's Delicatessen, which was on the corner of Gladstone and Twelfth Street. Jewish restaurants have always played an important part in the absorption and integration of Jews into mainstream American culture. In addition to nourishment for the body, they also provided a safe, comforting haven. Familiar foods and aromas were mixed with familiar faces and language. These were settings for reconnecting and obtaining news from the old country.

The Cream of Michigan was different from Boesky's for one very important reason: while the Cream was the central hub for those Jews struggling to become shareholders in the American Dream, Boesky's was where your presence meant that you were now living the American Dream. There was nothing fancy about the Cream of Michigan, with its functional furniture and no tablecloths. Only Yiddish or Russian were spoken by its regulars. It was an eastern European, non-*Yekeh* (a less than flattering term which Eastern European Jews used when referring to German Jews) establishment built for the common folk. Boesky's was much more upscale, with classy menus, uniform-attired staff, mixed drinks, and pink tablecloths. The common language at Boeskys's was English, with the exception of an occasional Yiddish-speaking senior. Boesky's catered to professionals, owners of mid-sized to large business, and their families. Boesky's was where I would frequently meet my most affluent friends.

The Cream of Michigan was well known for another reason, for it was there that one of Detroit's most infamous Jewish gangs, the Purple Gang, frequently gathered. Folklore was that they were given the name "The Purple Gang" by a disgruntled butcher who said that the members were purple like the color of rotten meat. The original founding members of the gang were the sons of Russian immigrants, the children of those who came to America thinking the streets were "paved with gold." What they found instead was heartbreaking poverty.

Led by the Bernstein brothers—Abe, Joe, Raymond and Izzy—the gang relied on the intimidation of new immigrants as their source for money and gratification. At a very young age they began beating up on other kids and stealing their money, until their violence escalated to the point where small business owners were victimized. With the onset of Prohibition, the Purple Gang switched from shakedowns to armed robbery, extortion and hijacking. Detroit's convenient location, directly across the river from Canada, gave them a strategic advantage over any party landing liquor along the Detroit waterfront. The usual procedure of the gang was to take over a shipment of liquor before executing the drivers and their guards.

During the late 1920's, the Purple Gang was the unchallenged leader of Detroit's underworld, holding the monopoly on gambling, liquor and drugs, as well as the local wire service which provided bookies with all of the data they required. For years the Purple Gang managed to avoid arrest and prosecution by hiring middlemen to handle the dirty work. Emulating the dress style of the most celebrated mobsters—Meyer Lansky, Joe Adonis, Bugs Moran and Al Capone—the Bernstein brothers kept well above the fray.

The brothers continued to frequent the Cream until a poorly organized and implemented gang killing led to internal discord and confusion. In 1933, the police sweep was completed and the majority of gang members were in prison or dead. The Cream of Michigan stayed in business until the early 1950's, by which time most Jews had moved further west. Boesky's held out for a while longer until finally joining the movement westward.

My going to Hutchins was made easier, I believe, by the fact that I would be returning to a location so rich in Jewish history and tradition.

I was determined that Hutchins would not be just another stopping place on the road to high school. I would not screw up what could be my last opportunity.

Hutchins was one of the older school buildings in Detroit, lacking a swimming pool, a well-stocked library, science equipment, or even a decent gym. However, what it might have lacked in amenities was more than compensated for by dedicated teachers and a student body interested in learning. In a short time I no longer felt like a newcomer or an outsider. I had quickly made friends with three classmates—Morty, Ralph, and Sammy. In addition, I was smitten by a lovely blonde Jewish girl named Flo. I would have felt great about my new prospects, except for one long shadow following me.

Prior to coming to Hutchins, I became involved with two older guys, Irving and Marty. I misinterpreted exploitation for acceptance and became a lookout in several purse snatchings and thefts from local shops. The thought of being apprehended was always there but was overpowered by the camaraderie and excitement.

As my new friends and related activities at Hutchins became a bigger and more satisfying part of my life, I wanted to end my relationship with my partners in crime, so I stopped showing up at places where I knew Irving and Marty hung out. I also made it a point of staying around my neighborhood and not wandering too far from home.

One evening, my mother answered the phone and said that I had a call. It was Irving, who had never before called me at home. He said that he and Marty were planning a few things in which they needed my help. I was clearly upset that he had dared to call my home and not certain as to how to respond to his request. I pointed out that between my schoolwork and bar mitzvah preparation, I really did not have the time to meet with them.

Irv's response was short and to the point: "Find the time." He added that he and Marty would look for me at the Leslie Bowling Alley on Thursday at 7:30 p.m. and slammed down the phone.

I had two days before the meeting. I was frightened and confronted with two unappealing and unacceptable options. I would be the loser no matter which choice I made.

The next morning in homeroom, Mrs. Boschan was talking about upcoming student council elections. She asked which of us wanted to be candidates for eighth grade council positions. I was only paying partial attention, being concerned with matters much more important to me than student elections. Mrs. Boschan looked over at me and said, "David, I think you would make a very good candidate and be a fine representative for this class." When I didn't respond, she repeated her comment. "No, I don't think so," was all I said in response.

The bell rang, and I was leaving the classroom when Mrs. Boschan called me over to her desk. She said that she could tell that something was bothering me since I was always eager to take charge of things and this was such a wonderful opportunity. I answered that I just did not have the time given my school work and daily after school bar mitzvah obligations.

As she reached out and touched my shoulder, I was finally unable to contain my distress and I blurted out, "Besides, I may not even be around after this Thursday!" Mrs. Boschan was taken aback by my outburst and immediately sought further explanation. She encouraged me to share what was on my mind. The warmth of her hand and the sincerity in her voice were all that I needed to pour out my story of crime and possible punishment. I shared all of the details, as well as my participation in the role of lookout. I was an accomplice and anxious about being apprehended by the police, or being knocked about by Irv and Marty, or both. Mrs. Boschan was an excellent listener as well as a sympathetic confidant.

It also turned out that she was in a strong position to provide a possible solution to both my problems. Her older brother, Eric,was a senior detective with the homicide section of the Detroit Police Department. She asked me to accompany her to the teacher's lounge where she would make a call to him. I had mixed feelings, since involving the police could lead to my arrest and possibly a permanent police record. She assured me that Eric would know just how to handle the situation.

Once in the lounge she called and explained to her brother all of the details that I had shared with her. She handed me the phone and said that Eric wanted to ask me a few questions. With more than a little apprehension, I took the phone and said "hello." Eric's voice was firm and authoritative. He asked my age as well as the ages of Irv and Marty. He wanted to know how many of these theft incidents I was in, what role I played, and did any of us ever carry a weapon. I answered all of his questions and added that in no case was any victim ever threatened with a gun or any other weapon. He asked me where and when I was supposed to meet Irv and Marty. I shared that information with him as well. He said that he would help me this time but that if I ever got into any further trouble, he would see to it that I was sent up to Jackson, a major prison facility nearby. I assured him that from here on in there would be no further problems.

He told me to meet him outside the Leslie Bowling Alley at 7:00 p.m. He would be just around the corner of the entrance in a police car accompanied by a uniformed police officer. I asked what would happen. "You just be there and we will take it from there," he said.

For the next several days I carried on an internal debate with myself as to whether or not I had done the right thing. On the day of the designated meeting, Mrs. Boschan took me aside and assured me that her brother was to be trusted and that I would soon have this terrible burden lifted from my back.

I arrived at the meeting place fifteen minutes early and waited. The police car pulled up to the curb at exactly 7:00 p.m. The back door opened and I was told to get in. Eric introduced me to the other officer and explained the plan. At 7:30 I would enter the Alley to meet Irv and Marty. Once the three of us were together, Eric and his partner would take over. I got out of the patrol car and walked toward the entrance, with the officers some fifty feet behind me. Upon entering I went directly to the pool parlor where I found Irv and Marty waiting. I walked up to them, and Irv said that he was sure I would show.

At that moment, Eric and the uniformed officer arrived and came directly over to us. The three of us were ordered to raise our arms and spread our legs and we were searched for any hidden weapons. It took only a few moments to clear the pool hall.

Eric took over on the talk side while the officer stood by with his hand on his holster. He said that the police had the three of us under surveillance for the past several weeks. We were all suspects in at least five cases of purse theft and shoplifting. In addition, Irv and Marty could be arrested for involving a minor in the commitment of crimes. The only thing saving their sorry butts was the fact that they were under the age of eighteen. He told them he was going to take them down to the police station for finger printing and photos, but he was letting me go this time because of my age. He also said that he had one final warning for Irv and Marty, and that was that if they ever tried to get in touch with me again, harm, or threaten me in any way, they would spend the next fifteen years in Jackson. He asked if he had made himself perfectly clear, and both Irv and Marty replied, "Yes, sir." I stood by as the officer placed handcuffs on Irv and Marty and led them to the patrol car.

It was some weeks afterward before I could begin to relax and really believe that I had escaped from my captors with my body intact and my record clean. I do not know whatever happened to Marty, but I know that Irv was later arrested for breaking and entering, this time carrying a gun, and was given a ten-year sentence to Jackson State Prison.

The next two years at Hutchins went fast and well. Though I chose not to run for a student council office, I accepted the job of campaign manager for my buddy Eugene Gentry. In part my motivation was that in that role, I could select classmates to work with me in the election-campaign.

My first choice was Flo. Flo was very attractive and very popular. I also figured that with her allegiance and appeal, Gentry would certainly gain the majority of the male votes. Furthermore, and more importantly to me, I would have the opportunity to spend some quality time with Flo. In addition to her good looks, Flo was a very smart young lady.

Each candidate was given forty-five minutes at a student assembly to make a case for their election. The traditional routine was a quick fight song, endorsements by several students, another song and a plea by the candidate. Flo had a better idea. She argued that we needed to come up with a new format, something with more appeal and excitement. Her suggestion was that we select eight or ten of the sexiest girls from the eighth grade and have them do a Radio City Hall Rockettes number, complete with skimpy costumes, high kicking legs, background music, and lyrics. This would be the opening act, followed by one pro-Gentry talk and then another musical segment. For the second number, she proposed an all-male cast performing a striptease-like routine.

I had good reason not to disagree with Flo. For one, I thought her ideas were dynamite, and also I would do nothing that might endanger the possibility of a long-term relationship.

I did however, have some concerns as to whether or not our departure from the norm would cause problems with the authorities, but I quickly concluded that, given the perceived rewards, it was worth the risk. To assure our chances of pulling off the plan, it was agreed that all our rehearsals would be held outside of school and that all involved would maintain confidentiality.

Flo and I then went about the business of recruiting dancers, musicians and production support staff. We had only one problem in selling the concept, and that, of all things, was with the guy for whom we were knocking ourselves out. Eugene Gentry had all the characteristics and attributes that could make him a successful candidate. What he lacked was a sense of humor and an appreciation for the unknown. Eugene was also a very devout Baptist and seriously questioned the morality of what we wanted to do. I did my best to reassure Gene that whatever we were going to do would be in good taste—no profanity, no sexual innuendoes, and nothing that would be in violation of school policies. Gene was not persuaded until Flo took over the negotiations.

Flo had determined that the big hurdle for Gene was not the fear of school authorities, but the fear of God. "Gene," she said, "I too am a very religions person, just like you. My religion is different than yours, but I do believe and I live by the Ten Commandments." She went on to share with Gene how the tablets were handed down to Moses on Mt. Sinai and how God had spoken to Moses. She also pointed out that all this took place long before Christianity came upon the scene. She added that there was nothing in those holy words that would be violated by anything we planned.

Before he could say another word, Flo quickly added that the girls would wear nothing less than bathing suits, while the boys would only strip down to gym shorts. Then came her closer and clincher: "Gene, by being president of the student body you could be a model for other students and a leader in keeping all of us on God's track."

No more needed to be said. Eugene Gentry was fully on board.

We held our rehearsals in a local Boys and Girls Club. We had no difficulty at all in gaining the support of student participants. In short order, however, it was apparent that the agreed upon code of silence had been lifted and the word was on the streets as well as in the hallways.

Once again, Mrs. Boschan came to the rescue. At her request I shared all of our plans with her, including the chorus lines, lyrics, and music. She was most complimentary and saw no reason for concern. She volunteered to share information about our production with the principal so that there would be no surprises. Later, she came to our rehearsal place and expressed her support of our efforts. She even congratulated us for our initiative and creativity.

Election Day came and it was time for our presentation. The auditorium was filled with students, teachers, and administrators. Lots had been drawn for the order in which classes would present; we drew the last slot.

The seventh and ninth grade productions were brief and wordy, with little if any entertainment value. Our time finally came. The curtain opened, and there was dazzling Flo in a glittering dance costume, high heel shoes, and fishnet stockings. As she raised her hands, the music began and, in perfect formation, ten of Hutchins Intermediate's most lovely young ladies began their routine. All were dressed in a fashion similar to Flo, with the exception that their costumes were silver and Flo was in gold. The dance number continued with high kicks, turns, twists, and lots of smiles. While the girls danced they sang a song which I had composed:

> Put your entry in for Gentry, right away!
> Hurry up, oh hurry up and don't delay!
> Such a guy you never knew
> and with such a guy you'll never feel blue!"

The words were less impressive and far less important than the high stepping dancers.

Their finale was met with wild enthusiasm and a standing ovation from students as well as teachers. I stepped onto the stage to say a few words on behalf of Gene, but was drowned out by the response from the male portion of the audience, who were all shouting, "Flo, Flo, Flo, Flo!"

I answered that there would be more Flo later but it was time for the Twelfth Street Boys. A high spirited musical introduction was followed by the entrance of ten of the eighth grades' finest boys dressed in black trousers, floral beach shirts, white scarves, low cut white sneakers, and skimmer hats. As the music played they began the disrobing act with first the hats, followed by the scarves, and then the shoes, one by one. With each piece of attire they would pause, wave it over their heads, and then throw it out into the audience. With each tossed item, the audience responded with increasingly louder shouts of "Take it off! Take it all off!"

Finally came the shirts and then, after prolonged audience encouragement, the unbuttoning of the trousers. After slowly steeping out of the trousers, the boys flung them with a dramatic flourish into the grabbing hands of the audience. The audience went wild with applause as the boys stood there in gym shorts. At that moment the dancing girls returned to the stage for the finale and unfurled a banner with the words, "VOTE FOR GENTRY AND GET MORE OF THE SAME!"

It was clear that, given the mood of the audience, it would be anti-climatic for Gene to attempt to make a speech of any kind. Instead I brought him from the left wing to center stage where he took more than a few sweeping bows before departing. Finally, we brought Mrs. Boschan onto the stage and presented her with a dozen red roses. The show had been an immense success, and Eugene Gentry won the presidency in a landslide.

Chapter 3

Life at Hutchins was good and I was not anxious to move up and on. Other than school, my activities included studying for my bar mitzvah, which meant being in Yiddish School each weekday afternoon at 6:00 p.m. My studies included the reading of the Tanach, a Yiddish translation of the Old Testament, and the writing of a speech to be delivered in Yiddish. Of all my Jewish friends I was the only one who was not attending a Hebrew School and studying with a rabbi.

The traditional bar mitzvah was held in a synagogue, with only Hebrew reading and prayers officiated by the rabbi, the president of the shul, and select elders. All in all, it was a highly structured, solemn and formal ceremony, with the fun and joy coming with the party that followed services.

The Yiddish bar mitzvah, as designed and produced by the teachers of The Shalom Alechim Folk Shul, was different in content, style, and mood. Far from solemn, the event itself was a time for joy, song, and celebration. It was not in any way a religious service, neither were we expected to wear skullcaps or a prayer shawl. There was no rabbi, no cantor, no congregational president or elders, and no separation of the sexes in seating arrangements.

The end goals were the same however, in that this ritual was to confirm the coming of age of the Jewish son. For my peers who had gone the traditional route, it meant that they would now be viewed as men and as religious Jews. For those few of us who pursued the Yiddish school course, bar mitzvah also meant that we were men, but more importantly, it was also our admittance into an ethnic culture. My peers were now men in the eyes of God, and I was a man in the eyes of our people, both past and present. Still, no matter the course we had taken we all had in common the happy anticipation that comes with being the recipients of the many yet to be opened bar mitzvah gifts.

In the days following my bar mitzvah I do not recall feeling any more or less like a man. For Ma and Pa, however, my having been bar mitzvahed was considered the end of childhood and the start of responsible adulthood.

"Now, you have no more excuses for your *mashigas* (craziness)," my mother would remind me. Pa, as usual, said very little with the exception of words to the effect that it was time I stop making both my folks crazy.

Another interest for me at the time was an organization called Habonim (Hebrew for the "Builders"). Habonim was a Zionist youth organization whose mission was to recruit young people in support of Palestine, which later became the State of Israel. The short-term goal was to educate and indoctrinate; the long-term goal was to encourage older youth to migrate and become settlers on Jewish collectives in Palestine. The major attraction for me was that Flo was a member, as was Gerry, another girl whom I found appealing.

The organization had rented a storefront facility where most activities were held. Habonim was a secular organization, free of all religious prohibitions. Its political posture was Socialistic with a strong commitment to labor and the idea that Jews could be farmers and pioneers as well as doctors and lawyers. The major weekly activity was an *Oneg Shabbat*, a Friday evening program celebrating the arrival of the Sabbath. All members were encouraged to wear white shirts or blouses with dark skirts or trousers. We learned Hebrew songs and dances and often listened to talks about the founding of Palestine and the struggle to build a Jewish state. I was usually indifferent to the intellectual portions of the evening, but enjoyed the singing and dancing. I realized that this was the first time in a long time that I had felt comfortable and confident with my peers. That sense of ease no doubt was enhanced by the fact that my closest buddies from school were also my closest *chaverim* (Hebrew for friends).

The appeal to Jewish youth of organizations like Habonim was in large measure due to the increasing awareness of the savage treatment of Jews in Europe. There was no longer any doubt of Hitler's commitment to the total destruction of European Jewry as increasing numbers of Jews were being deported to concentration camps. No worldwide or even regional force was willing to step forward as advocates or protectors. The United States did not shout out the words, "Give us your hungry and your poor!"

The one exception was the Jewish government of Palestine, which had few resources and minimal political clout. Young American Jews could at least feel some degree of identity and sympathy by learning more about the plight of our people and raising money for their cause.

* * * * *

My bar mitzvah was held in June of 1941. Six months later on December 7, a Sunday morning, the Japanese bombed Pearl Harbor. I was soon on the streets hawking my quota of the Detroit Free Press and shouting, "Extra! Extra! Pearl Harbor Bombed!" The following day, President Roosevelt and the United States Congress declared war on Japan. On December 11, both Germany and Italy declared war on America, and within a few hours we were at war with Germany, Italy, and Japan.

On our first day of class, the morning after the bombing of Pearl Harbor, we were brought to the auditorium for a presentation by the school principal and a speaker from the CDC (Civilian Defense Corps). The principal, Dr. Critelli, reviewed the events of the past Sunday when Japanese air and naval forces bombed Pearl Harbor. He pointed out that there was much loss of life, property, and military equipment. He went on to say that he knew of a Hutchins graduate who was serving in Pearl Harbor and prayed that he was safe.

He added that our lives would now be different, and we would all have to make sacrifices for the good of our country. "You are now the civilian force that will be needed as more and more of your older brothers and relatives are called into military service." He went on to say that every person in our country would now be required to become a part of the war effort. Then he introduced another speaker who told us that we must be prepared to defend ourselves in case of an enemy attack. In order to be prepared, all of us were expected to participate in air raid drills—both in school and at home. Civilian defense leaders would be designated for each neighborhood, and those who failed to cooperate could be sent to a federal prison.

Then the auditorium lights were dimmed and we were shown a training movie produced in England. The movie's focus was upon students from schools in London and how they responded to air raids. We were shown kids putting on gas masks and moving quickly to air raid shelters. We saw scenes of huge black balloons hovering over the city and heard the constant cracking of anti-aircraft guns and falling bombs. Our speaker left no doubt that what was happening in London could happen in Detroit as well.

The program that morning brought the realities of war to many of us for the first time. It did not highlight brave soldiers and fighting Marines. This was much more about kids like us and a war in our own neighborhoods. We were plenty scared and could not disguise our doubts and fears.

The realities of the war became more personal when my Uncle Abe, who had boarded with us for several years, registered for the draft and several months later was called into the Army. Like many of our neighbors, my mother hung a little white flag with red borders and a bright blue star in our window so that it could be seen by all who passed by our house.

Uncle Abe was hardly the ideal, poster boy candidate for the U.S. Army. He was middle-aged, heavy, stoop-shouldered, with a smoker's hacking cough. How and why he was ever classified as IA-combat ready we would never know. Uncle Abe left his civilian job selling ties to retail outlets and headed to Camp Custer for his basic training.

Two of my buddies, Ralph and Morty, had older brothers who were in the Marine Corps. Morty's brother Al was a career Master Sergeant serving with the First Marine Division stationed at Camp Pendelton, California. Morty had pictures of Al in his dress uniform and others that showed him with fellow Marines in combat dress. We all were fascinated with stories about Al and caught up with the war culture that presented soldiers and sailors as courageous heroes defending us from the "Japs" and the "Krauts."

Many movies of the time portrayed young men bidding goodbye to loved ones and going off to war. In real life we experienced the rationing of gasoline, food and nylon stockings. Conservation was encouraged and everyone was expected to do their part by collecting tin foil and aluminum. Citizens' efforts to support the war effort included the buying of U.S. Savings Stamps and Bonds. The slogan "Lucky Strike Green Has Gone to War" reminded us that even tobacco companies were taking the war seriously by no longer using tin foil for packaging. Of the current popular war songs, my favorite was "Johnny Zero," the tale of young Johnny who got zeros on his school tests but went on to become a pilot and now the only zeroes he got were the Japanese planes called Zeroes.

Yet despite the constant reminders about battles in the Pacific or Europe, brothers going into the service, the curtailing of luxury goods, and routine air raid drills, little change occurred in how my friends and I spent our time. There was school as usual and our after school jobs. There were weekly meetings of the Habonim youth group, movies, and, of course, baseball. We could read and hear about the bombings of major cities in Europe, the death march at Corrigidor, the slaughter of thousands of civilians, children being separated from parents and young soldiers being killed. But these events were not part of our lives. In reality, we were well insulated and protected from harm.

I graduated from Hutchins and spent the summer of 1942 working as a junior counselor at the same camp I had attended in previous years. My employment was made possible because many of the older male counselors were no longer available, having been called to military service. I enjoyed the switch in status from camper to counselor and being able to do unto the happy campers what counselors had done unto me.

The irony of all this was that I would now benefit socially and sexually from a war that had drawn the more eligible and mature men away and hence elevating my male stature and appeal. The title of "junior" counselor was no hindrance at all, and I had the best of summers.

Because no one in my own family was in a combat zone (Uncle Abe was still stateside), I paid close attention to what was happening with Morty's brother Al, who had left Camp Pendelton and was shipping out of some West Coast port. Morty and I spent hours trying to figure out when he would be leaving and where he was going. We knew that Al was in the First Marine Division and that his military operational specialty was light armor. All of our map reading and investigative efforts, as well as our speculation, were kept in confidence. We never shared any of Al's letters with anyone else, as we both took seriously the oft-repeated reminders that "loose lips sink ships."

There had been much in the news about a possible invasion of islands in the Pacific, but no word of specific landing sites. In June of 1942, there was a major naval battle near the Midway Islands, where the Carrier U.S.S. Lexington was sunk and the Japanese lost four carriers. With that news, Morty and I speculated that the First Marine Division would be going to the Island of Tarawa.

We were wrong. On August 7, Al and his Marine platoon landed at Guadalcanal. At the time, the best and most graphic source of news was Movietone News of the Week, seen each Saturday matinee at the local Dexter Theater. For Morty and me, the feature attraction was not the movie; our main interest was before the movie, when we would see real life battle scenes narrated by Lowell Thomas. Saturday after Saturday we watched as the battle of Guadalcanal unfolded. The struggle for control of that small island went on for months. Thousands were killed before the question of which side would be victorious was decided in February of the following year, when the Japanese finally evacuated.

During those months, Morty and his family had no word from Al other than a phone call from a fellow Marine from Al's platoon who had been wounded and returned to a state side hospital. He called to say that he was passing on a message from Al that he was doing okay and that the family should not be worried. For a brief period after that call Morty was relieved, but when there was no word even after the Japanese evacuation, he began to worry again. I tried my best to reassure him by pointing out that Al was a professional Marine and that he would know how to handle himself no matter the circumstances.

Finally, Morty looked at me and said, "Gottlieb, if it was your brother who was there and you knew how many guys were killed and wounded, would you buy the same crap you're giving me?"

I told Morty he was right and I would not believe it either.

In early March of 1943, Al called from Pearl Harbor to say that he was at an R and R center and hoped to be home sometime in April. Morty called me and shared the good news and invited me over for a family celebration. Morty's father opened a bottle of bourbon and said that on this special occasion even the kids should have a drink. We joined Marty's parents, and later that evening, when his folks had retired, we had several more.

We were soon drunk and unaware of how much noise we were making until Morty's father came in and caught us sitting at the table, spinning the remains of the whiskey bottle and playing our own version of Russian Roulette, with booze instead of bullets. Because this was a celebration of joy, we were forgiven our sins.

In that same year, my brother Bob was drafted and entered the U.S. Army. He remained in the states for the duration of his military service. But my other good friend Sammy's brother was drafted into the infantry, and on July 9 of 1943, participated in the Allied invasion of Sicily. He was badly wounded, awarded a Purple Heart and a Medal of Honor, and sent home. One year later, he committed suicide while being treated at a Veterans Hospital in Michigan.

* * * * *

Two days before the invasion of Sicily, I was celebrating my fifteenth birthday at Camp Kinneret, a camp owned and operated by Habonim, the Zionist organization I had joined several years ago. Most every job at Kinneret, with the exception of camp director, nurse and cook, was filled by teenage members in exchange for scholarships. My job at Kinnert was a combination of kitchen and maintenance assistant, two specialties for which I had neither experience nor skill. In addition to our assigned work, we were expected to participate in all camp activities and to adhere to all camp rules.

Camp Kinneret was a regional facility, which drew campers from Ohio, Illinois, andIndiana. The dailyactivities were much like you would find in any summer camp, with the exception of a strong emphasis on Jewish history and culture, Zionism, Hebrew, and Palestine.

One day we had a special visitor to our camp: Golda Meir, who was visiting the United States at the time and was in negotiations with the British mandatory government. She was also the head of the political department of the Jewish Agency in Jerusalem. There was great excitement, since Golda had grown up in Milwaukee and was being compared to FDR's wife Eleanor, "The Jewish Eleanor."

I was in the kitchen helping with the preparation of the dinner that was being held in honor of Golda. This was indeed a special event, as all tables were covered with white tablecloths, rented silver, and glassware as well as fresh floral arrangements. My job was kneading the meat and egg yolks for the meatloaf that would be served to more than a hundred people. My hands and arms were deeply immersed in a huge cauldron of ground beef and oozing sticky egg yolks when the doors swung open and Golda strode into the kitchen followed by an entourage of about a dozen people. She greeted each person with a handshake and "Shalom." As she approached me, she stopped and held out her hand.

I hesitated and explained that my hands were messy and it was best that she not touch them. "Nonsense," she answered, "Never hesitate to shake the hands of people with dirty hands if it is the result of honest labor."

With that she took my hand in hers, put her other hand on my back and asked my name and where I was from. I said my name was Dovid and that I came from Detroit. She was curious about the other ingredients in my meatloaf. Before I could respond, she volunteered that when she made meatloaf, she always included hard-boiled eggs, and wondered if we did the same. I glanced over to our kitchen director for some direction but she offered no help whatsoever. I answered, "Of course, with hard boiled eggs! That's the way we do it here."

Golda once again put her hand on my back and said she hoped that someday she would see me in Palestine, and with that went on to talk with others.

We promptly cooked a dozen hard-boiled eggs and included them in the many mounds of "Golda Meir" meatloaf.

After dinner there was much singing and dancing. Golda joined in with us as we made a large circle and danced the Hora. After she left a group of us sat around a table, quietly discussing what our lives would be like in Palestine.

* * * * *

By summer's end I had switched my affections from Flo to Gerry, who was a more serious student and very much committed to living her life in Palestine. In the fall we were both back at Central High School, where I would be with most of my closest friends—that is, my Jewish friends, as Central had a predominately Jewish enrollment.

Though the war was far removed from my daily activities, I could not escape the news that things were not going well for our side. Each morning in our study hall session we listened to radio broadcast reports from the BBC, followed by a class discussion.

Although I was far from being a dedicated, serious student, I was generally staying out of trouble and showing responsibility in completing all my study assignments. At the same time, I missed the excitement and popularity I had enjoyed at Hutchins. Central was a much bigger place with hundreds of students and numerous activities. I was now a much smaller fish in a much larger pond.

But by the end of the fall term I was once again in the kind of trouble that would certainly gain the attention of my teachers and peers.

After school I had a job at George V, a neighborhood drug store where I was a soda jerk, delivered prescriptions, and swept the floor at closing. One night while cleaning up, I noticed a red and white box with the word "Trojans." I opened the box and pocketed a half dozen packages of condoms.

The next day I took the condoms to school to share with my buddies Ralph and Morty. Ralph suggested we fill one with water and drop it from the window of the science room. "Great idea!" I said. "Let's also fill another and leave it on Mrs. Corder's desk. When she walks in and sees it, she'll go crazy!"

Ralph made it clear that he was willing to go for the window drop, but the desk was out of his realm of interest. That was all of the push I needed to go ahead with what I considered a far bolder and certainly more attention-getting act.

During the change of class period, I filled the condom with water and returned to the empty room where I placed it on Corder's desk. I made a quick exit just as the bell rang, then filed back into the room along with my other classmates. I watched eagerly as Mrs. Corder walked in and laid her books on the desk. The blood crept slowly up her neck as she noticed the condom. She closed the door and addressed the class. "I will say nothing other than to demand that whoever placed this on my desk must retrieve it immediately."

Of course, no one moved.

"Fine," said Mrs. Corder, "Then I will send for Dr. Drachler and request that he deal with this disgusting matter!"

The calling of the principal was not what I had anticipated, and I could see that escalation to a higher order would not be particularly helpful. I raised my hand and declared that calling Dr. Drachler would not be necessary since I was the one who had placed the condom on her desk.

"Well, Mr. Gottlieb," said Mrs. Corder, "You may now come forward, remove this from my desk, and take it with you to Dr. Drachler's office!"

"What about honesty being the best policy?" I desperately asked.

Her answer was short and to the point: "Obviously not in all cases, Mr. Gottlieb."

I carried the condom to Dr. Drachler's office and embarrassingly explained to his secretary that I was sent by Mrs. Corder to see the principal. She knocked on his door, entered, returned shortly and invited me to enter.

Dr. Drachler was short with dark hair and a small moustache. He spoke very quietly as he asked me to be seated and then asked my name. When I said, "David Gottlieb," it was clear from his expression that he was familiar with the name. "Are you related to Norman?" he asked.

"Yes," I grudgingly answered.

"Well," he said, "You must be the Gottlieb apple that fell far from the tree."

His observation really annoyed me, but I was determined not to let the situation get further out of hand. He went on to point out that he understood it was neither easy nor pleasant when you are constantly being compared with an older brother or sister. He even surprised me a little by saying that he was willing to let this incident go if I agreed to write a note of apology to Mrs. Corder.

I quickly agreed and stood to leave the room.

"Just one more thing, David," said Dr. Drachler, "If there are any future incidents, I will not be so forgiving."

I thanked him and hurried out of his office.

Though I was grateful and relieved for the reprieve I had been granted, I was not convinced that I could not talk my way out of future problematic situations. A test of my manipulative and persuasive skills was soon to come.

Meanwhile, I continued with my after school job at George V, spending most of my free time at meetings and social gatherings of Habonim. Gerry was well aware that I was having increasing disciplinary problems at Central and did her best to alter my behavior. Her approach was not unlike that of my mother: laying on the Jewish guilt. The difference was that my mother would always use, "Why are you doing this to me and Pa?" while Gerry would use the plight of the entire Jewish people. "David," she would say, "this is a time when we must all do whatever we can to prepare ourselves for helping our people. Educated Jews will be needed in Palestine if we are ever to build a Jewish homeland. Those Jews will not come from Europe because so many have been killed. Help must come from America."

It was clear to me that Gerry was deserving of a boyfriend whose stability and dedication to the cause was far greater than was mine. Although I enjoyed the camaraderie—the singing, dancing, and comfort provided by being part of something noble—my attachment to Zionism and a Jewish homeland was marginal at best. I was certainly not prepared to kiss off the material benefits of capitalism for a life of hard labor and sacrifice.

I told Gerry I would try to mend my ways and strive to exemplify the ideas that she so well expressed, but I had the feeling that Gerry was not persuaded.

Two weeks later I was back in Dr. Drachler's office. This time the incident would not be classified as an adolescent prank, but rather a serious violation of school policy.

I had borrowed Marty's 1932 Model T Ford, which was painted in bright psychedelic colors, and was driving without a driver's license on a street that circled the high school. I stopped and offered rides to my friends as well as students I did not know. For a while I was having a great time circling the school with a full carload of students, only stopping to let them out and pick up another eager group. After five or six rounds, I began to find the routine rather monotonous, so to add a little excitement, I drove over the curb and down the front sidewalk that led right up to the main school entrance.

My door-to-door service soon began attracting an even larger and more enthusiastic following. However, Morty's car was not in the best condition, with very old tires on wooden wheels. It had been years since any wheel alignment, and even at a speed of 15 miles per hour the car would wobble from side to side. It wasn't long before the left rear wheel came off the car and rolled across the school lawn. The car, filled with passengers, tilted severely to the right and came to an abrupt halt. Fearing that the car would turn over, my passengers started to panic and struggled to abandon the automotive Titanic.

Within minutes, police officers were at the scene of the disaster and took statements from several students and me. Morty was called to the scene and confirmed that the car was not stolen. Unfortunately, Morty's insurance did not cover any other driver. When informed of the incident, Morty's father announced that the car would be sold.

Having documented all of my offenses, including reckless driving, reckless endangerment of others, driving without a license, and destruction of school property, I was escorted to Dr. Drachler's office. Though still calm and soft-spoken, Dr. Drachler was a very different man than the one I had found to be fair, patient, and sympathetic. "David," he said, "We have reached an *impasse*. This is a situation where only one of us can remain at Central High School. It is to be either you or me. What is your choice?"

I answered that my preference would be that we both remained. But he was not to be moved, and informed me that our both remaining was not an option. To leave no doubt that there was only one choice available to me, he said, "One of us will stay and one will remain, and I have no intention of leaving. Now, what is your decision?"

I answered that I would leave.

He shook his head in agreement, extended his hand for me to shake, wished me the best, and commented that he would be in touch with my parents.

So once again I was a man without a country, or at least a high school.

The only thing that I had going for me at this time was that I was fifteen years of age, so without any felony conviction I could not be banned from the school system. The same age restriction would force me to remain in school no matter my personal preference.

Dr. Drachler met with my mother and told her the complete, unabridged story. This time my mother did not even attempt to argue and suggested that perhaps not going to school, at least for a while, was perhaps the best alternative for me. Dr. Drachler informed my mother of the age related policies and that going to another high school was the only alternative, at least until age sixteen. He attempted to comfort my mother by saying that perhaps in the next few months some miracle would occur and I would change my ways. Ma looked to the heavens and replied, "From your mouth to God's ears!"

My next school stop would be Northern High School. Here, too, my tenure would be short lived, and not because of hostile schoolmates or disciplinary problems.

Enrolling at Northern High School meant once again using Aunt Mindel's home as my registered place of residence. Northern was located way out on the north side of Detroit and required my taking two buses and a streetcar from home to school. Like Hutchins, Northern was located in a neighborhood transitioning from a blue-collar white to black. The building was very old, with even fewer amenities than Hutchins.

In my assigned study hall I was one of three white students. Though not overtly friendly, my fellow classmates were neither unpleasant nor inquisitive. No one, neither the teachers nor the students, seemed to care why I was there. Over the course of several weeks I formed a few friendships that were pretty much limited to time together in the lunchroom and between class breaks, since my home was a great distance from my classmates' neighborhoods.

What I quickly learned I could not handle were the daily four hours spent getting to and from school, which required me to be at the first bus stop at 6:00 in the morning. I would leave school at 3:30 and usually not arrive home until 6:00 p.m. In short order, I got into the pattern of either being late or skipping school. On several occasions, my Aunt Mindel would receive a call from some school clerk inquiring as to my whereabouts or reporting my being tardy. Having been instructed by Uncle Morrie not to talk with any school personnel she would respond in Yiddish, "*Ich veis from gornicht* (I know from nothing)."

That summer I reached the age of sixteen and had no further desire to attend school. State law no longer bound me, so I informed my mother that I quit. Her reaction was a combination of anger and relief. She was, of course, upset that one of her boys would not finish high school, but she also no longer seemed to have the energy to fight. But both she and Pa made it clear that as long as I lived in their home, I could not be a "bum just hanging around the house." I would need to find full-time employment in order support myself.

Through a lead provided by Morty Tobin's father, I found my first full-time job. My job was to remove the wiring from burned out electric motors. When that foul task was completed I immersed the wire-free motor into a sink filled with a powerful cleansing compound. The work was tedious, dirty and painful. The old wires would cut into my hands and arms. The compound would burn my skin and cause my eyes to water. I began on a Monday and quit on a Friday, five days later.

My first full-time employment was followed by a series of other short-lived careers, from a well digger's assistant to a wall plasterer for a building contractor. I was also a counterman at Buddy's Bar-B-Q, whose only redeeming feature was a middle-aged waitress seeking sexual pleasures from young countermen. This was followed by my brief career as a "shoe dog" at Burt's Shoes, a retail chain catering to women with little money or fashion awareness.

It was clear I was without any sense of purpose or direction. While all my closest peers were doing what was expected of good Jewish boys, I was a dropout and an embarrassment to my parents. Everybody else appeared to be on course and pursuing some socially acceptable goal. My brother Norman was completing high school and planning on enlisting in the Navy. My brother Bob had been discharged from the service for medical reasons and was enrolled in college. Morty's brother Hal had shrapnel wounds in his leg and was back at Camp Pendelton for R and R.

The tide of the war had turned and Allied Forces were aggressively pursuing the enemy in both Europe and the Pacific. In June of 1944, Operation Overlord, or "D-Day," began with a combined Allied Force invading Europe. Later in the year the U.S. Airforce would bomb Tokyo.

The constant in my life was my friendship with Gerry and my participation in Habonim. But even those relationships were now different since I had quit school. In Gerry's eyes I was not only an academic failure, but I had also failed the cause of the Jewish people. I would not bring to the Jewish homeland the skills and knowledge she thought were sorely needed.

I pointed out to her that the only thing needed to be a successful *chalutz*, or pioneer, in Palestine was a strong back and a dedicated heart. "It's not as if we are going to be doctors or lawyers!" I argued. "We are going to raise chickens and cows, plough fields, and fight for our independence as a Jewish state. Where does that require scholarship or a college degree?" On and on we continued without any satisfactory resolution.

My relationships with my male friends had also changed, since my status as "dropout" placed me well outside the high school student culture. I found their interests to be superficial and a waste of time. Whenever I began to talk about Habonim and my interests, there was little comment from any of my former friends.

I knew I had to do something to escape feelings of distance and isolation from my peers and family. I was still too young to enlist, and the idea of going back to school, any school, was not an option I wished to pursue. The many odd jobs, though providing me with discretionary dollars, were far from fulfilling.

In early 1945, our Habonim group had an important visitor. His name was Aaron, and he had come to us from the national office in New York. Aaron was in his early twenties but had already lived in Palestine. He told us about a farm in Cream Ridge, New Jersey, which was a training site for members of Habonim who had made the decision to migrate to Palestine. With the war coming to an end, opportunities for "*aliyah*" (a Hebrew phrase for moving up to our homeland) were once again possible. The farm experience would be our first serious test in determining our readiness for *aliyah*.

Aaron described a working farm where each member would be exposed to the day-to-day demands and challenges of hard work and collective living. The farm was modeled on the division of labor and socialist ideology of the kibbutz. Hebrew would replace English as our language. Everyone would be given work assignments and gender differences would not be a factor in work placement. Men as well as women would share kitchen duties along with the other tasks required in maintaining a large agricultural enterprise.

Life at Cream Ridge would not be like life at home. Rules and requirements would be strictly enforced. This was not going to be like our summer camp experiences; this was no nonsense serious business.

Aaron made it clear that he was not on a recruiting mission and recognized that we were high school students not yet prepared for "*hachsharah*" (preparatory training). His goal was to provide information and answer questions.

For me, it was as if Aaron's visit had been preordained by some *deus ex machina*, providing me with the direction I so badly wanted and needed. *Hacsharah* was my way out of the wilderness. By taking this path I would elevate my personal status with my peers and convince my parents that I was not a lost soul. I would be the child pioneer and the first of my comrades to take the big step. I would actually walk the talk. While my friends continued to live their sheltered lives with no hardships more demanding than exam preparation, I would be on my own in a strange new place.

After the meeting I approached Aaron and informed him that I was ready to make the move to Cream Ridge. Aaron did not act surprised by my comment. He did, however, have some questions about my age and current school status. I answered that I would be seventeen in July and that I was no longer in school. Anticipating his next questions, I volunteered that I had been out of school for some months, had been on my own and working, and would have no difficulty in obtaining parental consent.

Aaron stopped me from continuing. "Whoa, whoa, slow down, *chaver*! I don't even know your name."

I explained that I had been in the movement for two years and had also worked one summer at Camp Kinneret. I added that I was accustomed to hard work and was determined to live and work in Palestine. Aaron answered that he wanted to talk with several of the more senior members of our Habonim group before we talked again.

That evening I informed my mother of my plans and told her she might be getting a call from Aaron. Her reaction was one of reluctant acceptance. "At least you will be in a place with Jewish people who will be able to watch over you. Better than what you are doing now."

Two days later, Aaron called my home and spoke with my mother. Ma gave the venture her blessings, and within several days all arrangements were completed. There were several farewell parties and a Sabbath program acknowledging my courage and dedication. Gerry wanted me to know how proud she was of me and also to assure me of her devotion and loyalty. She promised to write and planned to visit me in the summer.

Chapter 4

On April 12, 1945, the same day FDR died, I began my journey without a road map or any really serious thought about the consequences of my impulsive action. I was the perfect American adolescent, living for the moment and confident in my belief that no matter what challenges the future would bring, I would overcome them.

I was met at the Trenton station by David, a tall, heavyset man in his mid-forties, accompanied by Magda, a young woman in her mid-twenties, of medium height wearing a large straw hat. They greeted me warmly, inquired about my journey, and told me everyone was eager to meet me. They had just finished their twice-weekly task of delivering fresh eggs from the farm to Trenton customers. The delivery truck was a sorry looking red, 1936 Dodge Truck. The three of us squeezed into the front seat and began the 25-mile trip to my new home.

As we drove out of the city, David talked about himself and events that had brought him to Cream Ridge. He was from Los Angeles and had gone to school at UCLA where he earned both a bachelors and master degree in business administration. After graduation he pursued a career in the retail business. His intent was to stay in that line of work until retirement. When the war began, he attempted to enlist but was rejected for medical reasons. Meanwhile all of his friends were either enlisting or being drafted into the service. Because there was nothing in his physical appearance or manner that would indicate a handicap, he felt others viewed him as a social pariah. He took a job working on the assembly line of a plant producing military vehicles.

It was during this period of time that he "rediscovered his Jewishness" and came to the conclusion that what was happening to the Jews in Europe could happen to Jews in this country as well. This was his motivation for undertaking *hachshara* and moving to Palestine.

While David kept up a constant stream of chatter, Magda paid little attention, but propped her feet on the dashboard and read a paperback.

Once we arrived at the farm I gathered my possessions and followed Magda into the lobby of the main building. It was a large, two-story building with twenty-five sleeping rooms, a massive kitchen and dining room area plus a spacious, comfortably furnished living room.

Magda served as my guide and showed me to my room. Each permanent resident had a private room with a washbasin. Bathroom and shower facilities were shared. My room was modest in size, with a small bed, a three-drawer dresser, a desk with a chair, a reading lamp, and a worn leather lounge chair.

After I had deposited my duffel bag, I was escorted downstairs where I met some fellow resident members. We walked through the farmyard, making stops at the various chicken coops, the dairy barm, heavy equipment shed, egg candling and carton packing rooms before heading back to the main house.

I was informed that all members were expected to attend a brief meeting at 6:30 in the evening before dinner at 7:00. That left me with about one hour to unpack and prepare before the meeting.

Just as I began unpacking, there was a knock at my door. I opened the door and was greeted with warm embraces from two young and rather attractive twin sisters. Their names were Sarah and Rosie, and they, like David, were from Los Angeles. Both were very energetic and highly animated. One would start a sentence and the other would complete it. They asked lots of questions, but never really appeared interested in waiting for my response.

I was grateful for their greeting and offer to answer questions and help me adjust to my new surroundings. I thanked them both and said that I would look forward to seeing them at the meeting. Sarah said that since they lived next door to me they would come by and accompany me to the meeting. I thought no more of the matter and headed for the shower.

As promised, my two escorts arrived promptly at 6:25, and we walked downstairs to my first meeting with my *chaverim* (comrades).

It took only a moment for me to make three demographic observations about my new family: first, women outnumbered men by three to one; second, the women were much younger than the men; and third, I was by far the youngest person in the room. The meeting was called to order by a guy named Bernie, whom I later learned was serving as the Rosh or leader of the group.

Bernie took a few moments to call the meeting to order and introduce me as the group's newest member. Following his introduction everyone present broke out into the Hebrew song of greeting, "Shalom Alechim."

Other business was covered, including reports on egg and milk production and sales as well as reports on the status of the corn and tomato crops. Then work assignments for the coming week were announced. I learned that my first job would be assisting in the laundry room. I was disappointed, since I had imagined myself in the driver's seat of the Farmall tractor I had seen on my tour of the farm. If not that, then at least working in the fields or milking cows.

As we headed into dinner, I recalled Aaron's words about how all work was equal in value if not in excitement or challenge.

During dinner Bernie told me that in the kibbutz, new arrivals start out in either the kitchen or in the laundry room, and that with time and evidence of dedication my choices of work would be expanded. I also learned that an exception had been made in my acceptance for *hachshara*. Because the war had taken the most mature and fittest males out of the recruitment pool, special efforts were made to achieve gender parity. During the next several evenings I quickly learned how my age and the overall shortage of males would benefit me in other ways.

My female co-workers in the laundry shop assured me that they would help me learn the routine and spare me any undue work stress. With the exception of folding clean linens, towels and clothing, I had no other responsibilities. No washing, no hanging of laundry, and of course, no ironing. I was treated like a king. They insisted that I take extra rest breaks, and procured special snacks and drinks for me.

But the greatest and most unexpected gratification I received was from the twins Rosie and Sarah in the late hours of my third night on the farm.

I was in a deep sleep when I suddenly realized that another person was not only sharing my bed, but also licking my ear. As I pulled away and grabbed my pants beside the bed, an arm pulled me back. As my night visitor pleaded with me to be quiet, I realized that it was one of the twins, either Rosie or Sarah. I turned on the lamp, and Rosie said she was sorry that she had frightened me and wanted nothing more than to "cuddle."

We were soon engaged in more intimate and passionate activity. Rosie recognized that I was still a novice in the business of sexual performance, but was pleased with how quickly I responded to her direction. After several hours of making love, we fell asleep. When I awoke at dawn I was alone and wondering if I had just had a wonderful dream.

I greeted Rosie at breakfast but there was no mention of the events of the previous night. After dinner she asked if I wanted to go for a walk. Rosie took my hand as we walked down the road. She wanted me to know how happy she was that we had become such good friends. I responded that I also enjoyed our relationship and hoped we would continue to be friends.

Rosie assured me that we would and so would Sarah. I was puzzled by her reference to her sister until later that evening, when Sarah appeared in my room.

For the next several months, the twins and I shared daily laundry chores and nightly trysts between the sheets.

* * * * *

On May 7, Germany surrendered. The war in Europe was over and thousands of men and women were being discharged from the armed forces. Within a few months the number of fit, mature males coming to the training farm increased the male population to thirteen. In short order I was dumped, gently of course, by Rosie and Sarah and replaced by the veterans. It was time for me to move on.

My work attitude and motivation were improved by my new assignment to what I considered to be more prestigious and more masculine tasks. My first assignment took me to the dairy barn where I fed and milked the herd as well as shoveled manure and cleaned stable areas. There were about 60 cows, a mix of Holsteins and Jerseys. We used milking machines, which involved placing a suction cup on each of the cow's teats. This was not a simple task, since the cows seemed to find little pleasure in my cold fumbling fingers searching for the connection points. Hardly a milking period passed when I did not get knocked off my stool by either a fat, smelly leg or the wet, piss-soaked tail of a cow.

The entire herd was given Hebrew names reflecting some symbol or hero of Zionism and the struggle for a Jewish homeland. There were Avodah (work), Palmach (the pre-state of Israel Defense Force), Trumpeldor (a Jewish patriot), Havlagah (restraint), Shalom (peace), and many others—too many names for me to remember, so I began assigning my own preferences. My selections were based on the behavioral and personality traits of select herd members that I would associate with people whom I felt best fitted the cow's characteristics. In short time, the herd was completely renamed with names like Colonel Dudley, Gerry, Dr. Drachler, Pushkin, Frankie (Sinatra), Vincent (Van Gogh), Moishe (for my father), Zippah (for my mother), and of course, one cow for each of my three brothers.

Having completed my dairy tour I went to work with the poultry group. The farm had thousands of chicken coops and houses. The task of collecting, cleaning, candling, grading, and packaging eggs was boring but easy; the cleaning of the coops and houses was the most distasteful of all work. The notion that all labor is good and equally important loses its credibility when it comes to shoveling chicken shit in an airless building filled with powdery dust that covers your clothes and fills your nostrils. After a few weeks in the barn and the chicken houses, I requested and was granted outdoor work.

The farm sold its tomato crop to the Campbell Soup Company, whose manufacturing plant was located in New Brunswick. The best soil for growing tomatoes is a sandy loam. Good, perhaps, for the crop, but not for those who plant and harvest. It was, once again, an experience of backbreaking toil and suffocating dust.

In July, on my seventeenth birthday, I was presented with a cake and the opportunity to select the work assignment of my choice. Without any hesitation I said working with field equipment—tractors, hay bailers, silage loaders or mowers.

The next morning I reported to Mandy. Of any of us, Mandy was the most experienced in farming. He was born and grew up on an apple farm in upstate New York and was a graduate of Rutgers University College of

Agriculture. He was tall, tanned, well built, and married to Chanah, who was born in Palestine. Together, they were the poster people for the youthful Jewish pioneer couple.

My notion that I would quickly be on the seat of a large tractor was soon dispelled. First came hours of instruction on function and maintenance. Mandy made it clear that he was not about to turn over an expensive and essential piece of machinery to a kid cowboy. I was also expected to take a course at Rutgers on field machinery and various aspects of crop planting and rotation. This was a four-week course scheduled to begin the following Monday.

Four of us left the farm that Monday morning and drove to the New Brunswick campus where I found myself back in school for the first time since Northern High. As in the past, my completion of a milestone or the start of a new phase of my life would occur on a date that I would long remember for other than private reasons.

On August 14, 1945, the day the Japanese government agreed to the terms of an unconditional surrender, I received my first ever-academic credentials: a certificate of completion issued by the Rutgers University Program in Agricultural Extension. I was now certified to operate tractors as well as other agricultural implements and equipment.

Several days later, my knowledge and skills were put to their first test. My assignment was to prepare a seven-acre field for a winter corn crop. Very early that morning, I checked out the big red Farmall Model C tractor. I attached the two-bladed plow to the lift and headed for the field.

The basic and most challenging part of plowing is being certain that the first row is perfectly straight. If your first row is uneven or wobbly then all the following rows will be uneven and wobbly. The old adage of "as you sow so shall you reap" should be changed to "as you plow so shall you reap." At Rutgers they instructed us to identify a guide point, such as a tree, and as you plow keep your eye on that destination point. In concept those instructions seem simple enough, but in reality the task is far more complex. What if there is no visible end target? How do you keep the target constantly in sight when you are trying to maneuver a massive piece of machinery over a rut-filled field?

Those were the thoughts and questions running through my mind as I approached the field. It was then that I recognized Mandy's truck parked near the center of the field, which would be the starting point.

Mandy was there to express his confidence that I would do well and to offer his assistance in seeing to it that my first row would be on target. He suggested he take a position at the far end of the field that would be my destination point. My job would be to keep Mandy in sight and head directly towards him. With that, Mandy took off and I waited for him to reach his destination. Mandy positioned himself and waved a large red cloth, which was my signal to begin plowing. I inched the throttle forward and lowered the plow blades into the soft earth. I increased my speed and was amazed to see the steel blades cutting into the surface as they turned the soil just as had been shown in one of our instructional films.

I maintained an even speed as I moved closer and closer to Mandy. When Mandy was less than fifteen feet from me I prepared to make my turn, which required lifting the blades just at the right time and dropping them again to begin the return trip. As I made the turn, Mandy gave me a "thumbs up" and shouted for me to keep on going.

My first row had been perfect and had given me the start and confidence I needed. I continued with my plowing until noon. At that point I stopped to eat lunch. But first I wanted to look over the work that I had just completed. I walked along the side of the field and, sounding like a veteran farmer and plowing authority, I shouted out and continued repeating, "Good job, Gottlieb! Bitchin' piece of work!"

When I finished lunch I was back in the saddle again, determined to complete my assignment by dinnertime. I worked until dusk and still was not finished. I turned on the headlights and decided I would go until it was too dark to continue. I was so into the flow of the work, the sounds of the motor, and the turning of the soil that I lost track of time and was not aware of how dark it had become.

Suddenly, across the field, in the direction in which I was going, the darkness fell away and the field was covered with lights. As I drew closer, I could hear people shouting my name and cheering me on. As I prepared to make another turn I saw that my *chaverim* had parked every available farm vehicle along the edge of the field and turned on the headlights so that I would be able to see what the hell I was doing.

As I made a perfect turn at the end of the furrow nearest the crowd, I gave thumbs up sign to my *chaverim*. Though I was exhausted and ready to quit, the shouts of encouragement, as well as the ego gratification that came with being in the spotlight, kept me going. The juices were flowing and I relished every moment. There was no doubt in my mind that under these conditions I could have spent an eternity plowing every field in New Jersey.

I continued and within two hours, the job was done. In parade style we all returned to the farm for a brief celebration. Most important to me was the toast offered by my mentor and stabilizer, Mandy.

"To Dovid," he said, "He came here as a kid and leaves as a man!"

Although I could not explain why, I felt that this one incident had a profound impact on me. If nothing else I sensed, for perhaps the first time, that my life had some direction and purpose.

* * * * *

Whatever celebrity I had enjoyed soon passed, as all our efforts were now focused on a much more serious issue.

With the end of the war, the international pressure was mounting for a resolution of the plight of the thousands of Jews who somehow had survived the Nazi death machine. Thousands upon thousands remained in concentration camps, many others were still in hiding, and even more were perishing in German labor battalions. It was not until Allied forces occupied most of Europe that we learned first-hand of what the German inferno had accomplished and the devastating condition of the remaining survivors.

During the War, the immigration effort (*Aliyah*) attempted to rescue Jews from Nazi-dominated Europe. Some came to Palestine with visas issued under a quota system, but the majority came as illegal immigrants in contravention to the British Mandatory Government orders, which restricted the number of Jews who were allowed to enter Palestine. For the survivors and those who participated in the rescue of the remnants of European Jewry, this illegal immigration was called *Aliyah Bet* (the going up to the Promised Land). When several boatloads of pitiful passengers managed to reach Palestine, they were sent back by British authorities determined to uphold the quota system. Many perished at sea and many others died in the concentration camps. Still, no matter the nobility and worthiness of the cause, all those who engaged were participating in an illegal activity.

It had also become apparent that none of the Allied nations held the rescue of Jewish survivors as a high priority. Further, it was also clear that the British government, which controlled the immigration policy, was not eager to support a mass migration of Jews to Palestine.

The only alternative for rapid action would require a massive and concerted effort by influential and wealthy non-European Jews, sympathetic government officials, and the Jewish governing bodies of Palestine. The immediate need was for funds to acquire transport vessels, crews to man the ships, and a network in Europe that would organize the movement of refugees and establish ports for vessel fitting and passenger embarkation.

Despite the consequences or dangers, a number of my male colleagues on the farm quickly volunteered for crew assignments. All had served in the military, some had combat experience, and several were married.

I sought to do the same, but once again was informed that due to my age I would not qualify for consideration. The age barrier in this case was not imposed by the organizers of this effort, but rather by the United States Coast Guard. In order to serve on a merchant ship whose port of departure is in the United States, you are required to have merchant marine papers. These papers, similar to a driver's license, are authorized by the Coast Guard and require an applicant to have reached the age of eighteen. I was some seven months shy of the acceptable age. My friends, as well as those doing the recruiting, were sympathetic and assured me that my age was the only barrier. I was very unhappy and angry that a variable over which I had no control, and one that was irrelevant to the task, would prevent me from participating in what I considered to be a most challenging and necessary mission. My imagination had already produced images in my mind of my coming to the rescue of my people, of protecting women and children from the British, of sailing into the port of Haifa, under a bright blue sky, with the flag of Jewish Palestine flowing from the mast.

Just as I had come to the point of reluctantly dealing with my disappointment, I was informed that all was not lost and perhaps there was a way to get me on board. It seemed there was someone inside the Coast Guard office who could facilitate the issuance of needed documents.

I had no idea who had made the arrangements or how the deal was cut. At a specific date and time, I was instructed to go to the appropriate Coast Guard office in Philadelphia and request a merchant seaman application. I completed the application and was interviewed by an ensign who asked me for proof of citizenship as well as birth date. I gave him a copy of my birth certificate, which he studied, and then wrote something on my application. I was photographed and asked to wait in the outer office.

I was certain that at any moment the FBI would come upon the scene and place me in custody for violation of some law or other. At one point I stood up and headed for the exit, only to be called back by a shore patrol officer who was serving as receptionist. He told me that I would have to wait until all of my papers were reviewed and processed.

An hour had passed, and finally the ensign called me back into his office. He asked me to raise my right hand and to repeat after him an oath affirming that all the information I provided was accurate, with the understanding that committing a falsehood would mean big trouble for me. After I affirmed the truthfulness of all I had stated in my application, I was given my official U.S. Merchant Mariners Document noting that I qualified for the lowest possible ranks, Ordinary Seaman or Wiper. Only later did I notice that the surname on the documents was "Gotlib" and not "Gottlieb."

Over the next several weeks, other crewmembers joined us at the farm. The group now included several guys from Canada, South Africa and Palestine. We were told that everything we learned about the mission and anything we observed were not to be shared with others. Failure to comply with this order could result in dismissal as well as placing the mission in jeopardy. Of course there was much speculation among us, but it was clear that we would only be given as much information as needed, and to ask for more would be fruitless. We did learn that two crews were being assembled for two different vessels.

Even though most of us had no previous experience serving on merchant ships, there was no instruction on anything related to seamanship or the onboard tasks we might be performing.

The uncertainty about the voyage made the waiting all the more difficult. I looked forward to the weekends, when young members of Habonim would come to the farm for two-day visits. They came mostly from the boroughs of New York, and their liveliness and loudness helped distract me from a very uncertain future. The girls struck me as somewhat more mature and sophisticated than my Detroit friends.

One of the girls who became a regular weekend visitor was Shoshonah. She was from upstate New York and attending NYU in downtown Manhattan. Shoshanah was of medium height, fair skinned with curly, light brown hair cut short. At the farm she always wore jeans and a long sleeved man's shirt. She was the most energetic folk dancer I had ever seen and was always the last to leave the dance floor.

Although Shoshanah was serious about the movement and living on a kibbutz, she was not a Zionist nut as were some of the kids who came to the farm. I liked her because she was fun, attractive, and not looking for a long-term relationship.

We spent our free time together at the farm and I began to make weekend trips into New York. New York was a whole new experience for me, the unsophisticated traveler. Beyond Detroit, my travel had been restricted to several days in Trenton, New Brunswick, Cream Ridge, and part of a day in Philadelphia. Shoshanah lived in a dorm in the East Village and was familiar with the locale of every jazz, theater, and folk dance club, as well as the most exotic restaurants. Worldly I was not, but I was more than eager to learn, and Shoshanah was a great guide.

In early October our volunteer crew group was called together for a special meeting. A representative of the organization responsible for the project chaired the meeting. His first comments were a stern reminder that whatever was discussed in this or future sessions was to remain confidential and that we were not to talk about it, even among ourselves. He also noted that what was being undertaken could easily be construed as unlawful activity.

While we had many friends who supported our cause, we had even more enemies who would find great satisfaction in halting our work.

"The task will not be simple," he told us, "There will be danger and no guarantee of success. You must be certain in your own minds that this is what you choose to do. Do not allow pressure from others to influence your decision. Once we go beyond this meeting the choice of leaving will no longer be with you alone."

Following his comments there was absolute silence and no one gave any indication of what they were thinking or what they might do.

After an extended pause, the leader thanked us for our commitment and courage. He said that we were not alone in this venture and we would be joined by Palestinian Jews who were members of the Haganah, the Jewish defense force of Palestine. Other allies included former partisans of Italy and France who had fought the Nazis.

Finally, he talked about the human cargo we would be transporting to *Eretz Yisrael* (Land of Israel). Those people were being refereed to as "DP's" for "Displaced Persons." They had not been given the title of "refugees" because refugees were identified with a specific place—a town, village, city or country. DP's were people without a place or a country. No country or state offered them sanctuary. Only the Yishuv (the Jewish authorities in Palestine) requested or rather demanded that all exiles be returned to the Promised Land.

I found it ironic that the same governments that would not allow entry into their countries were also most opposed to resettlement in Palestine. Most prominent in this case were the British, who had dispatched the Royal Navy to intercept any vessels carrying DP's into Palestinian waters. The chance of an encounter with the British would only increase the probabilities of a disaster at sea.

With those sentiments and ground rules expressed, our speaker got down to specifics. Our crew, along with others, would be assigned two ships. Each of the ships had been purchased, as surplus, from the Canadian Navy. The ships were similar in size and design to an American destroyer. Both ships would undergo renovation and refitting at a yet to be announced European port. We were to be prepared to report for duty in the first week of January, 1946. Meanwhile, we would remain at the farm and continue with our usual activities. Finally, we were informed that temporary housing would be made available in New York until the time the ship was ready to sail.

As soon as we left the room, participants began talking in small groups. One of the members of the Haganah angrily shouted that we were already violating our oath and that all talk must cease. Not being allowed to share thoughts and questions with my *chaverim* was difficult for me and, I am certain, for the others. My greatest concern at that moment was if I would have sufficient self-control to say nothing to Shoshanah. Although I had a compelling need to impress her with hard proof of my commitment and bravery, I made up my mind that I would say nothing.

The following weekend I traveled to the city to visit with Shoshanah. We had dinner at a small, Spanish restaurant. Shoshanah ordered a bottle of wine and suggested a mixture of different dishes. As we brought our wineglasses together she said that she wished to propose a toast. I was taken completely by surprise at her first words, which were, "I want to wish you the best of *mazel* (luck) and my love as you embark on this new adventure."

I made no response as I considered how I should react. I first expressed ignorance and said that I had no idea what she was talking about. She smiled and then gently informed me that everyone in New York knew about the ship that would soon be leaving for Palestine. I fumbled with my words, which were a mixture of denial and a request for the sources of her information. With an indulgent look she said, "David, no one can keep a secret in New York, especially Jews."

How I wished that one of the Haganah leaders was available so that I could ask for guidance. But that not being the case, I insisted that we drop the matter, and Shoshanah reluctantly agreed. Whereas before our conversation was endless with few pauses for silence, there was now a mutual sense of uncertainty as to what could and could not be discussed.

When dinner was over and we were outside the restaurant, Shoshanah said that she wanted to say just one more thing about the topic. She wanted me to know that she was very sorry about what happened and regretted any unhappiness she might have caused. She realized she should have said nothing about the subject but waited until I was prepared to share with her. Finally, she wanted me to know that she loved me and would do nothing to hurt me.

That was all I had to hear. I made it clear that all was forgiven and forgotten. We embraced, and the prospects for a long and enjoyable night were much improved.

Upon my return to the farm I quickly learned that there was validity in Shoshanah's observation that no secrets could be kept in New York, and most especially among Jews. Although the rumors lacked much in the way of accurate detail, they were on target about ships, crews, and preparations for ocean travel.

Once again we were assembled by the representative of the Jewish Agency and admonished for our failure to comply with the demand for absolute silence in all matters pertaining to the project. While all those in the room denied any responsibility, it was clear that there was a leak somewhere along the line. The major concern now was that the media not pick up any of the gossip. Our instructions were quite specific: "If anyone asks, you know nothing!"

Over the next several weeks we went about our usual tasks without seeing any indication that the public media had heard anything that was considered worthy of publication.

Toward the end of December, those of us selected as crew were informed that we would be moved to New York no later than the first of February of the coming year, 1946. Since I had been at the farm for six months and was not certain as to what my future plans would be, I decided that this would be the right time to take some time off. I planned to visit with family and friends in Detroit, as well as spend some quality time with Shoshanah.

Though my absence had been only a half-year, many things seemed to have changed. Norman was still in the Navy, but Bob had returned home. Harold was in school. My parents had moved again into a larger home in a very pleasant residential neighborhood.

Some things, though, had not changed. Ma felt the need to make up for the months I had been away by constantly offering me a multitude of foods. Although I was now in better physical shape than I had ever been, she insisted I looked sickly and undernourished. "What kind of farm is it that you look like you just came back from a refugee camp?"

My protests and pleas for a break fell on deaf ears. She not only wanted to feed me for the time I had been gone, but also for that undefined time when I might be absent in the future. Ma was very much into her own version of preventive health care. If you want to avoid a cold, you take pills prior to the onset of the illness. If you want to mitigate the pains of hunger in the weeks to come, you load up now. Ma was relentless and I was too easy a mark.

Pa was pleased that I was I home, even though he was not comfortable with expressing it in any physical way. He was never a kisser or a hugger. Most conversations with Pa never exceeded a brief exchange:

"So you worked hard on that farm?"

To which I answered, "Not too hard."

"That's good," he replied.

That about covered the six months of my absence. Despite my best efforts, the same pattern would occur whenever I tried to initiate discussion with him. Knowing better than to ask any question that could be answered with a simple yes or no, I asked, "Pa, what's going on at the store?"

"*Gornicht* (nothing)," he responded.

"Pa," I asked, "Tell me what you hear from your cousin in Palestine."

Again, "*Gornicht*." Pa always felt most secure when remaining on the margins of familial relationships.

Change had also occurred in the lives of many of my friends. Both Morty's and Ralph's brothers had returned, discharged from the Marine Corps, and both of them now in far worse condition than they had been when they left home.

Though Ralph was still seriously engaged in Habonim, Morty had moved on to other interests.

I called Gerry and we got together. She was pleased to see me and very much interested in what I had been doing and my plans for the future. I asked her the same questions. She confirmed what I had already heard, that after serious consideration she had concluded that the pioneer life was not for her. Gerry thought she could make a more global contribution to mankind by becoming a clinical psychologist.

She said that she had come to agree with my observation that the kibbutz and life in Palestine required strong backs rather than keen minds. I suggested that each of us had to make our own choices and do that which we feel gives us the greatest satisfaction. I told her that for the time being at least, my choice was to be a *chalutz* and live on a kibbutz. There had been an almost complete reversal in the positions we had taken only a short time ago. We parted, each wishing the other well.

Several times during my stay at home I attended Habonim events. I had anticipated that some may have heard the stories that were circulating among members on the East Coast, but I heard no comments of awareness, neither did there seem to be much more than polite interest in what I had been doing or my plans for the future. Perhaps one consequence of the long war was that my peers were turning more inward and away from concerns about what might be happening in other parts of the world.

Several of the more senior members and leaders told me that they were planning on going to Cream Ridge in order to begin their preparation for *aliyah*. They had questions about life on the farm, the accommodations, and how the place was governed. I tried to be responsive, candid, and accurate, pointing out that there was a significant contrast between the time of my arrival and the time I had left. The last six months had brought a dramatic change in the number and backgrounds of members. There were now older men who were married, and some with little children. At the beginning, I had viewed the place as I would a summer camp—people would be there for a given period of time and then return home. Because of political complications, passage to Palestine did not seem a reasonable option.

Now that the war was over, attention was shifting not only to the plight of the survivors, but to the actual establishment of a Jewish State, and the matter of *aliyah* was again a reality.

I told them when that you come to *hachshara*, the expectation was that you had already made your decision. Those who were not firm in their commitment should not waste the time and resources of the farm. I shared with them that though I had put myself on a path to Palestine, I was far from certain as to what I was doing now and what I would be doing in the future.

My final week at home was devoted primarily to time spent with my family, relatives, and close friends of my parents. Most of our gatherings took place around the dinner table, which was considered a neutral, no tension territory. Topics that might stimulate controversy were set aside while guests ate and enjoyed their meal. There were, of course, those rare occasions when the peace was, in the heat of the moment, abandoned. Still, we all understood that celebratory meals associated with bar mitzvahs, weddings, funerals, and farewells were to be spared expressions of family contention. Laughter, talk, tears, and countless toasts were shared. As each dinner ended and guests were leaving, I was presented with gifts, hugs, and kisses.

Because I did not know when I would see my parents again or where and how they might contact me, I felt I needed to tell them something of my plans. I also decided that since I could not come up with a believable cover story, I would need to get at close to the truth as possible.

The evening before I left, we sat around the kitchen table and I told them that within several months I would be working on a ship that would be taking Jewish refugees to Palestine. Since I had no hard information I could not tell them anything about specific destinations, logistics, or even the time we might be leaving. I did my best to point out that highly skilled and experienced professionals would be in charge of the ship. In anticipation of their major concern, which would be my safe return, I was prepared with what I considered to be the most reassuring of responses: "America won the war and we are the most powerful country in the world. No one will mess with an American citizen." I showed them my United States Coast Guard card, which I insisted was all the protection I would need.

"So what are you going to do when the British stop your boat?" Pa asked.

This was not a question that I had expected. I thought for a moment and said that is why my being an American citizen is most helpful; since they cannot arrest me, all they can do is send me back to America.

Ma started to cry. I expected Pa to step in with his usual charge of my wanting to send Ma to an early grave. But he did not.

What he did say took me completely by surprise. In Yiddish he told me that he was very proud of me and that what I was doing was a true *mitzvah* (a high and holy deed). With that he stood up and walked over to where I was sitting, leaned down, and kissed me on the head. I could not recall any prior time when my father had either praised my behavior or shown me such warmth and affection. Tears came to my eyes. I stood up and put my arms around him and pressed him close to me. The discussion ended with my saying that I would write to them whenever I could. They should try not to worry; I would be okay.

I did not ask my parents to keep whatever information I had shared to themselves. My main reason for not doing so was because I felt an expression of caution would add to their anxieties. I also knew that in a very short period of time the news would be moving quickly through the Gottlieb family network.

Early the next morning, my brother Bob drove me to the train station. My next stop was New York City and then the bus upstate. Shoshanah had invited me to spend a week or so with her and her family.

Shoshanah met me at the station and took me on a quick tour of Kingston. This was not only my first trip to upstate New York, but it was also my first exposure to Jewish life in an old American town. Downtown consisted of three blocks with small retail shops. There was one movie theatre, an old courthouse, and the local fire station. We drove by the Reform Jewish temple where Shoshanah had her bas mitzvah. Every structure seemed to be of a similar scale and every shop appeared to have been designed by the same architect. It was all picture perfect.

Prior to our going to her home, Shoshanah drove me over to the house where I would be staying. My host would be Rabbi Herb, Shoshanah's dear friend and mentor. I would later learn that Rabbi Herb was the one person most influential in guiding Shoshanah in her Jewish education as well as her membership in Habonim.

Rabbi Herb was a man in his mid-fifties who had been born with cerebal palsy. As a consequence of his condition, his conversation was occasionally interrupted by an uncontrollable hacking cough. His body was bent and he moved slowly but deliberately.

His wife, Blossom, was a small, roundish woman. Their greeting was so warm and sincere that I felt less like a visitor and much more like an old and dear friend. Having Shoshanah's endorsement meant the usual protocol in dealing with newcomers was waived and I was a welcomed guest.

Blossom showed me my room and the bathroom I would use, then gave me a key to the house. She said that I should feel free to come and go as I pleased and they had no fixed meal times. The exception was *Shabbos* dinner on Friday evening, when they would expect both Shoshanah and me to join them. Blossom poured us each a glass of wine and Rabbi Herb proposed a toast of welcome.

We left and headed for Shoshanah's home. Until this visit, I knew very little about Shoshanah's background or parents, except that she was an only child. On the way to her house I expressed my delight at how things had gone with Herb and Blossom and I thought they were really great folks. I also implied that I felt it would be asking for too much to think that I would receive a similar welcome from her parents. Shoshanah pulled the car over to the curb and turned off the motor. She said that perhaps it would be helpful if she gave me a little "pre-meeting" background.

I learned from her that her parents were both third generation Americans and had not been raised as practicing Jews. When Shoshanah was born, her parents were in their mid-fifties. Her father operated a small factory owned by one of her mother's brothers. It manufactured plastic products such as shower curtains and laundry bags.

Shoshanah's father had no living relatives, but her mother had many who were quite well off and residing in Manhattan. Shoshanah's birth was unexpected, and her parents considered her arrival as some kind of miracle. She was considered a precious gift and constantly pampered and protected. A major reason for their moving to Kingston was to escape what her parents considered to be the harmful environment of the big city. They wanted fresh air, safe streets, good schools, and proper playmates for their daughter.

I knew that "Shoshanah" was the Hebrew name for "Susan" and had assumed that it was the name given to her by her parents. But this was not the case; the daughter made the decision, much to the consternation of her mother.

Shoshanah's parents, Leo and Millie, were very pleasant and proper people. They seemed to have adjusted to the reality that their daughter would not be pursuing the lifestyle they had once expected. They were curious about my folks and family and gave no indication of surprise when I said my parents were immigrants. However, they were taken aback when I answered that I had not finished high school. Shoshanah volunteered the news that I was living and working on a farm in New Jersey in preparation for migration to Palestine. That seemed to do the trick—her mother heaved a huge sigh and her father went to pour himself a substantial shot of scotch.

I stayed for two weeks, with much time spent visiting with the Rabbi and Blossom, hiking, and driving around upstate New York. We said shalom and agreed that we would be seeing each other in several weeks.

On the bus trip to Manhattan, I thought about Shoshanah and our time together. It had been so easy and comfortable.

Chapter 5

In late February, members of our crew moved to a "safe" house in the Seagate section of Coney Island. We were moving one step closer to our ship and our journey.

I knew some of the guys from the farm, while others had arrived directly from their homes. We were a mixed group varying in age, geographical origin, marital status, and life experience. I was the youngest by one year, the other "kid" being an 18-year-old from Montreal. His name was Bunyetz. In our group of fifteen, only two had actual seafaring experience. We would soon be introduced to the pros of the crew.

With the exception of updates provided by our leader, the next two weeks were our own time. Bunyetz and I spent some time at the Coney Island amusement park and checking out local clubs

I also made trips into the city to be with Shoshanah. Our relationship was growing stronger with declarations of love and fidelity.

All of the guys, however, were getting increasingly impatient and were beginning to demand more precise information.

In mid-February we were told to be prepared to board our ship on the first day of March. I do not think any of us really believed that this information would be any more reliable than previous announcements. But this time it was true, and on the first of March we boarded a Staten

Island-bound bus with gear in hand. I had mixed feelings, which I believe were caused by my having learned the previous evening that Mandy would not be on my ship. I realized at that point just how much I had come to count on him as my guide and role model.

On the one hand, I was relieved that the waiting was finally over. On the other, there was the fear that perhaps this time I had carried things too far. I knew that once I got on that ship, like it or not, there was no way out. I looked around the bus at the others and wondered if they, too, were having self-doubts and second thoughts.

We arrived at the Todd Shipyard docks and walked over to our new home: a 750-ton ship, painted navy gray, with the name Beauharnois emblazoned on the hull. The ship had registered Panama City as its homeport. In this first leg of our journey we would be sailing under the flag of Panama—the explanation being that every merchant ship must be listed with and fly the flag of a nation complying with international regulations. Because Panama was among those nations most willing, for a price, to ask few questions and facilitate the bureaucratic process, Panama was frequently the flag of choice. The fact that the Beauharnois had never been anywhere near Panama and there was not a single Panamanian in our crew made no difference as long as the price was right.

The quarters for the crew were the warship standard for enlisted personnel. There were twelve of us in a section of four tiers with three levels of bunks. Bunk selection was not based on a lottery or first come first served basis. The older men took the lower and middle bunks and left the top bunks to the youngest crewmembers.

The same method of allocation was to be followed in the assignment of on board duties. With the exception of the ship's officers and those few crewmembers who had previous shipboard experience, the lowest status and least desirable jobs were assigned to the youngest crew members. There was no discussion of equity, nor any resistance;

it was rather the iron law of age-based oligarchy. I was assigned to the engine room and held the Merchant Marine job title of wiper with the rank of ordinary seaman. My buddy Bunyetz was assigned to the galley.

We were called for assembly and introduced to our officers. The captain and first mate were New Yorkers and both had extensive wartime merchant marine service. Both had also been on ships that had been torpedoed, and were veteran survivors. They were Jewish by birth, but hard-line atheists. The two had known each other for many years and were ex-Wobblies, members of the old IWW (International Workers of the World).

The captain was explicit in his instructions that the ship was neither a kibbutz nor a democracy. No matter our past accomplishments or our past experiences, we were all ordinary seamen, with the emphasis placed on "ordinary."

"You will become sailors and you will follow orders given to you by the officers of this ship," the captain said.

We were also introduced to our boatswain, a guy named Thayer, who was to be the boss of all on deck ordinary seaman. Thayer was by far the oldest man on board, and undoubtedly the most bizarre. His hair was a long, unruly mess, matched by an equally ill-kept beard. His sizeable pot belly hung over his trousers, which were belted with a piece of twine. Thayer was a health nut and carried his own supply of various grains, nuts, raisins, preserved fruits and vegetables. He drank only herbal teas, which he brewed in his own portable teakettle. In an earlier life, he had been a Jewish hobo, and eventually became a member of Jehovah's Witnesses. There was nothing in his appearance or manner that would give anyone a clue as to his profession. He was surprisingly agile, strong as a bull, and low key in manner, but he knew ships and he knew his job.

The chief engineer was a middle aged Swede with many years of maritime experience. He was not Jewish, and I felt that he was neither aware of our purpose nor ultimate destination.

Our ship's cook looked like he could have been the son of the boatswain. He was a Canadian with long, blazing red hair and a matching beard. He was large-sized and wore baggy jeans and a blue chef's toque, opened at the top to accommodate the overflow of his amazing hair. He did not look as if he could pass even the most liberal of personal hygiene requirements.

We were a very odd collection, and hardly reflective of what one would expect to find on an ocean going vessel. Our ineptitude and lack of experience would manifest itself soon enough.

Whether in port or at sea, an operational vessel is a 24-hours-a-day, seven-days-a-week enterprise. The crew's working hours were based on a schedule of four hours on and eight hours off. Work schedules were rotated on a weekly basis. My first week duty started at midnight and continued to 4:00 a.m., when I would go to the galley for a hot drink and a snack. I would sleep until about 11:00 a.m., take a quick shower, and be at my station at noon. After work in the afternoon I would try to find a comfortable place on deck to read or write letters before joining the crew for dinner. I would make an effort to get some sleep, but the activity below deck was such that the best I could hope for was a few hours of uninterrupted rest.

We remained on board for the next two weeks, with the reward of a 24-hour leave commencing at noon on Saturday. The time on board was dedicated to learning the most fundamental aspects of our jobs. My work was divided between on deck tasks such as removing old paint from the deck and bulwark surfaces and repainting. Below deck in the engine room, my job title described exactly what I did. As a wiper, I wiped. I removed oil stains from the engine room deck, polished and shined gauges, and pumped bilge remains from reciprocating engines. The work was not difficult but routine and monotonous. Knowing what Bunyetz's life was like in the galley was my only real source of comparative satisfaction. Poor Bunyetz was working for a tyrannical chef who gave him no relief or kind words. No matter how hard he tried, he could not remove the stench of fried foods from his clothing or body.

My leave time was spent in the city with Shoshanah. Because I was not yet certain as to when we would sail, whatever time we had together was considered a bonus. The second leave turned out to be the last, and in the first week of April, a tugboat maneuvered us out of port and into the Atlantic.

We were all on deck taking a last look at the New York skyline. One of the older members of the crew who had for many years been involved with the Zionist movement began to sing a song with these lyrics:

> "Good bye America, good bye forever,
> We're going to Palestine because we are so clever.
> Good bye America, good bye Yankee fashion.
> We're off to Palestine, the hell with the
> Depression!"

Several hours after leaving the calm port waters, we entered the rolling waters of the Atlantic. The sudden transition from relative calm to rocking waves was enough to bring forth an epidemic of seasickness. Grown men, who otherwise showed great self-control, were now literally brought to their knees in agony. Those who had been below deck scrambled to the top deck in hopes that fresh air would offer some relief. There was no relief, and the retching and misery continued.

Below deck, more than a few of my mates were lying in their bunks, holding firmly to the enclosing rails. Sammy, a man of about thirty, in what I imagined was a plea for healing and compassion, called out to his wife, "Chaneh, Chaneh, why did you let me do this? Chaneh, I need you now please, please help me."

I was among the fortunate few who had suffered only temporary discomfort. I had found that by adjusting my body's movement to the direction in which the ship was rolling, I was able to ease feelings of nausea. I tried to share with others what I considered to be a helpful preventive health hint. Bunyetz, who lay moaning in his sack, told me to "fuck off." Others, while less direct than Bunyetz, made it clear that they were not inclined, at the time at least, to take instruction.

By late afternoon most of the crew had recovered to a point where they were able to return to work assignments. Not surprisingly, few took part in the evening meal. Most limited their nutritional intake to crackers and dry cereal.

On the following day the ocean was relatively calm, the sky was a cloudless blue, and the sun shone brightly. The beauty of the day, as well as the greater ease in moving about the ship, did wonders for our morale. We had, as the first mate noted, found our sea legs.

The remainder of the week was spent routinely performing our duties. Entertainment was limited to chess, checkers, card playing, reading, or letter writing. Much to our delight and surprise, we discovered that our chef, Rueben, played the guitar and also had a magnificent voice. In the evenings we would gather on deck to listen and join with Rueben in singing familiar songs. Rueben's catalogue of songs was large and diverse. He could sing arias from the works of many of the major composers as well as the songs of Porter, Gershwin, and Carmichael. Swing was yet another of his favorites. Miller, Dorsey, Ellington—he knew all their songs. Seeing him and hearing him perform went a long way to help us forgive his many culinary shortcomings.

Unanticipated events during the second week at sea quickly changed both our morale and our travel plans.

Typically, dramatic changes of weather in the North Atlantic occur gradually over an interval of several hours. But as we watched the mid-morning, sunny blue day go quickly to gray and just as quickly to black, we knew we were in for some action. The almost non-detectable wind changed to a notable breeze and then escalated to a swirling wind that made topside work difficult as well as dangerous. The most startling contrast, however, was the ocean itself. A calm, almost mirror-like stillness rapidly became a raging, swirling cauldron, heaving our ship from port to starboard and aft to stern. We were not prepared for the suddenness with which the storm struck and took firm control of our ship.

Those not assigned to engine room duty were ordered topside and given the task of making all deck cargo and equipment secure. Like the others, I put on a slicker and knee length boots. On deck mobility was virtually impossible. To avoid the possibility of being washed overboard, each of us tied a length of rope around our middle and secured the other end to an on deck rung. Conditions had deteriorated to the point where visibility was limited to an arms length distance. Communications with others was out of the question, and we could no longer hear whatever orders might be coming from the Command Bridge. We were each on our own and uncertain as to what we should and could do.

Then all hell broke loose. The deck cargo we had secured had broken loose. More than a dozen huge, metal drums filled with fuel oil came cascading down the deck, tumbling in every direction. We were at the mercy of both the storm and these ricocheting metal monsters. Each time the ship was tossed by the sea, the drums would change their course as if seeking to increase the probabilities of crushing one of us. It was as if I was part of a large-scale pinball game. The difference, of course, was that instead of one harmless metal ball, I was confronted by a dozen, uncontrollable drums of death.

I was terrified, I was cold, and I was soaking wet. Suddenly I became aware that I was yelling, or rather roaring, like a madman. I was cursing God and uttering profanities from at least four different languages when I felt an arm on my shoulder. I turned and saw Thayer, the boatswain. He was trying to give me instructions, but I could not make out any words. Suddenly, he cut loose the moored part of my safety rope and began pulling me toward the below deck stairway door. How he could see and how he could keep both of us together I will never know. He managed to get us down the stairs to safety. I later learned that I was only one of four crewmembers who he had saved from what I will always believe was certain death.

As there is always a calm before a storm, there is also a calm after a storm. In our case, the old adage was only a half-truth.

The following day, though the sea was serene, a thorough inspection of the ship showed severe damage both above and below deck. At the same time, there was great relief and celebration since no member of the crew had suffered serious injury. The captain agreed that the occasion warranted several rounds of beer and wine, and he offered a toast in praise of the crew's performance. He also called Thayer up to the makeshift stage in order to commend him for his heroic efforts. The boatswain reluctantly came forward and was given a rousing standing ovation. When offered the opportunity to address the crew, he modestly declined. When offered a glass of wine, he graciously said he would stay with his own brew of herbal tea.

When the ceremony was over I approached Thayer and started to offer my thanks for his efforts on my behalf. Before I could complete more than a few words he held up his hand in a clear "no more talk" gesture. He said simply that helping one another was what being shipmates was all about. Later in our voyage I would witness yet another example of the quiet courage of this extraordinary man.

A final evaluation of the damage done to the ship forced a change in our plans. Rather than proceeding directly to the Mediterranean, we would sail to a port in the Azores. Ongoing engine problems, as well as damage done to our automatic steering equipment, would slow our pace considerably.

Three weeks later, we arrived in the port city of Ponta Delgata, the major ship repair port prior to entering the Straits of Gibraltar and the Mediterranean Sea. Although we were still miles from land, I was excited and a bit wild with anticipation of my first view of foreign soil. It was a glorious morning, the sun was shining brightly, the water a calm, clear blue. Off the horizon I could see the countryside dotted with small houses painted in an array of bright colors.

As we moved very slowly toward the port I noticed dozens of rowboats heading in our direction. Each boat held at least two men, and each was rowing furiously in order to be the first to reach our ship. The occupants of these small boats were muscular and well tanned from many hours in the hot Mediterranean sun. Most of the crew was on deck and looking down from the port side at the small craft swarming around our ship as if they were a horde of bees searching for a rich source of honey.

In fact, these were high-pressure salesmen hustling to sell a wide range of products. Their little "bum boats," as they were called, would meet every incoming vessel to push various products. The boat's occupants knew just enough English to communicate that their prices were far lower than the same item would be in town. A long pole with a basket lifted items up to us.

The hot item for crewmembers was cigarettes, all the more desirable given the cheap price. The guys in the small boats held up dozens of cartons of cigarettes of every popular American brand. Guys were shoving each other out of the way in order to place their orders. "I'll take five cartons of Luckies," shouted one guy. "Send up four Camels and six Kools," yelled another, and so it went until all the orders were placed.

The tallest of the bum boat band, a guy who seemed to be the leader, called for us to put our money into the delivery basket and he would return change as well as the cigarettes. To ease any doubts that this was a hustle, he held up a huge wad of what appeared to be U.S. twenty and fifty dollar bills.

We eagerly complied threw our money in the container. No sooner was the basket lowered than off they headed for shore. It took only a few seconds for us to realize that we had been screwed. Once the shock wore off, we yelled, we cursed, we threatened and even pleaded—all to no avail, of course. The remaining bum boat associates could hardly control their delight at witnessing the fleecing of Americans. They were overcome with laughter, slapping each other on the back and high-fiving one another.

What we least needed, but were not to be spared, was the suggestion offered by our first mate. "Why stop with cash? Why not go after them and give them your clothes and jewelry as well?" he taunted us.

Later that evening we had our first shore leave in the Azores. Several of the guys were determined to search out the "*goniffs*" and recover their lost merchandise. Knowing the odds were slim to non-existent, they nevertheless felt compelled to set out on what would be, of course, a fruitless search. Others headed for one of the local port bars. I joined Bunyetz and two others and we set off to explore the town.

We were no more than fifteen minutes from our ship when two kids who could not have been more than eight years old approached us with an offer: "Hey, Joe. I got nice young girl for you."

Pointing to his companion, he added, "It's his sister."

When we declined the offer we were asked for cigarettes or cash. Again we declined. They walked away a short distance, turned and said, "Fuck you, Joe, and your mother, too."

Unlike many of our older crewmates, we were novices, being quickly exposed to cultures, experiences, and human behavior that we had previously only read or heard about. There was much more to come.

That first evening we stayed within the port area, stopping for beer and a late snack. We learned that Ponta Delgada had been a major staging base for Allied ships bound for the Mediterranean. The two kids we ran into obviously had grown up in an economy and community virtually dependent upon military personnel. Unfortunate casualties of war, these kids learned at an early age that they must sell, hustle, cheat, and lie in order to survive.

We were to remain in Ponta Delgada for close to a month. Our daily duties were primarily in assisting contracted repair teams. There was much work to be done in the engine room as well as on deck. Unless assigned evening security watch, our time was pretty much our own. We usually began leave at 6:00 p.m. and were expected to be back on ship by midnight. Weekends offered us more time away, since we could leave as early as 7:00 a.m. and, again, return before midnight. As in the past, we were instructed to say nothing about our ultimate destination or our purpose—an order that would not be difficult to carry out since we could not speak Portuguese and we were still in the dark as to when we would be leaving for our next port of call.

For a few days I fell in with different groups of guys as we wandered around the town of Ponta Delgada. The beauty and color of the place as seen from the distance was not matched by the reality. The major feature and most imposing architecture was an old, huge, brownstone church located in the town square. The major business section of the town featured a small grocery store, pharmacy, butcher shop, and a modest family clothing store. What Ponta Delgada possessed in abundance were bars, cafes, and prostitutes—not surprising, given that it was a major port for ship repair and fitting as well as housing an Australian Air Force base. This was Mecca for service men as well as civilian merchant seamen.

The fact that our crew was primarily of Jewish descent seemed to be less important than our being sailors on leave in a foreign port. There was an abundance of whorehouses offering a wide diversity of choices. I could walk down the narrow side streets and be grabbed at by women literally hanging out of their windows. Pimps of all ages would pounce on us and compete to sell us their wares. In short order, most of the crew, married or not, found a place or places where they could feel comfortable and, of course, gratified.

Perhaps it was a need to compensate for their own guilt that the older, married guys felt a need to protect Bunyetz and me from being equal partners in pursuit of sexual pleasures. Whatever the motivation, for the first week or so different guys would take turns serving as our chaperones. We were allowed a beer or a glass of wine, but no access to houses of ill repute. We resisted, we argued, and finally we rebelled.

Our shadow for this particular evening was Marvin, an overweight, out-of-shape, middle-aged, ex-shoe salesman. By the time we had finished our designated one beer quota, Marvin had consumed three beers. Our plan was to get Marvin so drunk that he would either fall asleep or be incapable of chasing after us. To encourage his continuous drinking, we bought the beers. After he consumed more than ten beers, we abandoned our original plan. The more Marvin drank, the more alert and attentive he became.

It was Bunyetz who came up with a strategy of laying on a combination of pity and guilt. Bunyetz was brilliant in both concept and content. He placed his hand on Marvin's arm and began, "Marvin, good friend. You are a Jew. We are Jews. You are a sailor, and we are sailors. Most important, Marvin, you are a man, and we are men. You need a woman's companionship, and we need a woman's companionship."

As Bunyetz intoned, he stood eye to eye with Marvin and squeezed his arm gently. His final plea emphasized that this was a wonderful opportunity for Marvin to be a teacher and a mentor. He promised that no one else would know of the agreement made between us.

Marvin sat silently staring at Bunyetz. Finally, he said, "Bunyetz, that is the greatest crock of shit I've ever heard. You're good. You're very good. Now get your asses out of here!"

We threw our arms around Marvin, thanked him again and again, and took off for places unknown but vividly imagined.

Now that we had been released from bondage and were eager to move on, we were uncertain as to how to proceed. We decided that our best bet was to pick a house and come on as experienced and sophisticated customers. We returned to a street where we had been earlier and observed women soliciting passing traffic. We followed one of the women into a small, dimly lit, sparsely furnished house. A woman of about thirty to thirty-five years greeted us. She was wearing a bright floral outfit that reminded me of the gymsuits worn by girls at the Winterhalter Elementary School. She sat down next to me and put her hand on my knee. Bunyetz quickly jumped in and said that we were looking for a couple of young, pretty girls. Our hostess stood up, excused herself, and left the room.

We assumed that she was the madam of the house and would soon be filling our order. Moments later she returned with another woman who could have been her twin sister. She signaled that I should come with her and Bunyetz should go with her associate. Bunyetz grabbed my arm, pulled me out the door, and shouted to me, "No way am I going to fuck a woman who reminds me of my mother!"

It was now close to curfew time so we headed back to the ship, disappointed, but determined to do better at the next opportunity.

Our chance came a few nights later when we were able to leave the ship prior to our self-appointed guardians.

This time around we had decided that we would demand to see the merchandise prior to entering the establishment. We wandered around and fell in behind three Australian officers who were on a mission similar to our own. The difference between us was that they knew exactly where they were going. A block later, they knocked on the door of a house that was by far the largest in the neighborhood. A well-dressed woman opened the door and graciously welcomed us to her home. She apparently knew the Aussies and quickly summoned three very appealing, slender young women.

We looked at each other and smiled. Bunyetz, taking the initiative, conveyed our request for two of them. Her response in perfect English politely informed us that those particular young ladies were reserved for officers. I asked what might be available for us. Without another word she left the room and in a short time returned with two women, who were neither appealing nor slender but at least were young—too young. We thanked her for her time and effort. Once again, we had failed in our mission.

Feeling that the occasion warranted something stronger than beer, we stopped at a bar and ordered whiskey. We had not been at the table for ten minutes when two women, not too old and not too young, and not bad looking either, warmly greeted us. They asked if we would like some company and we answered in the affirmative.

Their English was sufficient for us to quickly learn that they could be available to us for, if we wished, any length of time we could afford. Little time was spent in chitchat or pleasantries; this was strictly a business negotiation. We settled on a price for a one-hour engagement.

On the way back to the ship, Bunyetz was in high spirits and expressed great satisfaction with his as well as his partners' sexual agility and stamina. I suppose he assumed that I was equally content, as he suggested that we return on the following evening. I declined the offer with the excuse that I had already agreed to switch deck duty with one of guys.

I knew that Bunyetz had greatly exaggerated his account of his accomplishments since the four of us had not only shared the same room but also the same bed. When we questioned the arrangements we were told that one room and one bed was the standard for the price that we had paid. There was little time for new negotiations since the girls were already pushing us into the room and onto the bed. I gave no resistance whatsoever and accepted my role merely as a student in a foreign country.

The next day, I found myself expressing words and sentiments similar to those voiced by the married crew following a night of house visits. They would lament their self-indulgence, plead for forgiveness, and pledge unswerving love and loyalty to their loved one. Like them, I felt that my need for instant gratification had temporarily gotten the better of my common sense, but also like my mates, this sense of guilt proved to be a fleeting sentiment, and soon we were all back on the streets again.

* * * * *

We departed Ponta Delgada in mid-April. Our immediate destination was the Straits of Gibraltar and the Mediterranean.

The four weeks we had been ashore were sufficient to erase whatever sea going adjustment we had made, and once again many of the crew were overtaken with nausea. For the first 24 hours, dry crackers were consumed and self-pity was the sentiment of the day. Again, I was blessed, but this time I made no effort to share my good fortune with others. I had learned that people suffering from seasickness seek neither companionship nor sympathy.

It took less than a day for a full recovery of the crew and we were quickly and smartly back at our jobs. The waters were calm and the ship was problem free. We made good speed and two days later we were able to make out the southern coast of Portugal. Visibility was excellent, and as we entered the narrowest point of the Straits we could clearly see the coasts of the most northern part of Morocco and the Tarifa, the most southern part of Spain. A short time later, we sailed through the Straits and into the open sea. As we progressed, it became more and more difficult to detect land, until eventually both coasts were lost from view. That evening there was a celebration marking both our entry into the Mediterranean as well as our having gone four full days without any serious mishap.

Two days later, we were informed that our destination would be Savona, Italy. Savona was a small port located just to the north of Genoa. We would be docked there for at least six weeks. During that period, the ship would be completely refitted in order to accommodate our human cargo of displaced persons.

Though this news had been anticipated, the announcement of specific destination and an actual time frame created a buzz. Now the speculation began anew as to who would take command of the ship, who might stay with the ship, and who might be transferred to another vessel. Though we had become accustomed to not asking and being grateful for any bit of news, we continued to talk among ourselves as if one of us had the answer but refused to share it with the others.

The voyage from Gibraltar to Savona passed quickly and took on the easy, carefree characteristics of a Mediterranean cruise, sans the amenities that come with a luxury liner. The waters remained deep blue, and our ship glided along our sea of glass. When not on duty I sunned on deck, read, and played cards. A couple of the guys, using makeshift fishing tackle, made a noble but less than productive attempt at deep-sea fishing.

Our tranquility was soon interrupted by the news that a British frigate had intercepted and boarded a small craft carrying 250 illegal immigrants to Palestine. The captain of the ship was ordered by British officers to reverse course and return to his port of origin. He protested the order, pointing out that the ship was in international waters and the demand of the British was in clear violation of established maritime law. But his protestations as well as those of refugee leaders were to no avail. The captain was given two choices: either turn about or his ship would be confiscated and his passengers returned by some other means.

The reaction of our crew to this news was predictable. There were cries of outrage and anger. But no one on board could match in emotional tone or content the comments of our captain. Using the bridge megaphone, he shared his sentiments of the Royal British Navy and the world with us. In a voice filled with rage and indignation, he damned the kings and queens of England from the time of Henry I to Elizabeth II. He placed a variety of curses upon the House of Lords, the British Parliament, The Foreign Office, and former Prime Minister Neville Chamberlain, who had sold out Czechoslovakia in order to appease Hitler. He spared only the working class people of England and Sir Arthur Balfour. (Serving as Foreign Secretary in 1917, Balfour had drafted what became known as the Balfour Declaration, which declared that his Majesty's Government "views with favor the establishment in Palestine of a national home for the Jewish people, and will use their best endeavors to facilitate the achievement of that object...".)

But the captain saved his greatest wrath for the Royal British Navy. In words that rang with defiance, he declared, "Royal Navy, my ass! If any of those Limey scum try to board my ship, I will kill every bloody one of them!" There was no doubt in my mind that he meant every word, curse, and profanity that he had uttered.

The most poignant observation came from a man whom I would consider the least likely source, our Swedish chief engineer. This man, who hardly spoke and rarely offered an opinion, noted, "I suppose the Brits believe that they are supposed to finish the job which Hitler started."

My own reaction leaned more toward bewilderment than anger. Why would the British or any other nation that fought against the Nazis resist the proposition of finding a safe haven for Jewish survivors? Why do the host countries in which the displaced find themselves encourage their quick departure, and then deprive them from going to the one land that welcomes them? Obviously there was no satisfying answer, since I was seeking a moral explanation for behavior which was politically driven.

As we continued on our journey, there was an uneasy awareness among us that we, too, might be faced with a confrontation with the British. Perhaps British intelligence already knew of our presence and our mission.

During the first week of May, we arrived at the port of Savona. As we were escorted to our designated pier by a small Italian tugboat, most of the crew was above deck, grateful that unlike Ponta Delgada, we were spared the bum boats. There were other ships of varying size docked nearby, including an American naval vessel.

The dock itself was a long, narrow concrete pathway leading into the city of Savona. We were assembled by the first mate and told that a brief six-hour shore leave was being granted. As in the past, we were reminded to say nothing other than we were in Savona for general repairs and supplies.

Since the older crewmembers no longer felt a need or perhaps a desire to watch over me, I decided to make my first leave a solo one. As I walked along the dock I saw that there were the usual bars, cafes, small groceries, bakeries, and fishing tackle shops that were typical of most European ports. Because the war had ended less than a year ago I expected to see some evidence of structural damage. I soon observed that while the war had left untouched the physical setting of Savona, the economic and social damage had been devastating. Many young men had been killed or wounded, hundreds of children had been evacuated, families displaced, and current employment opportunities were nil. Elderly women would gather around the docked ships pleading for the leftovers that we considered garbage. Children begged for food, cigarettes and money. Other kids served as pimps, assuring all takers they could provide "young virgins." Older men would follow behind us in hopes of picking up discarded cigarette butts. Schools had not yet reopened, and there seemed to be little evidence of any functioning social service organization.

In Savona, there were numerous parks and churches, as well as the retail shops you would expect to find in a mid-sized city. In spite of their hardships, the local people were friendly, and several waved to me as they walked by the table where I sat with a glass of wine, some bread, and a plate of cheese.

I was eager to see and learn more of the country. There was something about the language, the music, the style and gestures of the people that appealed to me. Though the Italians of the Mussolini era had been allies of Germany, I never felt the same contempt and hatred that I felt for all Germans. Admittedly, I viewed the German people as a monolith, all cut of the same cloth as Adolph Hitler. In the matter of Italy, I allowed myself to separate the Fascists from the masses of Italians I considered to be without guilt. Perhaps this was a naive view, but it was one that was only to be reinforced by my day-to-day experiences in Italy.

We had been informed earlier that new people would be joining us in order to prepare for the next and most important phase of our journey. Two of the four were former Italian partisans who had been active in the anti-Fascist, resistance movement. Both were dark, strong looking men whose appearance and manner were gracious and at the same time determined. Their role would be twofold: first, to oversee the work of the Italian crew who would be doing the required on board construction modifications;

second, to serve as liaison and deal with Italian governmental officials.

The third addition was a Sabra (a native born Palestinian Jew) and member of the Haganah (the defense force established by the Jewish government and considered illegal by the British). He was a young man, tall, blonde, and in his early thirties. His task would be to coordinate all organizational efforts involved in transporting our passengers from refugee camps to our ship. The logistics would be very complex and problematic given the number of people involved and the absolute requirement for secrecy.

The fourth and final addition came as a great and pleasant surprise for me. It was Mandy. For reasons I did not know, he had been transferred from our sister ship, the Norsyd, and would now serve as an officer with the Beauharnois. His presence on the ship did wonders for my morale and self-confidence. We greeted each other warmly, and I took great pride in being his tour guide. Later, I learned that the reason for his transfer had been an unexpected delay in the departure date of the Norsyd. It was great having Mandy as a mate.

Every morning I would start my workday by standing on the deck and watching the Italian workers as they approached our ship. En route, they would stop at a local bakery/café to buy warm rolls and hot coffee. They ate, drank, and chatted among themselves as they came down the dock and up the entrance plank to our ship, the scent of fresh bread and coffee following them.

The work to be done aboard the ship was significant and time consuming. The goal was to take a ship with a passenger capacity of 175 and expand those quarters so they could accommodate more than 1,200 people. It would require every inch of available space below and above deck. Finding sufficient sleeping space was only one of the challenges. The passengers—men, women, and children—would need to be fed and provided with adequate toilet facilities. Finally, because of the uncertainty as to how long our voyage might take, we would need to carry more than the usual amount of required provisions and fresh water.

Though there was much onboard work and activity, there was little that required the fulltime attention of the ship's crew. My own regularly scheduled mainatence duties took no more than three hours of each day, which left me time to explore this vibrant city.

I became increasingly aware of how the death of Mussolini and Italy's surrender opened the door for a feverish outburst of political campaigning and elections—the first open national elections held in many years. Like most things Italian, the elections were far different from any I had ever experienced in the United States. For one thing, there were many more political parties, something to suit and satisfy every political taste.

There appeared to be few ground rules and certainly no restrictions on recruiting party loyalists. High unemployment, the shortage of public school facilities, and limited options in leisure time choices all gave everyone a foothold in getting in on the campaign activity. It was not unusual to have candidates for multiple parties touring Savona at the same time. Party workers would claim a town square's plaza or a churchyard and declare it as their turf. Large, brightly colored banners were hung, bands would play, and free food and drink contributed to the festive atmosphere. After the dark years of oppression and exploitation, of war and defeat, people were eager to bust out and celebrate.

It did not seem to matter who the candidate was or the ideology of the particular party. Every part of the political spectrum, with the exception of the Fascists, was represented. My favorites were the Communists and the Liberal Socialists. Their celebrations offered the best entertainment and refreshments. They also seemed to attract the most spontaneous and energetic segment of party faithful. The dancing, singing, music, and drinking were almost endless and speeches were kept to a minimum.

After a few glasses of wine, I would join in with others and shout, "*Finito Benito, Viva il Socialismo, alla Libera!*"

Another important factor contributing to my special enjoyment of these events was the abundance of beautiful young women who were friendly, outgoing, and easy to be with. Language differences were rarely a barrier, and much of the time was a spent in group dance, eating, drinking, and just watching others. I got to know a very attractive 17-year-old girl whose name was Anie. In appearance and dress, she looked like a typical American adolescent. She wore skirts with a blouse or sweater, penny loafer shoes, and bobby socks. She lived with her mother, who during the occupation had lived with an American Army officer. Anie had managed to acquire just enough English that we were able to communicate. Our time was spent together attending political campaign parties, going for walks, swimming, and frequenting one of the two local music clubs. We became good friends and enjoyed each other's company.

There were a few occasions when, through the courtesy of one of the Italian contractors, we were given the loan of a small car. With four other members of the crew, we drove down the coast to San Remo. Along the way we stopped at family-owned cafes and bistros where there was cooking unlike anything I would ever experience again. The freshest seafood with a wide assortment of pastas and delicious vegetables were simply prepared with wonderful red wine, which, for some reason I never understood, was referred to as "*vin ordinaire.*" To my taste, there was nothing ordinary about the wine, but its taste helped explain why wine was the beverage of choice for most, if not all, Italian families. This was certainly wine that was a wide cut above the Mogen David and Thunderbird that I had consumed as an adolescent. After eating and drinkin*g, we would make our way to the beach and spend the rest of the day swimming, reading, and relaxing under the bright, warm sun.

One evening the boatswain asked several of us if we had any interest in driving to Milan and visiting La Scala. I knew nothing about Milan, though it was only a two-hour ride from Savona. I had never even heard of La Scala. Thayer explained that La Scala was an old and most magnificent opera house. He spoke to us about the great conductor Arturo Toscanini, who had fled Italy because he refused to live under a Fascist regime. After years at La Scala, this most favored son of Italy had abandoned assured comfort and security and fled to America. In America, he continued to be a vocal critic of Mussolini and raised funds for the partisans. For these reasons he had become an important symbol for the Italian resistance movement. Now, at seventy-nine years of age and after many years of exile, Toscanini was returning to La Scala.

As we arrived in Milan, there was great excitement throughout the city, for in the evening Toscanini would be conducting the first of his concerts. Tickets for this celebratory event were available only to citizens of Milan, with priority given to students and seniors. To make up for not being able to attend the concert, that evening Thayer arranged to have a recording of Toscanini played over the PA system.

The work of renovating our vessel was progressing without serious impediments. The major task was to find the space required for installing more than 1,200 bunk beds. In addition, sanitation facilities, as well as additional storage to hold the passengers' baggage, were needed. Finally, the galley required the installation of several large stoves and serving counters. I was amazed by the creativity and innovation of the Italians as they increased by sixfold the number of below deck bunks.

The word now was that we should be prepared to board our cargo within two weeks. The immigrants we would be transporting to Palestine were currently living in Displaced Person camps approximately fifty miles from Genoa. We had inquired of our Haganah leader if it might be possible for us to visit one of the camps. He said that he would explore the matter and let us know.

One evening he informed us that a visit would be possible, but that we would need to go in groups of no more than five. Each group would have a guide provided by camp officials and, of course, we were to say nothing of our reasons for being in Italy. I was in a group with Mandy, the boatswain, Bunyetz, and one other guy. We left at dawn and headed in the direction of Genoa. Ironically, until less than a year before, the camp had been a basic training installation for Italian Army recruits. It was now being leased from the Italian government by an American-based organization. This particular camp held 600 refugees; the majority were Jews from Poland and Czechoslovakia.

When we arrived, we were taken through several of the barracks, which had been modified in order to house families. There were separate barracks for single men and women. U.S. Army surplus cots were placed in long rows on each side of the barracks. There were few, if any, amenities. Windows were bare of curtains; overhead lighting came from a bare bulb attached to a socket hanging from the ceiling. There were no chairs, desks, dressers or closets. The few personal possessions people had managed to bring were kept in old suitcases and canvas bags stored beneath beds. There appeared to be more women than men, and about a third were elderly people. There were young children as well as some teenagers.

What impressed and surprised me was that despite all they had endured, despite the meagerness of their surroundings, these people were neither somber nor defeated. It was as if being a survivor had left them with an attitude of "no matter what more comes, I will not be broken."

Most of the refugees spoke their native tongue or Yiddish. Thanks to those many years at the Shalom Alechim Folk School, it turned out that I was the only one in our group who spoke Yiddish. The first person I spoke with was a 38-year-old man born in Poland. His name was

Avram, and he had a wife, Lisa, and a daughter, Golda, age two. We sat in the dining room, where we drank hot tea and talked about how he and his family had come to this place in Italy.

Avram was born and lived for many years in Warsaw. After completing high school he had enrolled in a technical college where he wished to study civil engineering. While in college, he and another student roomed together and became close friends. When the Germans occupied Warsaw, all Jewish students of every grade level were prohibited from attending school. All Jews were forced to abandon their businesses and professions. Avarm's parents and young brother were among the thousands of Warsaw Jews who were sent to concentration camps. In a voice that had now become almost a whisper, Avram went on to tell me that his survival was not an act of God but of a friend who was not even a Jew. His good friend from school had arranged with his aunt and uncle for Avram to live with them on their farm outside of Warsaw. He had stayed with them until the Russian Army occupied Poland. When he returned to Warsaw, he learned that his entire family—parents, brothers, uncles, and aunts—had all been murdered. Avram was the sole survivor.

While in Warsaw, Avram made contact with a Zionist organization assisting Jews who might wish to migrate to Palestine. Up to that point Avram had not really given any serious thought to what he wanted to do with his life. He told me he knew that he did not want to remain in Poland. It was not so much a burning desire to live in a Jewish homeland that motivated him, but rather the need to make a life somewhere else. When he came to Italy for orientation and training, he met his wife Lisa. He did not say much about Lisa's past except to point out that the child, Golda, was Lisa's daughter. I said something about how grand it was that he had met and fallen in love with Lisa and now he had a family of his own.

Avram looked at me as if I had completely missed the point and said, "*Du farshtesit nit vos ich zog. Es it nit from lib vos ich hob Lisa und Golda zu mir gemacht a mishpocah* (You do not understand what I am saying. It was not because of love that Lisa and Golda became my family)." Rather than love, it was the unbearable pain of loneliness that brought them together. Like Avram, Lisa and Golda were homeless, without family and without any clue as to what they would do with the remainder of their lives. No matter, they were now a family with a common destination and purpose. The child had been given the name "Golda" in honor of Golda Meir.

Our conversation ended with Avram asking me why I was there since it was apparent that I was not a refugee. I did not know how to answer and certainly could not share my real purpose for being in Italy. I replied that I was a sailor on an American ship and that we were in port for several days. While there, I had learned of the camp and, being a Jew, I wanted to visit.

As we stood to say goodbye, I could not resist embracing the three of them. It was as if they had now become part of my family and I was saying "shalom" to loved ones. We hugged, and Avram's final words to me were spoken in Hebrew: "*Loshana habab nYerushiliam* (Next year in Jerusalem)."

Each of the crew had brought boxes of candy bars to share with children in the camp. Prior to leaving, we were taken to a play area where there were a dozen or so kids from ages seven to ten. We were instructed to give each child no more than a couple of chocolate bars, and the remainder would be given to other children. I offered my two Milky Ways to a little boy who was playing on a swing. He took both bars, placed one in the pocket of his trousers and very carefully unwrapped the other. He then took one small bite off the top of the bar, rewrapped the remainder, and placed it in his pocket.

I could not believe my eyes. Every American kid I had ever known, including myself, would have immediately and quickly devoured both bars. A nearby teacher provided an explanation. There had been so many times in the short lives of these kids when they were never certain as to when or whether there would be another meal. They had mastered at a very early age the difficult task of self-control and self-imposed rationing, so that even now, after weeks of regular and uninterrupted meals, they would still hoard and hide their food.

Soon after, we left and returned to Savona. There was very little conversation on the way back to the ship. I believe each of us needed our own quiet time to deal with what we had experienced.

Chapter 6

Over the next several weeks we made final preparations that brought us closer to our departure and mission. Meetings were held with our captain, Haganah representatives, and an Italian partisan responsible for all ship-related logistics. His name was Salvatore, and he had been a major figure in the Italian underground. I never knew how he became involved with the *Aliyah Bet*, but the locals as well as the Haganah leader treated him with great respect.

The Haganah members were all very serious young men, concerned primarily with their assignment of insuring that all passengers and crew safely reach our destination. In the next few weeks we would all have a much clearer picture of just how problematic, frustrating, and dangerous this mission would become.

In the third week of June, all construction and refitting was completed. We were now prepared to take on passengers and provide them with sleeping quarters and adequate feeding facilities. Drinking water fountains had been installed topside, and extra canvas was stored until needed to protect people from the hot sun.

We departed Savona in the early evening and headed south, down the coast to the port of La Spezia. We were to remain in La Spezia for no more than a few days before moving on to a place where we would be boarding our first passangers. The run from Savona to La Spezia had two purposes: first, to be certain that all engines and new equipment were fully operational; second, to take on food and other needed supplies. The short trip was problem free, and upon arrival a pilot ship escorted us to our berth.

Over the past week, the crew's impatience and tension had been increasing with each passage that brought us closer to our ultimate destination. It had been several months since we left New York, and we were still in transit. Morale, which was at its lowest ebb, was worsened by the fact that no mail had been forwarded to us. We were hot, tired, anxious, and getting to a point where it was too easy to find fault with others. Most frustrating was the belief that our leaders had the answers to all of our questions but chose not to share the information with us.

In quick order all required provisions, including canned goods, powdered eggs, fresh bread, and water, were brought on board. On the evening of our third day in port, we were informed that we would depart the following evening to pick up passengers. The trip would take no more than three hours. We were also given instructions as to the procedures for assigning passengers to their sleeping quarters. Each refugee would be given a piece of paper containing information on sleeping section, bunk row, and a bunk number. On deck quarters would be given first to the elderly and handicapped. Men and women would have separate sleeping arrangements. Meals would be done on a rotation basis, with special provisions made for those who would eat only kosher foods. All crewmembers not assigned to a special duty participated in distributing information and acting as escorts. Yiddish speaking crewmembers were requested to move about the ship offering assistance wherever we might be needed.

The depression and discontent we felt only a few days earlier completely vanished. Now there was excitement, high energy, and a strong feeling of solidarity. Finally, after all the delays and frustrations, we would fulfill our mission of bringing 1,200 refugees to *Eretz Israel.*

Sometime after sunset we traveled further down the coast to a point offshore from where the refugees would be gathering. Soon we were able to see a long caravan of trucks proceeding down a hill onto the stone-covered beach. We waited for the signal to move into the inlet and drop the gangplank. A few moments later, an onshore light sent the coded message we had anticipated. We moved slowly forward, quietly drifting to the inlet, and dropped our gangplank

Just as the first passengers were about to board, a dozen or so *carabinieri* (Italian police) drove up. In the darkness we could hear a commotion, but we could not see what was happening. The passengers moved quickly and quietly up the gangplank. Another hour passed, and finally the cars with the *carabinieri* drove away and the last of the passengers boarded. Though exhausted by the long trip to the ship and the additional uncertainty and delay caused by the arrival of the police, they appeared relieved and happy to finally be on board. The crew greeted them with enthusiastic cries of *shalom* as we welcomed and escorted them to their sleeping quarters. The arrival process went quickly, and within an hour we had boarded the first half of the expected 1,200 passengers.

Daylight came and there was a growing concern that the Italian police might return and either interrupt or stop the ship from departing. The second group of refugees was now two hours behind schedule. Our captain, the lead Italian partisan, and the Haganah liaison were attempting to make contact with the camp from which the refugees were coming. An hour later, we could hear trucks approaching. One truck had broken down, causing a delay while they shifted the passengers to the other trucks. The second group to arrive included many more elderly people. Those already on board joined in greeting the newcomers and were helpful in getting them to their quarters.

The children were the first to adjust to being on a ship and were soon running around the deck.

Crewmembers and passenger volunteers undertook the first meal service. As large containers of food were brought to the deck, two lines were formed, one for those preferring kosher food, another for all others. Each person was instructed to keep his or her bowls and utensils for the remainder of the voyage. Tubs, for dishwashing and garbage disposal, were placed in several locations.

As the final truck departed and we prepared to leave, several police cars approached. The captain gave the order to depart immediately. The engines rumbled, the gangplank was cast off, and we were on our way.

It would be one year later, through a chance encounter with I.F. Stone on a train to New York City, that I was able to learn what had occurred that prior evening when the police showed up. *

At the time, I.F. Stone, who preferred to be addressed as "Izzy," was a reporter for PM, a New York tabloid. He had managed to gain permission from the appropriate Jewish sources to be the first American reporter invited to sail on an *Aliyah Bet* vessel. His plan was to travel to Europe, where he would visit several displaced person camps, and then make the trip to Palestine with either us or our sister ship.

I had met Izzy once before when he visited with our crew while we were still in New York. He was of average build, in his early forties, and spoke Yiddish plus a scattering of several other languages. Though easygoing in manner, it was apparent that he considered his assignment more as a mission and a tribute to his people than an objective journalistic inquiry. His resentment and anger at the British and the role they were playing in preventing Jewish refugee migration to Palestine were well known.

According to Izzy, just as we were beginning the boarding process the Italian police arrived and moved

* For those who would seek more detailed information, as well as the full story of Stone's adventure, I would urge them to read his book, Underground to Palestine, Pantheon Press, 1946.

toward the gangplank shouting that they had come across a bunch of Jews. In an effort to intimidate the police, Izzy stepped forward and flashed his impressive looking reporter's State Department card. He asked for the officers' names and ranks, informing them that he would be sending a cable to America with a full description of the encounter. The lead Italian officer refused to give his name, so Izzy tried a different tactic.

He asked them why they should risk getting a bad reputation with Americans by doing the dirty work of the British. As this exchange was going on between Izzy and the Italians, the refugees were quietly coming up the gangplank and boarding our ship. The Italian officer proposed as a compromise, that the ship remain in port while Izzy came with them to the prefecture. Izzy drove off with the officer and several of the other *carabinieri*. Meanwhile, the loading continued.

At headquarters, Izzy threatened that with one phone call he could end all American aid to Italy. The fact that the Italians were not fond of the British and uncertain as to how much influence Stone could really muster seemed sufficient to delay any serious actions.

Izzy finished his story as we entered the tunnel at Penn Station. I had in my wallet the blue card that had been issued by the Yishuv (Jewish Community of Palestine) and served as an entrance visa. I asked Izzy for his autograph, and he wrote, "To David Gottlieb, a fellow traveler in the *Aliyah Bet*, in memory of an exciting night in Italy."

On our second day at sea I had more of an opportunity to walk about the deck and have a closer look at our passengers, who were of all ages and origins. Most were originally from Poland, Czechoslovakia, and Russia. Some were Jews who had fled Germany and had lived in Holland; others were Jews from France, Italy, Lithuania, Turkey, and Hungary. Some were strident Orthodox Jews; others were openly atheistic. There was a large group of young adults, who intended to live in kibbutzim (collectives) once they arrived in *Eretz*. Many of them were already affiliated with a Zionist organization and had been studying Hebrew. More than a few had relatives in *Eretz* and planned to stay with them until they were able to establish their own homes. The remainder had no plans, but seemed to believe that even an uncertain future would be an improvement upon the life they had been living.

As I walked around the deck through the throngs of people, I was amazed with the number of different languages being spoken, the backgrounds and ethnicity. On the port side of the ship, a group of Orthodox men wrapped in prayer shawls were swaying back and forth as they *davened* (prayed). Not far from them, a small group of Turkish men had removed their shirts and were performing a very fluid, sensual dance. Two men accompanied them—one played a balalaika, the other a wooden flute. A short distance down the deck, a group of Polish Jews was having a heated political debate about Communism and the future of Europe. At the bow of the ship, a group of young women were sunning themselves and speculating on whether or not all *Sabras* would be as handsome as the ones on board. On the starboard side, mothers were breastfeeding their infants, and elderly *bubbies* (grandmothers) were chatting among themselves while darning old clothing.

On Friday evenings the aft deck was converted into a temporary shul (synagogue) where those who wished to participate in services could do so. The Sabbath was celebrated with the lighting of candles and a beautiful blessing sung by a woman from Poland. On the other end of the ship, a group of youthful *chalutzim* would celebrate their own *Oneg Shabbat* by dancing the hora and singing Hebrew songs.

If America, because of its diversity, could be called a "melting pot," then our ship, because of the limited space and crowded conditions, could pass as a "pressure cooker."

That evening, as I stood by the deck rails, someone patted me on the shoulder. I turned around and there was

Avram. He, Lisa, and Golda were among the last of the refugees to be boarded. He took me down below to where his family had been assigned. Like everyone else, they were in cramped quarters, the three of them sharing two small bunks. To provide some privacy, they had hung a blanket in front of their bunks. The front of each bed served as storage space for their few pieces of baggage and Golda's small doll.

As I embraced Lisa and kissed little Golda, I felt as if I had rediscovered *mishpocah* (family) that I believed had perished in the Holocaust. I asked if there was anything that they needed—food, extra blankets, anything. Avram smiled and assured me that they had all they needed and wished no more than what others received.

Over the next several days I was able to spend time with Avram. He told me that for so many years, he had not given serious thought to his future, and felt as if his fate was in the hands of others. He had accepted the fact that he would ultimately migrate to Palestine; beyond that, he had no plans. Now as we drew closer to *Eretz*, he recognized that there were decisions that had to be made. Since he had neither family nor personal contacts, he felt that it would be best to settle on a kibbutz, although he had little interest in agriculture and could not see himself spending a lifetime "feeding chickens and cows." I asked him if he had a choice of any occupation what that might be. He thought for a moment and answered, "Bus driver."

Avram could see that my reaction was one of complete surprise and bewilderment. "*Ich vil dir derzelin varum ich dos arbet* (I will tell you why I wish that kind of work)," he said.

He told me that he wanted a job where he could be free to travel throughout Palestine and not restricted to a limited space. For so many years he had lived in confined spaces with many others. He did not want to be tied down to any one place. He longed for the freedom that comes with mobility. He said that he believed once he was in

Eretz he would find employment as a bus driver. I found myself caught up in his optimism and said that I knew that one day I would board a bus in Tel Aviv and find him in the driver's seat. Avram laughed and said that I would still have to pay my fare.

Great weather and calm waters kept seasickness to a minimum, although life below decks was far from pleasant. Ventilation was poor, and the constant sounds of infants crying, people coughing, and the disturbances caused by people living in close quarters added to the tense atmosphere. Most would have preferred to be topside, but that was not possible. We did our best to make the elderly and ill reasonably comfortable. There were times that the Haganah liaison had to take the megaphone to persuade the male passengers to go below deck.

A doctor on board—as well as a group of men and women with first aid instruction—was kept busy night and day. The doctor's office was located in what had been the officer's mess. For this voyage, formal rank became secondary to necessity, and officers ate with the crew. During the course of the voyage there were two births, two weddings, one bar mitzvah, and fortunately, no deaths.

We were always on the lookout for other vessels, and when one was sighted all passengers were quickly sent below. We made every effort not to be detected by the British or any other ship that might pass on the news of illegal immigrants at sea.

On our final full day at sea, everyone was called on deck for announcements and instructions. The Haganah leader first informed us that we would be arriving in Haifa the next day. The reaction to his message was one of wild enthusiasm, laughter, embracing, and shouts of, "*Eretz, Eretz, Eretz, Israel!*"

As the tumult subsided, the Haganah leader went on to say that we could not be sure as to what would occur if and when the British tried to stop us. "Many of you will once again have to go to camps for a while. The difference is that these camps will be in *Eretz* and friends will surround you."

One older man turned to his wife and said in Yiddish, "So, once again they put us in a prison camp, even in our own land!"

Our instructions were that if the British were to board our ship, we should follow orders given by the Haganah, who had wide experience in these matters and could be trusted and depended upon. We were than told that each of us would be given an entry visa. We formed two lines and proceeded with the business of obtaining our entry documentation.

A blue card, smaller than a passport, was given to each of us. The card was a permit to enter Palestine, with Hebrew written on one side and English on the other. We were to add our names, the names of our parents, our date and place of birth, and our nationality.

Authority to enter Palestine was granted by the Yishuv (the Jewish Community of Palestine). There were several sources cited in support of this action by the Yishuv. The one I found most appropriate was from Ezekiel:

> "And they shall abide in the land that I have given unto Jacob my servant, wherein your fathers abode, and they shall abide therein, even they, and their children, and their children's children, forever."

Crewmembers were told that employees of the Yishuv who would be serving as entry agents would collect the cards.

As expected, that evening there was much excitement among the passengers and crew. The major problem we faced was getting all the passengers below deck to their quarters. Our chances of getting our passengers and ship into Haifa would improve the longer we remained undetected. Precautions were taken to eliminate all lights other than those required for navigation.

After my watch at midnight, I was determined to remain on deck as long as possible so that I would be among the first who would see the City of Haifa and the shores of *Eretz.*

On my way to the galley to get some coffee, Mandy stopped me and asked if I had a little time to talk. I was more than happy to have his company, as well as any information he might want to share with me. I knew that Mandy was involved in all discussions and decisions affecting our mission. We both took our cups and went topside.

It was a beautiful night. The sky was filled with stars, and only the churning of the propeller broke the silence. Mandy began by saying that this would be our last night at sea, and the next day would demand the complete cooperation of all those on board. He expected that the British would attempt to stop us prior to our entering the port of Haifa. He could only speculate about what the British would do with the ship and passengers. If we got close enough to Haifa, the chances were good we would all be transferred to a detention camp in Athlit near Haifa. The other far less desirable alternative would be having the ship and passengers escorted to a camp in Cyprus.

I told Mandy that I was curious about what would happen after we left the detention camp. Mandy's response was quick and to the point: "You will not be going to any camp. Once you leave the ship and go through immigration, you will be met and taken to another ship. That ship will be sailing for Italy, and from there you will obtain passage back to the States."

I was stunned, and before I could reply, Mandy offered an explanation. He reminded me that I had not reached the age of eighteen and that I had not yet completed high school. Given my experiences, I would be more valuable returning to the States and working for Habonim. The movement needed many new and youthful leaders. Since I had experienced *Hacshara* at the farm in New Jersey and had also participated in *Aliyah Bet,* I would be a perfect candidate. Returning to the States would allow me to complete school while I worked for a Jewish state.

Mandy knew me well enough to recognize that flattery would be the most effective form of persuasion with me. "David," he said, "not many guys your age have accomplished so much. For a lot of people, you will be a hero."

To argue with Mandy would have been fruitless, and I was quickly finding real merit in his argument. I was starting to miss my family, and I was eager to be with Shoshanah. Although the completion of school was not among my top priorities, I knew it was the right thing to do. However, I must admit it was the idea of celebrity that carried the most clout with me. The image of being the center of attention with my peers, brothers, parents, and others captured me. Of course, I shared none of that with Mandy. Instead I said something about my willingness to set aside my own desires if that was what was required of me.

Mandy smiled and said, "Good. Now let's get this ship into Haifa."

On July 6, 1946, our ship was less than 30 miles from Haifa. The Haganah leader did his best to encourage everyone to remain below decks, but no one wanted to miss the opportunity to be the first to see Mount Carmel. It seemed as if all of our 1,250 passengers, no matter the age or physical condition, were on deck. The collective excitement and tension produced an almost electric current that seemed to run through every person on the ship.

A short time passed, and then there was a sudden roar from the refugees as they first saw the vague outlines of the city of Haifa. At that very moment, the Captain called for the Panamanian flag to be lowered. With all eyes looking to the sky, the blue and white Star of David, flag of *Eretz Israel*, was raised. There was much cheering and the singing of "Hatikvah," the Jewish national anthem, followed by a few seconds of silence. Even though there was little available space, people managed to form a huge circle and dance the hora. There was much shouting, hugging, kissing, and crying as a huge banner was raised proclaiming the return of the exiles to the Promised Land. Another banner noted that our ship had been renamed the Josiah Wedgewood, for the British military officer and statesman who had supported the Balfour Declaration for a Jewish state in Palestine.

While the celebration continued, a British frigate drew alongside our ship. After a short exchange between our captain and an English officer, it was announced that a pilot ship would guide us safely into the Haifa harbor. As we moved closer we could see and hear the thousands of citizens of Haifa who lined the dock to welcome us to *Eretz* and to make certain that no harm came to us. They waved and shouted "shalom" and "*baruch habba*" (welcome the holy ones).

After all of the secrecy, speculation, and apprehension, our arrival was smooth and anti-climatic. In an orderly manner, we departed the ship and walked up the dock to the immigration clearance building. There was a long row of desks staffed by Jewish representatives of the Yishuv. Each of us presented our entry card, which was stamped as we exited the building.

Mandy was there to escort our Swedish chief engineer and me to another office to meet our contact. The other passengers and most of the crew boarded buses to the Athlit camp. I did not see Avram or his family, neither was it possible for me to say "shalom" to my mates. Mandy and I embraced and said our farewells. I promised him that I would return to *Eretz Israel.*

After waiting less than an hour, the Chief and I were taken by one of the Haganah workers to an Italian ship docked at a nearby pier. The ship was an old freighter scheduled to leave that evening for Naples. We walked up the gangplank and were escorted to the captain's quarters. The Haganah liaison, who spoke Italian, introduced us and gave the captain an envelope, which I assumed contained payment for our passage. The captain had one of his officers show us where we would be bunked and the galley area. Our quarters were small but comfortable, and compared to the accommodations on the Wedgewood, these were first-class quarters.

We extended our thanks to the Haganah leader and took a stroll along the deck. At dinner we were invited to dine with the captain and his officers. We relaxed for the first time in many days with good food and excellent wine.

In the week it took us to get to Naples, time seemed to go very slowly, as I had no work assignments, nothing to read, and no one I could talk to other than the Chief. Most often I would sit on the deck and reflect about the past months and wonder about the status of my former crew-mates. I regretted having left without any explanation or farewell, but I assumed that Mandy had informed them why I was not in the detention camp with them.

We arrived in Naples on the morning of July 16. We had anticipated that our contact would meet us at the docking pier. We waited for several hours and still no contact. The Chief suggested we walk into the city and find a place to stay for the evening. Between us, we had a few Italian lire and about twenty American dollars. Not far from the port we found a flophouse of a hotel which catered to beached seamen. After renting rooms for the night we sat down to dinner and discussed our next steps.

The Chief had already decided that for whatever the reason, there had been a screw up and that there was little likelihood any contact would be made with us. Our best bet would be to find a berth on a ship going to the States. Given the circumstances, I could think of no reason why I should not follow his lead. He proposed that in the morning we go to the American Embassy and see what help they might provide. We would, he pointed out, have to tell them how we came to be stranded in Naples.

The next morning we took a taxi to the consulate. The Chief told our story to an English-speaking receptionist and we were referred to a consular official. He was a young man, pleasant, and eager to be of assistance. As the Chief predicted, after examining our passports and Coast

Guard papers he inquired as to how we came to be boatless in Naples.

Without a moment's hesitation, and in less than a few minutes, the Chief summarized our entire voyage and mission. The young man asked us several questions and then excused himself, saying that he would return shortly. He returned accompanied by a more senior official. The older man asked the Chief to repeat his story.

We were asked if we had been detained by the British military and answered no. The Chief volunteered that we had remained in Palestine for less than three hours. The consular official asked about our financial status and if we could obtain funds for commercial flight or ship passage to America. I responded in the negative and the Chief added that he would prefer to work his way back to the States. "Me, too," I added.

We were told that the Embassy kept a roster of American ships in the Naples port and data on berth availability. Not surprisingly, there were many more openings for lowly ordinary seaman and wipers than for officers. I was given a clearance and exit form from the Embassy, as well as the name and location of an American ship looking for a Wiper. Since it was early afternoon and I was anxious to get closure on this issue, I thanked both consular officials, bid farewell to my mate, and headed for the docks.

The vessel was an early World War II Liberty Ship named the Belvedere, and its homeport was Beaumont, Texas. It was painted dark gray and still had the mounts on deck that one time secured anti-aircraft gunnery. As I came aboard, I gave my name and purpose to a deck hand and asked if he could escort me to the officer of the day. His lack of response was my first indication that this ship and crew would be far different from the Wedgwood. This guy was about fifty years of age, potbellied, with a bulbous red nose and stubble which covered much of his face. I repeated my request, and this time he gave an irritated jerk of his head. He informed me that the officer I needed to talk with was the first mate and that he was currently having breakfast.

I commented that I had not eaten and asked if he would show me the way to the crew galley. Graciousness and hospitality were traits not possessed by this man. His answer was a brisk "no," but he said he would inform the first mate of my presence.

When he returned he was accompanied by the first mate, who in both appearance and manner stood in dramatic contrast to the deck hand. He introduced himself as Mr. Morgan. He was in his mid-forties, tall, well groomed and articulate. He even inquired as to whether or not I had eaten and showed me the way to the galley. Once at a table, he asked to see my Merchant Marine card and passport. He did not ask why and how I came to be stranded in Genoa. It seems that losing crewmembers during a trip was not at all uncommon, particularly on the Belvedere. Sailors taking shore leave after a long voyage were known to drink too much, get rolled, and even find themselves in the local lockup. That was the case with two crewmembers of the Belvedere.

The First also told me how three other crewmembers had returned from a shore leave in Liverpool drunk and looking for trouble. Once back on board, they went to the galley and threatened to kill the only two black men on the ship. A wild and brutal fight led to the stabbing of one of the black sailors before the captain and other officers arrived and put an end to the chaos. The three troublemakers were thrown into the brig and then turned over to the U.S. Navy Shore Patrol to be deported to the States. As a result of the arrests and the desertions, any live and willing body, no matter the circumstance, was eagerly sought and accepted on board the Belvedere.

My anxiety about my new ship and crew was not eased when the First offered the advice that I make a real effort to steer clear of other crewmembers. "Do your work and keep to yourself," he told me.

My job was to replace one of the oilers in the engine room, even though my papers did not qualify me for that position. The First showed me my bunk and then the engine room where I met the Chief. The Chief explained my duties and watch time.

Since this was the return trip to homeport following four months at sea, much of my effort and that of the crew would be devoted to chipping and painting. In my case, it would be painting virtually everything in the engine room other than the engines and the steel deck.

My fellow crewmembers were a mixed lot. I would guess that the average age was about forty, most were from the South, and with the exception of the officers, few had gone beyond high school. The lack of a high school diploma was the one thing we seemed to have in common.

From brief discussions with the Chief I learned that he and several other crewmembers had been on merchant ships that were sunk by Nazi submarines.

My first non-work related encounter with some of the crew occurred in the galley the morning following my coming on board. We were at breakfast, and having introduced myself, I was asked what kind of a name was "Gottlieb." Previous experience had taught me that inquiries about my last name were to determine if I was Jewish. Seeking to avoid any unnecessary conflict, I answered that it was a German name. I went on to explain the meaning of my name: "The first part is 'Gott,' meaning God, and the second part is 'lieb,' for love, put them together and you have lover of God."

My hope that my response would be sufficient to move us to another topic was quickly dispelled. The meanest looking guy at the table, with scrawny arms sporting numerous tattoos, declared, "Boys, we got a Jew here!"

Not knowing what response to make I sat there and said nothing. I kept thinking of the advice that the First had given me and hoping that he would magically appear upon the scene.

He did not, but someone else finally broke the silence. It was the same guy who had treated me in such an indifferent and less than helpful manner when I first came on board. His comment, though I am certain not meant to aid me, managed to move things in a different direction. "No, he ain't a Jew," he said, "If he were a Jew, he would be in college, not on this tub."

His observation provoked some supportive comment and affirmative head shaking. However, my antagonist was not completely satisfied. "Well, if he ain't a kike, what is he?"

Without hesitation, I responded, "I'm Maltese." The speed and firmness of my statement seemed to gain me some acceptance. Also, the fact that none of the crew was certain he had ever met a Maltese, and hence had no basis for comparison, was, I think, helpful for my case. The issue of my ethnicity now being resolved, the table conversation turned to less controversial topics, such as women, tattoos, and hunting.

The work I did was both monotonous and physically draining. For the first few days I was painting the overhead sections of the engine room. We used a whitewash mixture, which meant that one coat was never adequate. Because the overhead was some twenty feet above the deck, it was necessary to use paint rollers attached to fifteen-foot extension poles. The routine was to first apply paint to the roller, attach the roller to the pole, climb a ladder, then, stretching your arms upward, apply the whitewash. The task was made all the more difficult because of the rolling of the ship, the noise and heat of the engine room, and the non-adhesiveness of the whitewash. More of the stuff dripped down on my face than remained on the overhead. If this miserable work was to be something other than temporary, I was likely to be among those sailors who would jump ship at the first opportunity.

When not working I usually kept my own company, but one day out of boredom I agreed to sit in on a poker game. I had the misfortune of beginner's luck, and several hours later I found myself with close to $350 in winnings. It was then that my troubles began.

My shift began at midnight, it was now 10:30 p.m., and I needed some sleep before taking on the whitewash battle. As I gathered in my winnings and prepared to leave, the guy sitting next to me grabbed my arm and made it clear that I could not just walk away from the table. Further, there was still plenty of time before midnight. I sat down intending to be done and gone as soon as possible, but my winning streak continued. Finally, at five minutes to midnight, I asked to be excused. This time there was no argument, only a firm reminder that the game would be continued when I came off duty.

At that moment, I decided that I had no other option than to be a gracious, though cowardly, winner. "Guys," I said, "here are all my winnings. Take it and divide it among yourselves, okay?"

I considered myself fortunate when they quickly accepted my offer.

The one blessing of the entire journey was that we had nothing but excellent weather. The waters were relatively calm, there was minimal rain, and we were making good time. We were to reach our destination, Beaumont, Texas, within 48 hours.

Because we were running ahead of schedule, it was necessary for the crew to work extra duty shifts. Each crewmember was to receive double time as added compensation. Since I was working in order to pay my passage, there was some question of whether I was to be paid anything at all for my overtime. Whoever had final say on the matter determined that my labor was not worthy of monetary reward.

It was also at that time that I began to give serious thought as to how I would get from Beaumont to Detroit. I had less than $30, and the idea of calling my folks, with whom I had not spoken for months, and asking them for help was not acceptable. I decided that my only other choice was to see if I could find Shoshanah and ask her for a loan.

I was contemplating both of these undesirable alternatives when the arm-grabbing poker player came up to me. He told me that they all had heard about my being shafted and not getting the bucks to which I was entitled. "The shits should have given you your money," he said, "They didn't, so we will." He counted out $168, exactly half of my poker winnings, and handed the money to me. I thanked him and rambled on about what good mates they were and how much I had learned from them. As he turned to walk away he added, "You're a good Jew boy."

Chapter 7

That evening we stopped just outside the port at Beaumont to await the pilot ship that would bring us into the harbor the next morning. It was a hot humid night, so I chose, as did others, to sleep on deck. At about 2:00 a.m. I was awakened by the buzzing and stinging of swarms of mosquitoes. All over the ship you could hear the sound of hands slapping bare arms and necks. It was a bizarre scene of chaos as we scrambled around the deck scooping up our belongings in a wild dance that could only have been created by a mad choreographer.

Welcome to Texas.

At daylight we were brought into our mooring place. I headed for the railroad station and learned that there was no direct route from Beaumont to Detroit. I was advised to take a bus to Houston and then travel by train to Atlanta. From Atlanta, a train to Chicago would take me to Detroit. The journey would take two full days by coach. I calculated that after expenses I would arrive home with my original $30.

After completing my travel arrangements, I placed calls to my folks and Shoshanah. My mother answered the phone and was, of course, surprised to hear my voice. I quickly assured her that I was in excellent health and would be home in two days. My mother kept insisting on assurances that I was "really alright." I concluded that all of the time I had been away and she had not heard from me, she assumed I was fine. But now that I unexpectedly called, she was convinced that I was afflicted with some horrible illness. "Swear on my life that you are in one piece," she said.

Shoshanah was not at home, but her mother told me that she was working as a counselor at a summer camp in Connecticut. I knew that she would be the Habonim camp at Killingworth, Connecticut. Her mother agreed to pass on word that I was back and that I would soon be in Detroit.

My bus to Houston was scheduled to leave at 4 p.m., leaving me with about two hours to kill. With the exception of some bars, a few dingy cafes, and a pool hall, there was not much in the way of tourist appeal. The only advantage I could see between Beaumont and the foreign port cities I had recently visited was that there were no small kids begging or pimping.

The bus station was located in the downtown area, and other than the people in the waiting room, there was little street activity. The temperature was in the upper nineties, and within a half-hour my shirt was soaking wet. I decided to head back to the station where I could at least escape the heat. I was mistaken. The few overhead fans only managed to push more warm air around the smoke-filled room.

I sat down on a long, hard wooden bench and began to read a paperback I had purchased. My fingers were so damp they stuck to the book's pages. I looked around the room at my fellow passengers and was struck by how they all seemed to be victims of exhaustion and frustration. There were no animated discussions, no goodbye hugs and kisses, and no laughter. The heat had sucked the energy and spirit out of everyone in the room. The people moved as slowly as the time, and I began to have doubts that I would ever make it to Houston, much less Detroit. Every few minutes I would go over to the information counter and check out the departure schedule. Finally the clerk lost patience with me and suggested that I sit down or be thrown out. He appeared to be the one person in the station with sufficient energy to generate anger. Soon the announcement of the departure of my Houston bound bus came over the loudspeaker.

The Gulf Coast bus was of pre-World War II vintage, painted in the red, white, and blue colors of the Texas state flag. I gave my ticket to the driver and made my way to the rear of the bus, thinking that since there were only a few other passengers, I would take advantage of the last full row of unoccupied seats. I was exhausted and laid down across the length of three seats to take a nap. As soon as I closed my eyes, the bus driver tapped me on the arm and said in a pleasant enough manner, "The back of the bus is for colored passengers only."

I had anticipated that he might find fault with my having occupied a full row of seats, but not because I would be crossing racial barriers. He seemed to sense my bewilderment as he once again repeated his message, this time pointing out the well-worn but still visible yellow line that served as the border between the white and black sections of the bus.

It was then that I noticed that the five or six blacks on the bus were all seated together in the rear of the bus. White people, of whom there were about ten, had the choice of sitting in any of the remaining seats.

No one seemed to be particularly interested in what was happening, and the few blacks sitting nearby struck me as making an extra effort to avoid eye contact. I collected my belongings and moved to the front of the bus.

It took me some time to fully internalize and understand what I had just experienced. Obviously, I already knew that there were laws, mainly in the South, which prohibited blacks from attending the same schools or eating in the same restaurants as whites. I was also aware of physical conflict between the races. While I was a student at Hutchins, Detroit experienced race riots so severe that curfews were imposed and tanks patrolled the streets.

During the course of the War that had just ended, blacks and whites were segregated, and blacks were assigned the lowest status jobs, such as working the mess aboard ships or burial detail in the Army. Despite the many contributions made by black officers and enlisted men, it was not until the end of the War that segregation in the armed forces was eliminated.

But this was different. This was the very first time I felt personally involved and affected. I had attended schools with black enrollment, but I had no black friends. I had never been in their neighborhoods, much less their homes. Most of the time when my parents or relatives would refer to blacks, they would use the derogatory word "*schvartzehs*," the Yiddish word for the color black. Derision of others was not restricted to blacks alone: non-Jews were "*goyim*" and German Jews were "*yekehs*."

The only black person I knew was Lilly Mae, who was our weekly maid, and of her I knew very little. I knew Lily Mae lived many miles from our home and she washed and ironed all of our clothes and linens. On some special occasions such as a bar mitzvah or High Holy Days, Lilly Mae would be there to help with the cleaning up. Whenever I needed a shirt washed or ironed, my mother would tell me to ask Lilly Mae, who would tease me by requesting a hug in return. We would hug, and soon I would have my clean, ironed shirt.

As the bus moved along, it came to me that during all of that time that I was in Europe, I never felt out of place or alienated from those cultures. Though I knew very little of the history, norms, or language of these foreign places, I was without anxiety or apprehension. I believed that I understood the rules of everyday life and that I could successfully cope with any unforeseen problems. Now I found myself feeling like a stranger in my own country, where, supposedly, I knew the cultural and behavioral ground rules. Instead, I was totally unprepared and uncertain as to how to react.

Two hours later, we arrived at the downtown Houston bus terminal. In order to save a few dollars on taxi fare, I decided to walk the mile-and-a-half to the train station. It did not take me long to realize that I had made the wrong decision. It was the first of August, and the boiling rays of the sun were bouncing off the concrete sidewalks. Having to schlep my seabag added another fifty pounds to my burden. I finally made it to the railroad station, which was located in what had to be the seediest part of town, next to a mission center for homeless men.

The next available train for Atlanta would be leaving at 11:00 in the evening, arriving in Atlanta at noon the next day. Once again I found myself with time to spare and no place to go. There was a bar in the waiting area and I had no problem in buying a beer. I killed time by reading and walking around the lobby.

I was on my way to the men's room when I saw a sign indicating the bathroom was for "Colored." There were also two separate waiting areas, one for whites and one for blacks. The white lobby was more spacious with better interior lighting. I later discovered that there were duplications in drinking fountains, restaurants, and newspaper stands.

I returned to the bar for my second beer. The bartender inquired as to my destination and I answered that I was on my way to Detroit through Atlanta. Having decided that he seemed to be a reasonable and pleasant person, I asked him the one question that was most on my mind: "What would happen if I went into the restroom set aside for colored men?"

"Probably nothing," he said. As if anticipating my next question, he went on to say that if a colored went into the white man's bathroom he would be asking for serious trouble. "That ain't likely to happen here because people know the rules and they don't want any trouble. They don't want to mix with us anymore than we want to mix with them, so it all works out." He indicated that he saw no value in pursuing this topic any further, and I returned to my warm glass of beer.

If someone had told me that someday I'd make Houston my permanent home, I would have said they were crazy.

As the time for my departure neared, I walked downstairs to the boarding platform. Once again, I saw a sign noting that blacks would board those cars at the rear of the train, hence having the longest distance to walk. Having coaches closest to the entrance of the boarding area would, of course, better accommodate whites. Several hundred passengers were boarding the train, including a large group of soldiers and sailors.

The coach that I selected was about a fourth of the way down the loading platform. I took an aisle seat next to a middle-aged man and across from a soldier and his young female companion. Once the train left the station, the lights were dimmed, making it difficult to read. The hour was late, there was little talking, and most people were making an effort to sleep. The only sounds were coming from overhead fans and the occasional blast of the steam-driven warning whistle. I tried to sleep but could not find a comfortable position. I spent some time walking back and forth through the various cars in hopes that the activity would make me tired enough to sleep. I finally returned to my seat, determined to get some rest. I must have fallen into a deep sleep, as it took me some time to realize that the train had come to a halt. There was loud shouting and activity coming from the car directly behind mine. Two uniformed train employees rushed by my seat to the next coach.

A soldier who was sitting in the aisle seat across from me had just returned from the troubled coach and informed his buddies what he had learned. It seems that a young black soldier had entered one of the prohibited coaches and was stopped, cursed, and threatened by a group of white soldiers and civilians. An elderly woman was so terrified by the commotion that she pulled the emergency cord, bringing the train to a sudden halt. The offending black soldier attempted to explain that he had become confused and mistakenly wandered into the wrong car. Fortunately, train personnel had arrived in time to avoid any serious physical harm being done to the young soldier. The soldier across the aisle from me concluded his commentary by noting that colored people were becoming too pushy and that a good beating was the best preventive medicine.

The train ride from Chicago to Detroit was a significant improvement over the others I had ridden through the South. The seats were more comfortable, the lighting better, and there were no race-related instructions. As we moved closer to Detroit I began to imagine what the arrival scene would be like. I tried to imagine my first encounters with peers from Habonim whom I had not seen for many months. There would have to be some dramatic contrasts, since my most recent experiences were so different from those of a high school or college student.

My most serious concern was that after all I'd experienced, I still had no idea what I wanted to do with my life. What troubled me more than anything else was my inability to make a choice. I was far from secure in my convictions that Palestine was the life for me, and I was equally hesitant about getting back on the formal education track. I could think of no occupation or career that really excited me. It seemed that rather than controlling my own destiny, I was allowing events to determine my direction. In this case the movement would choose what to do with me and I would comply. It was not a rational or reasoned decision but rather a failure to find a viable alternative. I found myself once again just going along for the ride.

At last we arrived in Detroit. I hurried up the ramp to the exit and ran up the stairs to the lobby. Ma, Pa, and my brothers Bob and Harold met me. Until that moment I had no idea how much I had missed my family. Ma, of course, was quick to point out that I had lost weight and looked undernourished. Bob put his arm around my shoulder and said how proud he was of what I had done. Harold was curious about what I was carrying in my seabag. Pa awkwardly responded to my hugs.

It was late when we arrived home. I was tired and wanted to get to bed. Ma, however, insisted that I have a "*nosh*." Not having the strength to take on a losing struggle, I agreed on eggs and a bagel. Pa sat with me as I ate, and asked only one question. He wanted me to tell him about the refugees–where they came from, what they looked like, what they wore, and what would happen to them in Palestine.

It was a discussion I would have preferred at a later time, but I knew Pa's reasons for asking the questions. Pa had several cousins whom he knew had gone to Palestine as part of the *Aliyah Bet* project. Whatever secondhand data I could provide was better than nothing, and I felt could offer him some relief. I told him of my visit to the camp and the family I had met. He was visibly moved when I shared with him my meeting Avram and his family on the Josiah Wedgewood and how we sailed together to Palestine. I added that like himself, Avram was from Poland. I shared with him what I knew about the origins of the refugees and how they were dressed. I told him about the living conditions on the boat and how grateful everyone was to see the hills of Haifa. Finally I said that although I was not sure what happened to each of them, I was convinced that they would all find happiness and security in *Eretz*. Pa said only on other word, "*Alaviy*," which can best be summed up as, "From your mouth to God's ear."

That night was the first in many that I slept soundly without any interruption. Late the next morning, Ma woke me to say that there was a long distance phone call from a girl.

It was Shoshanah, and it felt great to hear her voice and her assurances that she loved me and missed me. We agreed that I would come east in a week and visit with her at Killingworth.

Norman had been out on a date the previous night and off to work before I awoke. He came home in the early evening and we spent the next few hours exchanging experiences. Norman had applied and been accepted at the University of Michigan, where he planned to pursue a law degree. Meanwhile, he was working part time at a men's haberdashery shop. If Norman had doubts about anything, they were rarely made public. He knew he wanted to be a lawyer, where he wanted to go to school, and even where he wanted to practice law. Having decided the kind of social life he preferred, Norman quickly went about the business of choosing a workplace to meet his needs—hence the haberdashery store, where his employee discount would allow him to wear the snappy clothes his social life demanded.

My brother Harold was more like me when it came to matters of direction and focus. Harold was in his first year of high school and had an after-school job working with the Boys Club of America. I was surprised and pleased to hear that he had recently joined Habonim. From my mother, I learned that Harold's involvement with Habonim was quite recent and not without the influence of a pretty girl he had met in school. It would seem that Harold and I had more in common than I had ever realized.

For the next several days I visited with relatives and friends. Since it was summer, there was little in the way of Habonim activity. I did, however, meet with several of my closest buddies: Ralph, Morty, and Sam. Of the three, only Ralph remained firm in his plans to eventually live on a kibbutz in Palestine. He had completed high school and would be taking carpentry courses at a local community college in the fall. This would be followed by work as a carpenter, and then off to *Hachshara* at the farm in Cream Ridge. Morty had also graduated from high school and was working at his father's junkyard. While uncertain as to his future, he was convinced that Palestine was no longer in the picture.

"If I am going to work hard I want to make money," he said, "The idea of sharing my hard-earned cash with everyone is not my idea of a good time. No thanks." Sam, who had been only marginally involved with Habonim, had moved completely out of the circle. He had enrolled at Wayne State University with aspirations of becoming a pharmacist and eventually having his own drugstore.

They were curious about my adventures and asked many questions. Everyone was eager to know what would be next on my agenda. I said that other than doing work with Habonim, I was not really certain. I told them that I would know more in a couple of weeks, as I would soon be going to New York to meet with organizational leaders.

On my fifth day at home I received a call from a guy named Artie, from Habonim in New York. He was calling me to firm up my meeting time in New York and also to request that I give a speech to a Jewish woman's organization here in Detroit. The group I would be speaking to was a branch of a national organization. Artie made it clear that this was less a request than an order. He explained that the talk was scheduled for that evening and the original speaker had cancelled. I protested, saying that I had never given a public speech, that I had no idea what to talk about, and that I did not own a suit. Arnie proceeded to knock off each of my arguments. "Look," he said, "they are Jewish women, and you are a Jewish kid who just came back from Palestine. They will love you. Just tell them about the ship, the refugees, and how they were brought to *Eretz*. You do not need a suit; you are a *Chalutz*. You can wear dark pants and a white shirt."

He went on to give me some additional advice that I have never forgotten. He said that when you talk to a group of Jewish women, always pick out one that is sitting close up. That woman, he went on, should be your target and your challenge. You keep talking, always looking at her. Your goal is to get her to cry. Once she cries you will know that your talk is a success and you stop. There's no more to say.

He gave me the name and phone number of the woman I was to contact. We agreed that I would be in New York on the following Wednesday.

Once my mother heard about my speaking engagement, she placed calls to Mrs.Salmanov, Mrs.Goldberg, Aunt Mindel, Aunt Fagel, and Aunt Chanah. "Dovid is doing a speech at the Arbiter Ring on Linwood, seven o'clock. Bring a friend!"

I arrived at the hall at a few minutes to seven and was met by my hostess, Mrs. Gorenstein. She appeared to be out of breath and quite excited. "A wonderful turnout!" she exclaimed, "So many more ladies than we had expected!" She escorted me down the aisle and onto the stage. There were about a hundred women in the audience.

After being seated I was able to get a better view of the hall, and it was then that I understood why Mrs. Gorenstein was impressed with the turnout. Ma had not only solicited her sisters and dearest friends, but also the entire membership of the Detroit Chapter of the David-Horodoker Women's Organization. These were women who had all migrated to Detroit from the small *shtetel* of Horodok in Byelorus, Russia.

The Horodoker ladies were active in raising funds for numerous Jewish causes, orphans, the elderly, refugees, and now assistance to Mogen David, the Jewish Red Cross in Palestine. They rotated their monthly meeting at the homes of members. We would always know when it was Ma's turn. That would be one of those rare occasions when she would take her best china out of a locked dining room cabinet and create elaborate, multi-colored Jell-O molds, along with a variety of salads and pastries. Competition between the ladies was intense and each would seek to outdo the others in menu and décor. But the greatest degree of status would be given to the mother whose daughter married well, whose child won a scholarship, or whose son earned a professional degree. Success as a mother was confirmed by the achievements of the offspring.

No greater "*nachas*" (self-gratification) could be bestowed upon a parent than the highly visible success of a child. This was Ma's moment to "*glieb a bissel nachas* (gather a little public self-esteem)." It was also the first time since my bar mitzvah that I could recall my mother taking such delight and pride in anything I had done. I was determined not to let her down.

Mrs. Gornestein called the meeting to order and I was introduced. As I approached the lectern, I remembered Artie's advice about identifying the most vulnerable woman in the front row. My dilemma was that my mother, my aunts, and the dear ladies of the Horodoker occupied the front row. Before I even began my talk, Ma was crying, soon to be joined by Aunts Chaneh, Mindel, and Fagel. I decided instead to focus upon a woman sitting in the second row.

Once I started to talk, I disregarded my prepared thoughts and, as Artie suggested, just told my story. I talked for about a half-hour, and when I reached the point where I felt I had nothing more to say, I stopped and returned to my seat. There was a moment of silence, and then one woman (not the one I had targeted) stood up and began to applaud. Others did the same and soon they were all standing and some were even cheering. Mrs. Gornestein took my hand and brought me to the center of the stage. I made some kind of bowing gesture and looked over at Ma. She was standing with the others, holding a handkerchief to her eyes and trembling. I left the stage, walked over to her, and put my arms around her to comfort her, which only intensified her crying. She finally regained some control and whispered, "I am crying not from sadness but from happiness."

For me, it was a good night and I had enjoyed every moment of it. I felt that this was exactly the kind of thing I was cut out to do. I loved the attention and the accolades. I made up my mind at that moment that if there were more speeches to be given, I could be counted upon.

There was one more thing I was determined to do before leaving Detroit. I had to see Hank Greenberg.

"Hammering" Hank had enlisted in the Army Air Corps in 1941, immediately after the Japanese attack on Pearl Harbor. He was the first American League player to enlist. A month after the formal ending of World War II, Hank returned to the Tigers. His return was fortuitous, since the Tigers were battling for the American League pennant. They needed only one win to beat out the Washington Senators. Hank came through in the ninth inning of the last game of the season. The Tigers were behind 3 to 2, and the bases were loaded. Hank hit the third pitch and drove the ball deep into the left field stands for a dramatic, pennant-winning, grand slam home run.

The 1946 season was winding down and there were rumors that this would be Hank's final season with the Tigers. He was having a great year, leading the league in home runs and runs batted in. We were both going to be leaving Detroit, and there was no way that I would go without saying goodbye.

I went to the game with Morty and his father. The Tigers were playing the St. Louis Browns. In the eighth inning, Hank came up to bat for the last time in that game. I stood up alongside Morty and thousands of other devoted fans, pleading and begging for Hank to hit one out of the park. I honestly believe Hank looked right up to where we were standing. Hank was not known for showboating and was never one to call attention to himself. Yet at that moment, I could swear that when he looked in our direction and pulled down the bill of his cap, he was sending me a message.

Hank took two strikes and a ball, and then slammed his thirty-ninth home run of the season way up into the centerfield bleachers. Though the Tigers lost the game, it was a perfect farewell, as Hank left for Pittsburgh and I headed for New York.

Chapter 8

The Habonim office sent me my train tickets and a fifty-dollar money order. Once again I said my goodbyes, and Bob drove me to the train station. This time there was little in the way of emotional angst or cautionary comments from Ma. My leaving home had become routine and, even if reluctantly, accepted by my parents.

I arrived in New York the following morning and took a cab to the Habonim office at Union Square. I was happy to be back in Manhattan but eager to finish my business so that I could get to Killingsworth and see Shoshanah.

I met with Artie and a woman named Reva. They quickly outlined the next two years of my life. First, I would spend three weeks at Killingsworth and assist in the seasonal closing of the camp. From mid-September until May of the following year, I would be enrolled in a Habonim leadership program, where all participating students would live and attend classes at The Jewish Teachers Institute located on Manhattan's East Side. During the course of the training, a decision would be made as to where I would be assigned as a "*madrich*" (a messenger and coordinator of a local Habonim group). While at the Institute, all of my school-related expenses would be taken care of, and I would also receive a weekly stipend of $20. Curriculum and studies would be intense and demanding. In addition to formal curriculum offerings, there would be Hebrew language instruction, select field trips, and hands-on experience working with New York area Habonim members. There would be a total of thirty students coming from all different sections of the United States and Canada. Artie added that they would also expect me to share my overseas experiences with the other students.

The meeting ended and they both walked me to the outer office. After handshakes and "shaloms," Artie mentioned that he had received a phone call from Mrs. Gorenstein. According to Artie, Mrs. Gorenstein was delighted with the talk and asked if arrangements could be made for me to speak at the national convention. Arnie smiled and said, "I told you to make one lady cry, not the whole bunch of them!"

I took a cab back to Penn Station, bought my ticket, and was on my way to Killingsworth by way of New Haven.

I arrived at New Haven at about 2:00 in the afternoon and was met by a staff member who drove me to Killingworth. It was a short drive on a wonderfully cool day. The countryside of Connecticut was lush and green and the landscape was unlike anything I had ever seen.

The camp itself was located on seven acres with a nearby small, private lake. It was co-ed with 125 or so campers, the majority coming from the New England region. The staff was made up of college students who were active members of Habonim chapters. This camp was not too different from the one I knew at Kinneret in its layout, organization, and mission to provide campers with a mixture of work, learning, and recreation.

The learning was directed at instilling in campers an understanding and dedication to *Eretz* and the labor Zionist philosophy. Each Habonim camp was modeled on the kibbutz concept of shared labor and socialistic collective living. The work portion of the program was confined to grounds clean up, kitchen and dining room duties, touch up painting, and so forth. Obviously, in order to attract middle-class Jewish kids it was important to also offer the usual athletic, social, and crafts activities found in most residential camps.

As we pulled onto the campgrounds we were met by a large group of campers carrying a large white banner with blue printing reading, "SHALOM DOVID." When I stepped out of the truck, Shoshanah was there to greet me with a warm embrace. Her hug seemed to be the signal for the group to begin singing, in Hebrew, the song "Haveynu Shalom Alechim," a touching melody of love and welcome.

Shoshanah walked me over to the tent that I was to share with three other staff members. We sat and talked for a short time, mostly exchanging comments affirming our love and dedication to each other.

At dinner that evening I was formally introduced and serenaded with yet another song of welcome. I also learned that evening that campers and staff had been informed of my recent participation in *Aliyah Bet* and that I would be expected to share my story with the staff and campers. I readily agreed.

For the next several weeks, most of my time was spent in small group discussions and supervising work teams. I enjoyed the setting and the lack of a demanding schedule. The kids were easy to work with and the staff was friendly and cooperative.

Most satisfying were the opportunities to spend relaxed periods of time with Shoshanah. We had much to discuss—not only events of the past several months, but plans for the future. The good news was that both of us would be living in Manhattan for almost a full year; I would be at the Institute, and she would be enrolled at NYU and living in at Judson Hall, a student residence in Washington Square. The only uncertainty was that I had no idea of what my assignment would be once the *madrich* training was completed.

If the inability to defer immediate need for gratification is a mark of adolescence, then we certainly passed the test. We thought of ourselves, compared to our peers, as being if not worldly then at least cosmopolitan. After all, Shoshanah was from New York and I had been to Europe. What other proof was required? We were completely caught up in our love and being future pioneers in *Eretz*. If the Jewish people could wander in the desert for years and years and still make it to the Promised Land, what could possibly stop us?

Ironically, we were totally oblivious to current events in the Promised Land. In late 1946, Palestine was an armed camp. Conflict between Arabs and Jews was compounded by a mutual distrust of the British. For many years, the Jews of Palestine had practiced great restraint. During the War, Jewish citizens of Palestine had volunteered for service in the British Army as well as the Jewish Brigade. Only after the War, the imposition of quotas on immigration, and increased threats by the Arab Legion, was organized resistance implemented

While the British viewed the Haganah as an illegal organization, Jews saw it as being essential to their survival. The Holocaust was sufficient proof that Jews could not count on others for protection or comfort. The Haganah had grown from being a small and informal collection of volunteers to a well-organized, highly disciplined organization with three branches, each of which included women. A report issued by the Anglo American Committee of Inquiry estimated the total force as being in excess of 60,000. Impressive numbers, perhaps, but only a slight fraction of the trained and better-equipped forces of the Arab Legion and the armies of Egypt, Lebanon, and Syria.

Yet another factor exacerbating the already dangerous and potentially explosive situation was the emergence of two Jewish extremist groups. The Irgun Zvai Leumi was formed by dissident members of the Haganah. The Stern Group broke away from the Irgun, claiming the organization was a passive tool of the Haganah and the British. The Stern group had engaged in acts of assassination of British soldiers, ambushing of Arab civilians, and the bombing of both British and Arab offices.

As the gulf between Jew and Arab increased, the British sought to appease both sides by employing a tit-for-tat policy of mutually ineffective sanctions. It had also become clear that the British Government, as Mandatory of Palestine, was seriously considering the withdrawal of all British troops from Palestine. Neither Jewish nor Arab representatives expressed displeasure with such an outcome. Still, both were uncertain as to what would happen once that formidable military buffer was removed.

The kids left camp in the third week of August, and most of the staff took off within the next few days. Shoshanah and I were among a handful that remained to clean up and close up.

After camp, we both took the train up to Kingston to stay there for a week before returning to New York. As during my first visit, I would stay with Rabbi Herb and his family. Since neither of Shoshanah's parents drove, we took a cab from the train station to Rabbi Herb's home.

Blossom answered the door and gave me the warmest of welcomes. We went into the study, where Herb was working on a Sabbath sermon. He slowly stood up from his chair and embraced me. "I am so very proud of the great things you have been doing," he said, "*Baruch Habba*, and you will always be welcome in this home."

Blossom went into the kitchen to get refreshments while Herb invited us to sit and make ourselves comfortable. Herb said he wanted to know about my trip and experiences in great detail, but before that, he wanted to ask me for two favors. First, he asked me to give a talk to the congregation at the coming Friday night services. Second, he asked if I would accompany him to a nearby state prison, where I would meet and talk with a small group of Jewish inmates.

Besides his other duties, Herb was the visiting rabbi at two penal institutions. One housed serious criminal offenders, the other was a minimum-security facility. I was invited to the latter. Herb explained that most of the thirteen Jewish inmates had committed white collar crimes such as fraud, stock trading violations, passing bad checks, and book making. Herb thought an informal session with the group would be of interest to them and to me. "These are not your run-of the-mill crooks," he told me, "All of the men are well educated and all had been successful. They just fared poorly as *goniffs*." He went on to say that most of the men were serving relatively short terms, all the more reason for keeping them informed of current events. I readily agreed, and that Saturday we set off for Albany.

As we entered the grounds I expressed surprise at how nice the place appeared. My notion of a prison was armed guards in towers, high walls with electric wiring, and drab cinderblock buildings. I kidded Herb by asking if he had perhaps made a wrong turn and taken us to a country club. He laughed and then added, "There is one big difference: once you're here, you stay until they let you leave."

All the guards knew Herb and politely waved us in to the visitors parking area. The services were held in a small non-denominational chapel. When used for Christian services, a large wooden cross was placed at the foot of the pulpit. For Jewish worshipers, the cross was removed and replaced with a Star of David that Herb had brought along with prayer books and a Torah.

The men were already present, and we exchanged "Good Shabbos" greetings. Herb moved to the lectern, and after another greeting in Hebrew, he introduced me. He informed the men that following the service I would be talking with them.

The services began, and I was impressed with how familiar these men were with the ritual and how responsive they were in recital of prayers. To be sure that no one was left out, Herb recited prayers in both Hebrew and English.

When the Sabbath prayer portions were completed Herb delivered a short sermon. His talk served as a segue to my comments. His focus was on the plight of the Jewish survivors in both Europe and Palestine and how critical it was for American Jews to recognize that we are all one people. Calling me to the lectern, he told the group that I had worked with the survivors and served as a sailor on a ship that took refugees to Palestine.

The men sat silently and were attentive as I told them about what I had seen in the camp in Italy and about our voyage. I spoke for about fifteen minutes, and then asked if there were any questions. One of the older men raised his hand and asked me my age. I answered that I had just turned eighteen. He continued to stand as he looked around at the other men and said, "Look, he's just a kid, and see what he's already done, and we don't do shit!"

I looked over at Herb, but he was not about to help me out. So I plunged ahead on my own, saying things like it was never too late to get involved. My firm response seemed to gain their attention, so I continued with suggestions as to what they might do. I mentioned learning more about the issues, writing letters to President Truman, telling friends and relatives they should also learn and help. When I completed my suggestions, another man raised his hand. He, too, had a message for his peers.

He suggested to his associates that they could be most helpful by raising money for the refugees. Each of them had plenty of contacts, people who knew where the money could be found. His comments set off others and, typical among Jews, they began competing among themselves as to who would be the highest giver. Things were getting out of control when thankfully Herb took over. He praised them for their interest and generosity. He told them that he would be pleased to see to it that their contributions were turned over to the proper charity. At that point, the man who had originally proposed a group contribution insisted that they decide on a total before anyone left the room. His tone and manner were most effective, and he got an answer that satisfied him. The men would pledge $500, which would be turned over to Rabbi Herb two weeks from that day.

I shook hands with each of the men and expressed my appreciation for their interest. As we left and walked toward the car, Herb stopped and said to me, "If you can get $500 from these guys, you should get at least $1,000 when you speak to the congregation." We drove back to Kingston, both still very much enjoying the special joys and blessings of the Sabbath.

My next speaking engagement in Kingston turned out to be my Waterloo. The expression "you cannot win them all" had a new meaning for me. As Shoshanah would later say, "Your gig at the Temple was a bomb!"

By now I had given at least half a dozen talks to mixed groups which all had been well received. It was the Friday evening service, and attendance was around 175, including Shoshanah's parents and a visiting aunt. The demographics of this crowd were very different from the good ladies of David Horodoker. These were second and third generation Jews, mainly of German descent. These were not the people of the *shtetel*, neither had they endured the trauma and displacement of the European Jews. The majority had come to America well before the Nazi regime came to power. They were a highly educated congregation—professional and affluent. I was also later to learn that few would consider themselves even mild Zionists, and fewer would regard *Eretz* as a place for themselves, much less their children.

Herb gave me little indication of what I might expect other than a side comment of, "Some of these people may be a hard sell."

We followed our usual routine with one modification that should have given me a clue as to what to expect. This time, when he gave my introduction, Herb played down the idea of all Jews being one people. Instead he said, "We must learn that we are all one people." As he called me up to the lectern, he put his arm on my shoulder and said, "This is David Gottlieb. He is my friend and he has a story to tell you."

I looked out at the congregation, searching for that one sympathetic face to which I could direct my comments. There were several elderly women sitting in the front row, but I doubted if they were the crying kind. I felt my best ploy was to play upon their sympathies, so I told them about the refugees, where they had come from, what they experienced, and what they hoped to find in Palestine. I shared with them how I had met Avram and his family in the camp and later, by chance, on our ship. There was little movement among the audience and I felt they were being attentive. I shifted to the subject of Palestine. My first words on that topic were sufficient to cause some visible stirring and quiet whispering. I pushed ahead saying, "No matter who we are, where we live, whatever our political orientation, we are all Jews and we have an obligation to support a Jewish homeland in Palestine." I also picked up on Herb's suggestion and added, "If a group of Jewish men in prison can contribute $500 to the cause, there is no reason why this group cannot do at least the same."

That one line escalated the level of sound from murmur to audible commentary. I looked back to Herb, hoping for some sign as to how and if I should proceed. Herb merely smiled and raised the thumb of his right hand in what I took as a signal to continue.

I talked about my future job, where I would encourage young Jews to become pioneer *Chalutzim* in *Eretz*. "Together, we will transform the desert into a flourishing garden," turned out to be the final words of my talk. About a quarter of the congregation stood up and headed for the exits. Those who remained seated carried on heated discussions among themselves. The remainder, including Shoshanah's family, sat in silence, waiting, I assumed, for words of closure from Rabbi Herb.

Rabbi Herb approached me, placed his hand on my shoulder, and called for silence. He said that he considered what happened that evening as being a healthy experience for the congregation. He went on to explain that it is good to have a diversity of opinions and an honest exchange of beliefs. His closing comments were that he hoped in the weeks to come, the congregation would consider my talk as part of an ongoing dialogue. With that, he thanked me, blessed the congregation, and wished all a happy Sabbath.

I was desperate for feedback, especially concerning what Herb, Blossom, Shoshanah and her folks had thought. I walked out and saw Shoshanah standing with her parents and aunt. I considered it best not to join them, so I waited until they left for home.

My first question to Shoshanah consisted of one word: "Well?"

She answered that I had done a good job of stirring things up, which she considered a positive outcome. "You knocked them off their complacent, smug asses and that's good." As for her parents, "My mother believes you are much too radical, un-American and a bad influence on me." Her father, on the other hand, thought and hoped that with time I would forsake some of my wild ideas. I was looking for something more definitive, and so I asked Shoshanah what she thought. Her response, I thought, was part hedging, part diplomatic, but mainly evasive: "Since I love you, I cannot be altogether objective, but I think you did a great job of keeping their attention."

Later that evening, when we were home, Blossom said that she agreed with Herb that it was a healthy and lively presentation. I could detect that she had more to say, and so I asked what changes, if any, she would propose. She quickly responded with, "Well, now that you ask, I would suggest a less confrontational and belligerent presentation." My feelings were hurt, and I was prepared to come back with some kind of defensive comment, but Blossom was a remarkably perceptive woman and quickly inserted, "Remember, you did ask, and more importantly, I love you as if you were my own son."

Herb felt that he had placed me in a difficult situation and he should have given me more information about the congregation. Still, he believed that even those who were offended or upset would hopefully benefit. At that moment the phone rang, the first of a dozen complaint calls from Temple members that evening.

Now I was the one who felt guilty and lousy. I knew what I was doing when I had shifted from telling a story to lecturing and moralizing the congregation. Now Herb and Blossom would have to deal with the consequences of my being a hot shot, smart-ass. Herb dismissed my attempts to apologize and insisted the matter would soon blow over. "I know there are people in the congregation who would rather have a different rabbi. I know that some consider me too liberal and too outspoken. There are also others who are made uncomfortable by my cerebral palsy."

He went on to tell us that this was a familiar pattern that occurs whenever there is a controversial issue. "One of the ringleaders will call others and encourage them to call me or, preferably, the President of the Board."

Herb sighed, and looking to Blossom he said, "Not to worry. This too shall pass."

Somehow, I was not comforted or assured by his words and wished more than anything else that I could undo the damage I had done that evening.

* * * * *

It was time to pack up and move on to Manhattan for the start of my Habonim leadership training. I was determined, however, that before leaving I would attempt to reach some kind of civil accommodation with Shoshanah's parents.

For counseling on this sensitive matter, I chose Blossom. She pointed out that my goal was to convince Shoshanah's parents that I was responsible and would do nothing to ever hurt their daughter. It was important to let them know that while Shoshanah was studying at NYU, I would be enrolled as a student in another school. Both of us would take our studies seriously and behave in an appropriate manner. Most of all, I should tell them that although we were very fond of one another, we both recognized that it was far too soon to talk of marriage. We both had much to accomplish before taking such a serious step. "Just try to be charming, something you are especially good at with middle-aged women," she teased me.

Of course, the truth was I was more than fond of Shoshanah, and there was no doubt in my mind that we would marry. I assumed we would migrate to Palestine. Clearly, if the goal was the pacification of her mother, then revealing the complete truth would not do the job. I would tell her mother what she needed to hear; I would heed Blossom's advice.

Shoshanah was not convinced that the heart-to-heart talk that I was proposing would be a wise move. "You both get so emotional so quickly that things could become even more difficult."

"They could not be any worse than they are now, and I have to do this before I leave," I replied.

So it was settled that the night prior to my leaving, I we would all meet at a local restaurant in Kingston.

Everyone had ordered drinks, and we were on our best behavior. No mention was made of the events of the other evening, and the discussion somehow shifted to families. I was asked about my family and responded with a brief biography of my parents and brothers. I made a special point of mentioning my Uncle Morris, who was professionally a lawyer.

I started to get a little irritated when Shoshanah's parents began asking questions concerning the size of my parents' home, my father's store, and whether or not I came from an Orthodox home. Much to Shoshanah's relief and surprise, I retained my cool and initiated a change of topic. I reminded them that I would be leaving in the morning and that I was aware that they had concerns about me and my relationship with their daughter.

Now having their full attention, I proceeded with my rehearsed script, addressing the issues that Blossom had identified. I was calm, coherent, sincere, and, I thought, very persuasive. I concluded by reaching across the table and touching the hands of both parents, asking for their trust and acceptance.

Shoshanah's father spoke first and said that he was impressed with my comments and he for one was willing to keep an open mind. Her mother remained silent and finally said something to the effect that she was also willing to keep an open mind. These were not precisely the words I wanted to hear, but I felt—and Shoshanah later concurred—that I had made some progress.

The next morning, having offered one more apology and my thanks, I met Shoshanah and we walked to the bus station. She would be coming down to school in a few more days, and we agreed to meet during the coming weekend.

I was among of the first to show up and sign in for the Habonim leadership-training program. The Institute, located on the Upper East Side, was in an impressive four-story building. The neighborhood was primarily commercial along Lexington Avenue, and mostly brown stone residences throughout the East seventies. This was affluent uptown property and considered prime real estate. Magnificent stained-glass double doors led into the building to a large, high-ceiling lobby. The first floor was mainly offices and a beautiful library with long oak study tables and row after row of volume-filled, ten-foot high shelves. Classrooms, study areas, and a conference room were located on the second floor. Dormitory-style quarters, as well as a kitchen and a dining room, were located on the third and fourth floors.

While life at Cream Ridge was labor intensive and the milieu reflective of a proletariat lifestyle, this place was, in comparison, aristocratic. Both places spoke to a necessary contradiction in youth-centered, labor Zionist organizations. The central purpose of these movements was to somehow persuade Jewish kids to abandon a life of privilege and comfort for one of hardship and struggle. The need was for a division of labor that would consist on the one hand of *Chalutzim* and on the other *Madrichim.* The Institute's aim was to produce the intellectuals and organizers (*Madrichim*) while Cream Ridge would generate the dedicated bodies (*Chalutzim*). No one spoke of "them and us," and never did I hear any talk of a status differential between the two groups.

Because I had now experienced both sides of the organizational coin, the contrast for me was both dramatic and apparent. I did not, however, feel any sense of guilt or a need to question or protest. As far as I was concerned, the arrangements were just fine.

Within the week, all expected students arrived and we were called together for orientation. Although most of my classmates were closer to me in age than those on the farm or the ship, I once again was the youngest. More bothersome to me was the fact that I was the only one who had not completed at least two years of college, much less high school.

We were each asked to state our name, where we were from, and a brief bio. By the time it was my turn, I had learned that more than half had graduated from college, many from prestigious universities. About a fourth were fluent in Hebrew, and some had already served as *Madrichim.* These were bright, articulate, well-educated and very self-assured young men and women. My hope was that I would say nothing that would set me apart from the others. For that reason I did not share with them that I had not completed high school. I hoped they would just assume that, like them, I was a college product. To gain a little edge, I declared that I had spent some months at Cream Ridge, but said nothing about my *Aliyah Bet* period. If the information about that experience was to be made public, it would need to come from another source.

Following orientation there was a further, more informal exchange of personal data and experiences. It took little time for me to feel that I was already outside of the circle. Clearly, living uptown would not erase the differences between me and this very sophisticated group of affluent young adults.

The same factors that had previously made school involvement difficult for me existed here in an even more pronounced fashion. As in the past, I was impatient with traditional teaching methods and could not abide boring teachers, forced readings, exams, and required papers—in short, everything I considered irrelevant and tedious. I had made a mistake in coming to the Institute, but saw no alternative other than seeing it through no matter how trying.

I also found it extremely confining to spend so much time indoors when just outside my window was all of the excitement and adventure offered by Manhattan. What I most enjoyed and always welcomed were the field trips that were tied in with our studies of the history of the Jewish experience in New York. Now we were on my intellectual and emotional turf. These were my people. In this setting, I had an advantage, since I spoke the language and was familiar with much of the literature, music, and culture of the Lower East Side. And what I did not know I was eager to learn.

For example, I knew that the Lower East Side was the major destination for hundreds of thousands of Jews from Eastern Europe. What I did not know was the magnitude of that migration and what these people, confronted with so many barriers and challenges, were able, in such a short time, to accomplish.

In 1892, the area east of the Bowery contained more than three-fourths of all the Jews living in New York City. The mobility of the Jewish population was such that by 1915, that figure had dropped to less than twenty-five percent. When the first Jewish immigrants began arriving in New York in the late 1800's, a large number earned their livelihoods by working as peddlers or in the garment industry. The title "garment industry" is misleading, since it seems to imply a high tech, brightly lit, air conditioned, comfortable workplace. A more appropriate and accurate image is portrayed by the term "sweat shops," so named because hot stoves were kept on continuously in order to heat the flatirons used by the pressers.

The narrow and crowded streets of the Lower East Side were reflective of the places where people worked and lived. Tenement buildings that housed as many as fifteen people in two rooms were dark, dingy, crowded, and frequently without running water or heat. So miserable were these dwelling places that many people chose to remain on the streets. Much of the daily and evening social interaction was conducted on the front steps of these wretched buildings. Working conditions were no better. Advocates for the workers were few, and laws protecting them from exploitation were never enforced. Children were employed along with adults, and worked more than 60 hours per week. In 1909, the average weekly wage was twelve or twenty cents per hour. It was not uncommon for employees to take piecework home, spending additional hours sewing by candlelight.

It was extraordinary that despite these deprivations and the barriers the Jewish immigrants created a vibrant community, rich in social, cultural, and intellectual activity. Places like the Henry Street Settlement House and organizations such as the Hebrew Immigrant Aid Society provided aid and counseling for immigrants. And of course there were synagogues. One of the first in New York was the Norfolk Street shul.

Two things that thrived were Yiddish theaters and Yiddish newspapers. It was almost as if each new wave of immigrants and each emerging social and political organization had to create their own new theaters and newspapers. Among the major Yiddish newspapers by the turn of the century were The Dag (The Day), The Forvertz (The Forward), The Morning Journal, and The Arbiter Schtime (The Worker's Voice). Newspapers represented a potpourri of ideological positions, including conservatism, anarchy, socialism, communism, and religion. Each of these groups generated splinter organizations, further increasing the quantity and diversity of available newsprint.

The Yiddish Theater, primarily located along Second Avenue, was the catalyst for producing a wealth of great playwrights and performers. By the year 1918, there were twenty-eight theaters, with a diverse body of work ranging from Shakespeare to Shalom Alechim and including, among others, Bernard Shaw, Y.L. Peretz, Clifford Odets, and Shalom Asch. The list of actors and actresses with roots in or ties to the Yiddish Theater included Jacob Adler, David Kessler, Boris Tomachevskey, Stella Adler, Herschel Bernardi, Lee J. Cobb, Paul Muni, Celia Adler, Jacob Ben Ami, and of course, Molly Pichon. Many of these performers would move on to Hollywood and Broadway.

Yiddish theater was of particular interest to me, since my Uncle Hyman (husband of my mother's sister Chaneh) was both producer and director of the Littman's People's Theater in Detroit. Uncle Hyman was short, thin, intense, and fully dedicated to the preservation of Yiddish culture. His theater was located on Twelfth Street in a former burlesque house. There were 250 seats on the main floor and a balcony with 125 seats. When Uncle Hyman and a partner acquired the venue, renovations were minimal, mainly boarding up the "peep room" where male customers were able to look at silent flicks of scantily clad women. Of course, they also changed the name on the marquee from "DARE BURLESQUE" to "LITTMAN'S PEOPLE'S THEATER." Uncle Hyman often invited me to the theater for Sunday matinees. I was allowed to go backstage and see all of the activity related to performance preparation. The hanging of scenery, the checking of light and sound, the costume room, and an occasional rehearsal, fascinated me.

Littman's presented a wide range of entertainment, live as well as film. Live performances were a mix of tragedy, comedy, and musical—all the works of primarily Yiddish writers and composers. Uncle Hyman faced the challenge of presenting entertainment that would be responsive to the tastes of the Yiddish purist as well as to those looking for something lighter. I recall two examples.

On the more severe side was a drama based upon a poem written by Y.L. Peretz, entitled "*De Bezeh Groyeh Noit* (The Angry Gray Devil)." Briefly, this is the story of a large, motherless, impoverished family that lives in Brooklyn. The home lacks a roof or walls. Early each morning, before the light of day, the father would "*gehen by foos kein in New York fardinnen epes gelt* (travel to New York by foot to earn a little money)." During his absence the children would cry for a piece of bread, but there was no bread, for in that home lived the spirit of a mean, wrinkled old woman (*Deh Beyzeh Groyeh Noit*). While the children cried, she would laugh, because her happiness came from the miseries of others.

Up to this point we have a typical Yiddish story, but now comes a twist that makes it rather unique. For this tale has a happy ending. One day the father returns unexpectedly and begins to wake his children. He is laughing and joyful as he calls to the children, "See what I have brought you!" What he has brought them are fresh warm rolls and sweet milk. The kids are delighted and happy. The scene of joy is too much for the *Noit*, and so she goes up in a puff of smoke. Only in such an innocent age could one believe that a few warm rolls and sweet milk would bring delight and the demise of misery. In the *shtetel* as well as the tenements of the Lower East Side, even the most modest of gifts could have a magical impact.

On the lighter, more Americanized side was a musical entitled, "*Hesse Tropics* (Hot Tropics)." "*Hesse Tropics*" was a Yiddish carbon copy of a film that featured Carmen Miranda, a statuesque South American woman who wore outrageous colorful costumes and fresh bananas piled high on her head. Her acting ability was minimal, but she could wiggle her hips and belt out a song. Indeed, "*Hesse Tropics*" was a Yiddish adaptation of one of Miranda's most popular movies. To hear performers take the lyrics of South American melodies and sing them in Yiddish was a riot. However, the audience loved the show, especially when the female lead sang the theme song, "*Oy-Yoy, Oy-yoy, host do einmal gedanzed in de Tropics?* (Oh, Oh, have you ever danced in the Tropics?)." The entire performance was done in Yiddish, and the choreography for the mamba looked more like the hora.

My favorite of all time was a drama dealing with the Jewish uprising in the Warsaw Ghetto. The featured actress was the extraordinary Molly Pichon, whose remarkable versatility I had seen in both dramatic and comedic roles. The typical Yiddish Theater audience did not sit passively, but offered plenty of comment, sharing unsolicited outbursts with the cast. Occasionally, audience members became so agitated they had to be removed from the theater. But this time, not a sound is uttered. The play comes to an end when the Nazis put down the uprising and occupy the Warsaw ghetto. A few of the youthful survivors meet at center stage and the lights are dimmed with the exception of a single spotlight. That light follows Molly as she turns directly to the audience and sings in Yiddish, "Never say that we have gone our last mile. Never say we have perished for nothing. Tell the world, they dare not forget." With that Molly turns and walks offstage. There is a brief silence and then, to a person, the audience stands and applauds wildly, shouting for Molly to return to the stage. I look over at my Uncle Hyman, who is standing with Molly in the wings. They are embracing and crying. So am I.

Our first Institute visit was to the location of the scene of a massive tragedy that occurred on March 25, 1911, and is still considered the worst fire in the history of New York City. The Triangle Shirtwaist Company occupied the top three floors of a ten-floor building where 500 women were employed, mostly young Jewish immigrants. The youngest was thirteen, and the eldest twenty-three. To assure a constant flow of uninterrupted work, the owners locked all doors leading to exits.

It is believed the fire started on the eighth floor cutting room and quickly spread to the higher floors. As billowing clouds of choking smoke drifted across the floor, the women panicked and rushed to find some way out of the building. Many who worked on the lower floors were able to escape, but those on the ninth floor were trapped. Though they desperately tried, they could not force open the bolted metal door. Some tried to slide down an elevator cable but were unable to hold on and fell to their deaths. Others, with their clothes on fire, jumped from open windows in hopes they might survive. They did not. It is reported that Pump Engine Company 20 and Ladder Company 20 were prompt in arrival but were impeded by the bodies of those who had jumped to their deaths.

One hundred and forty six young women perished. The public outrage and editorial criticism that followed did little if anything to improve working conditions in the industry. The owners of the company were charged with manslaughter, and three years later were ordered to pay $75 to each of the families who had sued. Our guide informed us that this fire eventually became the rallying symbol for the formation of the International Ladies Garment Worker's Union.

A week later we had the opportunity to tour and meet with the staff of the three major surviving Yiddish newspapers. Where once there had been more than a dozen dailies and weeklies, there now remained only The Forward, The Day, and The Morning Journal. At one time the editorial position of each was strongly socialist and supportive of the labor movement. With the ensuing change in the composition of more recent immigrants and the acculturation of earlier immigrants, the newspapers also changed their political orientation, format, and language.

The Forward was the first to introduce a Sunday supplement with photos, reduce the number of Yiddish pages by adding English, and shift to the political center. The Day held on for a little while longer but eventually followed a similar pattern. The Morning Journal, however, was determined to maintain its original format and continued to be the voice for the Jewish proletariat until 1970.

The interiors of each of the three offices reflected where they stood in the Americanization process. The best furnished and most technologically advanced was The Forward, which had nicely lighted offices, soft music delivered by Muzak, and the fast-paced activity of a major metropolitan newspaper. The Day, with high aspirations, was in the transition process with longtime writers retiring and being replaced with the first generation of college-degreed journalism majors. Their facilities were adequate but not quite as impressive as at The Forward.

What the two had in common was the bottom line. It was clear that the Yiddish market was dwindling and dramatic change was required. The order of the day was to recruit new readers with less Yiddish, more English, cut the ideological stuff, and go with lighter features, more pics, more entertainment news, and, of course, an advice column. Needless to say, proficiency in Yiddish was no longer an employment requirement.

Life at The Morning Journal, on the other hand, continued as it had in the past. It was located in a distressed building with little in the way of amenities. I was immediately struck by the contrast in the ages of employees of the Journal with those of the other two papers. Here the journal staff was much older, more blue collar, and certainly more Yiddish. Type setting was still being done by hand. Printing and page compilation was a tedious and time-consuming job. The presses were of an early 1900's vintage, unreliable and prone to breakdowns, with parts difficult to come by since the machines were no longer being manufactured. All the printed pages were assembled by hand and tied in bundles. The workers and their machines were old, tired, and growing obsolete together.

I stopped at the stand where one of the typesetters was at work. There must have been a time many years ago when he could work with great speed and self-assurance.

Now, however, he paused to bring the type closer to his eyes and peer through his thick lenses to make certain that he had the correct letters. He looked at me and asked, "*Canst sprechen Yiddish* (Do you speak Yiddish)?"

I responded in Yiddish that I could speak it as well as read it. I do not think he believed me, since he reached over, grabbed a page off the press, and said, "Read!"

I read out loud, and after a few sentences he seemed satisfied. "*Vos is dine nomen* (What is your name)?" he asked.

I answered, "Dovid." He then asked our guide to call all of the members of our group to where he was standing. Once we assembled, he asked me to find out how many others in the class could also speak or read Yiddish. I asked the question, but there were no takers. The expression on the old man's face was not so much a look of sadness but rather confirmation of what he already knew.

He took me completely by surprise when he began to address the group in perfect English. "You are a group of some thirty young Jews, and only one of you can speak and read Yiddish. That, my young friends, is why this newspaper will soon be out of business."

He went on to say that only one out of thirty would soon mean the demise of the Yiddish Theater and the loss of the great works of Yiddish poets and authors. We stood quietly awaiting words of either challenge or guilt, but there were none. He simply smiled, thanked us for our attention, and wished us a good and healthy life.

The reality of his prophecy became more apparent when we went to visit Second Avenue, founding street of the Yiddish Theater. The sites of former theaters far outnumbered those that were still in business. Like the Yiddish newspapers, the Yiddish Theater was struggling for survival. Further, similar to the Yiddish press they, too, were searching for ways to retain and recruit audiences. They came to the same conclusions—less Yiddish, more English; less tear-producing drama and more comedy;

fewer plays, more flicks; and when all else failed, free give-aways. At one theater they gave away dishes and glasses, at another it was two-for-one tickets, and at a third, discount meals at the Second Avenue Deli.

The Second Avenue Deli, a large, single-floor place with the simple goal of serving as many people as possible within the shortest period of time, was the one establishment on Second Avenue that did not appear to be suffering from a lack of Yiddish enthusiasts. There were no frills, no fancy décor; it was, as my mother would say, "plain and *poshet*" (without any pretensions). The wait staff consisted of men in their mid-fifties and early-sixties who felt that they had no obligations whatsoever to the drop-in customer. Regular customers, however, were a different story. They were always the first to be seated and the first to be fed. Yiddish was not only the language of choice, but also almost a service requirement.

Fortunately, reservations for our group had been made in advance and we were seated at a long table. One of the waiters approached our guide and asked who we were and where we were from. The waiter had asked his question in Yiddish and the guide did not understand. Seeing yet another opportunity to gain stature, I answered in Yiddish that we were members of Habonim, a Labor Zionist Youth organization, and that we were studying at the Institute. He was not impressed and suggested that in his opinion none of us looked like we could survive a full day of hard work.

Before I could come up with a response, our guide asked if we could get menus. His request brought not only a look of dismay, but also a stern response from the waiter, "No menus. *Mir vesen vos ir vet essen, zog nicht meher vos do vilst* (We know what you will eat, so no more about what you want)!"

Wishing to somehow ease the situation and establish myself as an effective leader, I said, "*A tiren dank and vos do bringst velen mir essen* (Sincere thanks and whaever you bring we will eat)."

His response was short and less than reassuring: "*Mir velen zen* (We shall see)." With that, he turned and walked away.

The Second Street Deli feeding strategy, at least for the occasional diner, was based on the pyramid concept. The foundation is established with large servings of bread, plates of sour pickles and tomatoes, and pitchers of ice cold water. Being very hungry, we quickly devoured the bread, the pickles-tomatoes, and several pitchers of water. Then we waited for more than 20 minutes before the foundation was served: large bowls of chicken soup encircling the largest matzo ball I had ever seen.

Our pace of eating slowed down considerably and by the time the soup had been consumed we were stuffed. We had now completed the first two levels of the pyramid-feeding plan—a firm foundation of bread, water, pickles and tomatoes, followed by a hefty yet reasonable bowl of matzo ball soup. Next up was a mixed vegetable salad covered with a heavy dose of oil and vinegar. The salad, when compared with the preceding portions, was quite modest. It didn't matter, since the best we could do was random picking. Few even finished their salads.

The main attraction followed. This was the entrée, and true to the pyramid concept, the smallest portion of all: a plate with a meager serving of broiled chicken, a little rice and two small carrots.

We gave it our best effort but we could do no better than we had done with the salad. More food remained than had been eaten. Dessert was neither offered nor requested.

Our waiter, noting how little of the entrée we had consumed, could not resist a final comment, "You don't look like workers, and you certainly don't eat like workers." I thought it best not to attempt any response, and prepared to leave with the others.

It was at that moment that a member of our group, a guy who from day one I had considered a pure schmuck, loudly announced, "Places like this are what give Jews a bad name."

He went on to say that the operation was a rip off, with lousy service, deliberately serving large portions of the cheapest, most filling stuff, and miserly offerings of the main course. "This kind of place only perpetuates further the stereotype of the conniving and exploitative Jew." His comments were heard not only by us but by other customers as well.

I was shocked and outraged, as were other members of our group. Several expressed their anger, and one girl yelled out, "Allan, you are a complete and total asshole!"

Now we had the attention of everyone in the deli. I was not certain how many people might have heard or even understood Allan's comments, but it soon became apparent that at least one person had heard and understood.

An frail-looking elderly woman approached our table and asked if we would all sit down for a moment. Although she had an eastern European accent, her English was excellent. She addressed her first words to Allan, asking him if anyone had forced him to come to the deli. He answered no, but added that that was beside the point. She held up her hand and said, "Please allow me to continue."

Her next question was along the lines of the first, only this time she asked if anyone had forced him to eat. Understanding where her questions were leading, Allan chose to remain silent. She now turned to the entire group and repeated her question. The group response was clear, no one had forced us to eat, and the choice was our own. She smiled and said, "I want to share something with you I learned long before I was even your age. When I was a child my grandfather taught two rules about eating. In Yiddish my grandfather said first, '*Ah mensch est un a Chazer frest,*' and second, '*Ah bissel un a bissel macht a fullen schissel.*' "

My first reaction was what a small world it is, since my own grandfather had taught me the same truism. Her wisdom, of course, was lost on a youthful audience whose

Yiddish was limited to kid nasties like, "*Ge Kaken* (Take a crap)." I asked her permission to translate, adding that the rhthym and true feel of her words would certainly lose something in the translation. She nodded her head and I proceeded. " '*Ah mensch est un a chazer frest.*' A man eats and a pig overstuffs himself. '*Ah bissel un a bissel macht a fullen schissel.*' A little and a little makes a full plate."

As some in our group grasped the analogy and the message they began to laugh. But the wise, elderly lady was not yet finished, and this time her words to Allan were direct and without warmth. "I have also learned that the worst anti-Semite is a Jewish anti-Semite." And with that she walked away.

Chapter 9

Other than studies and field trips, I spent most of my free time with Shoshanah, who had her studies at NYU as well as her participation in Habonim. Because so much of my day was devoted to the movement, I had little interest in spending my evenings in organizational activity. My own preference was to see more of Manhattan, particularly the Village. Fortunately, there were many free programs, concerts, and events offered through NYU and uptown at the YMHA.

It was only a few more weeks until May, when both of us would complete our studies, but I was finding it increasingly difficult to stay focused. Field trips were over, replaced by an intensive Hebrew language program and organizational leadership skills. I could not buy into the idea of learning a foreign language while sitting in a classroom surrounded by English speakers in an English-speaking society. The Hebrew language as a currency in the United States was of little if any value. I was certain that once in *Eretz* I would quickly pick up the language, since Hebrew was the language of the people and the land. A major reason for my being able to learn Yiddish was that my teachers would accept no other alternative and Yiddish usage was the language of my home.

Neither my teachers nor the Institute principal were persuaded by my rationale and I was given a grade of "Incomplete".

A week before our graduation, we were each informed of our assignments. No one shared with me the criteria employed in determining who would go where. I was simply informed that Hartford, Connecticut would be my next place of residence. The only thing I knew about Hartford was that it is the headquarters of the Fuller Brush Company.

Housing arrangements had already been made and I would be staying in the home of a middle-aged widow. My hostess, Mrs. Lapman, was an officer in the Hartford Chapter of the Labor Zionist movement with responsibility for youth-related activities. My job would be to organize a new "*ken*" (local group) for West Hartford, a middle class suburb of Hartford.

For the summer I would have my choice of Cream Ridge or a return to Killingworth. I was inclined to Cream Ridge but chose Killingworth since that was where Shoshanah would be for the summer.

Our graduation took place in the third week of May, 1947. There were few guests other than instructors, Institute officials, and select national leaders of Habonim. Five of my class graduated with honors, twenty-three with full recognition, and two of us with "Incompletes." I immediately jumped to the conclusion (with some justification, I would later learn) that "Incompletes" were sent to the farm teams, the others to the majors. I was being shipped to Hartford, and the other semi-qualified graduate to Green Bay, Wisconsin. The honor students were headed for the Big League of Jewish communities—Detroit, Chicago, Milwaukee, L.A, Brooklyn, Atlanta, and the Bronx—all the high payoff places. We were going to the low risk places, those communities with a scattered handful of Jews. They were going to cities with well-established Habomim organizations, places where there was already a history of infrastructure and culture.

I had been to *hachshara* at Cream Ridge. I had sailed on a ship carrying refugees to *Eretz*, and I had knocked the audiences dead in Detroit. But that was then and this was now. Now I was headed to the desert of the Diaspora. I was not a happy Habonim messenger.

On the way up to Killingworth, Shoshanah did her best to put a positive spin on my dismal exile. "Look at it this way," she said, "They are giving you the challenge because they know no one else could possibly make it in Hartford."

"Where does one go after making it big in Hartford?" I asked. Before she could reply, I came back with my own answer: "Fargo, North Dakota!"

* * * * *

The summer turned out to be a pleasant interlude, and I was fairly successful at keeping thoughts of the immediate future at an emotional distance. By now, counseling had become routine, and the senior staff had found new ways of shifting our duties to the junior staff.

The biggest change in my life was that Shoshanah and I had become engaged. It was clear to both of us that, while marriage was perhaps premature, a public engagement announcement would somehow convince us and others that we were adults to be taken seriously.

We had also agreed that since Shoshanah had not met my family we would travel to Detroit as soon as camp ended. First, however, we would share our news with her parents. The big issue was who, when, where, and how.

We decided we would tell them on our visit in September. The "how" and "where" would be in Rabbi Herb's study with help, we hoped, from Herb and Blossom. We were able to negotiate the "when" and "where," but Herb adamantly refused to be the "who." He agreed to be present and as helpful as possible, but insisted that it was my duty and obligation to be the message carrier. I dreaded his next words, which were about my asking for Shoshanah's hand in marriage. I made it clear that we were not speaking of marriage but an engagement, and I was not seeking parental approval. Herb suggested that we could avoid a great deal of potential trauma by omitting the word "engagement" and declaring that we were going steady. We rejected that idea, since our intent was to show that ours was not just another adolescent fling. We were not talking about being pinned or, even if I had one, exchanging high school rings. We were serious about being engaged.

It was agreed that I would be the one that would share the news with Millie and Leo.

The deed was finally done during the Labor Day weekend, with Blossom, Herb, Shoshanah present. I wasted no time on pleasantries and came directly to the point. "Shoshanah and I have become engaged," I began. "We have no definite plans for the future other than we will eventually make our home in Palestine. We have not decided on a marriage date."

My brief comments were followed by complete silence, with the exception of Blossom, who came to the rescue with a hearty "Mazel Tov!" as she embraced Shoshanah and me. She attempted to do the same with Leo and Millie, but they sat motionless and stunned. Finally, Millie spoke. "I do not see an engagement ring."

A ring was the one subject we had not even thought about. Was her mother implying that without a ring this topic was dead in the water? Was the ring the thing that would get us over the parental hurdles?

I was just about to make some kind of reply when Shoshanah jumped into the fray. "We do not need a ring," she said, "or any other material token to show our dedication to one another. We will need whatever money we can save for our passage to *Eretz*."

Leo made a vague attempt to calm the waters, but it was too late. Millie began to sob and heave while expressing her distress and disappointment. For years she had looked forward to the moment when her daughter's suitor would seek marriage approval from her father. There would be a lovely engagement party, an announcement in the New York Times, and the making of plans for the wedding. Now, she concluded, there would be nothing.

I did my best and—without prior approval from my fiancée—assured both parents that there would in fact be a wedding. I went even further, promising that only after we were married would we leave for Palestine. Herb added that he would be more than happy to officiate. Shoshanah, recognizing that disagreement at this point could be fatal, came in with her most helpful comment. She told her mother that she was ready to begin discussing plans for both an engagement event as well as the wedding. Slowly, Shoshanah's mother regained control of herself and became a calmer participant. She said that though this was not what she would have wished for, her main concern was for her daughter's happiness.

With that, she stood and gave me a light, glancing cheek kiss, and hugged her daughter. Leo shook my hand and at the same time slipped me a fifty-dollar bill, whispering, "For heaven's sakes, get her some kind of ring."

Several days later I arrived at Hartford. Mrs. Lapman turned out to be a very pleasant, well-intentioned woman who lived in a modest ranch-style home bordering West Hartford. Within several more days I was able to gather hard intelligence, which I stored in my West Hartford mental database.

Fact 1: There was neither a Habomim organization nor any Habonim members in West Hartford. Further, there was not a local adult Labor Zionist organization or auxiliary, neither was there any evidence of any real interest in or support for such an organization. It turned out that Mrs. Lapman had been a most effective and optimistic advocate for a Habonim group in West Hartford. I do not know her motivation, but she was persuasive, and convinced New York that if you send someone, the people will come. I was the someone.

Fact 2: West Hartford had a small and very affluent Jewish population. They had a nice little Jewish

Community Center and one synagogue, a reform temple, and one rabbi. The rabbi was a young man, pleasant and cordial. We were quick to recognize that we were both recent graduates on our first assignments. We had little else in common. He had a clearly defined job, a well-furnished meeting place, membership, financial resources, volunteers, and community acceptance. I had none of that.

I considered none of these to be barriers to my doing the job expected of me. No, the deal killer was to come in just a few more moments.

The rabbi pointed out that his membership included virtually every declared Jew in West Hartford. He added that the children of his members, pre-kindergarten through high school, all attended Sunday school. I quickly got the point: all the teenagers were members of NFTY, the National Federation of Temple Youth. Similar to Habonim, NFTY had year-round activities and summer camps. NFTY camps provided the usual camp recreational and social activities with a strong focus on Judaism. Though sympathetic to the need for building a Jewish state in Palestine, NFTY was not a Zionist organization. More importantly, it was not an advocate for American Jewish *aliyah* to *Eretz.* The Rabbi also wanted me to understand that his was a fairly conservative congregation and would not be supportive of any competing Jewish youth group. He did say, however, that if I liked he could arrange for me to talk about my Palestine adventures with the older kids. I thanked him and said that I would consider his kind invitation.

West Hartford was Kingston without Rabbi Herb.

I talked with Mrs. Lapman and shared with her my belief that attempting to build a Habonim *ken* in West Hartford was pure madness, a waste of time and money. She was, of course, disappointed, and said that she hoped that I would consider giving it a few more weeks. I reluctantly agreed.

The next day I called New York and reported on what I had learned and added that if they had any ideas on how I might proceed I would appreciate the help. No advice was forthcoming other than my making certain that Mrs. Lapman was in agreement with any decision I made. I tried once again to explain that I had no clue as to what else I could do and that I needed help. The response was an infuriating "do the best you can."

My response was a loud "Up yours!" as I hung up.

A few days later I got a call from New York. The message was that I had proven, by lack of deed and vulgar word of mouth, that I was not yet ready to be a full-fledged *madrich*. My options were immediate dismissal or taking an associate position (junior *madrich*) in Boston. I seriously considered just walking away, but since I had no place to go and Boston had at least some appeal, I chose Boston. What was left of my wings had been clipped and I slid further down the organizational ladder.

I explained as best I could to Mrs. Lapman that I had been reassigned and regretted that I was not able to deliver. Kind soul that she was, she suggested that perhaps after more training in Boston I might return to West Hartford. My advice to her was not to count on it.

When I was given more specifics on my new posting, I discovered that I was not really going to Boston but rather to Dorchester, a fringe city area of Boston. The movement magicians had done it again—Hartford becomes West Hartford and Boston becomes Dorchester.

The good news was that I would be back with my people. In the spring of 1947, I arrived at Dorchester, a heterogeneous, blue collar, hard-working and hard-living community. The Jewish population was composed mainly of first and second generation Jews. The majority was trades people and service workers with a smaller number of white collar workers and professionals.

My home in Dorchester was a flat in a four-family, walk-up apartment. I roomed with a son who was about my age and a member of Habonim. His given name was Nachman, but he was called "Nucky." Nucky was built like a medium-sized icebox. Short and solid with bulging muscles, he had blond hair and an almost cherubic face. His parents had emigrated from Russia and settled among other newcomers in Dorchester.

Nucky was a young, carbon copy of his father. His father had two jobs. One was riding on a small motorbike with a trailer as he sold and delivered industrial soaps. His second job was delivering the daily Yiddish newspaper, The Morning Journal. Nucky's mother was also of short, stocky build, and was the loving fulfillment of the traditional Jewish mother. The kitchen was her domain, and her mission was to bring an abundance of *shtetel* style delicacies to all that entered her home.

I was welcomed into their home as if I was a member of the *mischpocah* (family). It was, as my mother would say on a hot summer day, placing her foot in the refreshing waters of Cass Lake, "*ah mechiah*" (a pleasure).

My favorite part of the day was the early morning, when the three men would sit at the kitchen table drinking hot coffee with cream and eating fresh bread with sweet butter and scrambled eggs smothered in onions. All conversations were held in Yiddish, with the exception of an occasional, "You better believe it!" uttered by Nucky's father. No matter the frustrations and irritations of the day, no one could take away the sheer delight of a weekday morning at Nucky's.

My Habonim job was to assist with the organizing of new members for the Dorchester chapter. Because the amount of time required was minimal, I was able to help Nucky's father with his delivery rounds. Other time was spent with Nucky and friends in Boston and Cambridge. Several evenings we went to Fenway Park to watch the Boston Red Sox.

I talked with Shoshanah on a regular basis, and she would keep me posted on news from the home front. Everything seemed to be going reasonably well and her mother was busy planning our engagement party.

Long evening discussions with Nucky's father were devoted in large part to the deteriorating political situation in Palestine. Violence between Jews and Arabs had reached a level where the British could no longer maintain control either by threat or force. Now Ben Gurion, who had always been a moderate, stopped talking about a "homeland" and insisted on a full blown Jewish state.

The Mandate giving governance to the British was without support, and in February of 1947, the Foreign Secretary, Ernest Bevin, referred the Mandate to the newly formed United Nations. The UN produced a new partition plan, which was readily accepted by Jewish leaders. There would be a Jewish state in parts of the Galilee, Upper Jordan Valley, the Negev, and portions of the coastal plain. The remainder would be for an Arab State. Jerusalem and Bethlehem would fall under international control. The Jews embraced the new plan, which was rejected by the Arabs. Predicted violence followed, leading ultimately to the death of many Jews and Arabs. Clearly, there would be even more terror, struggle, and casualties when the Jewish state was declared and the British would depart Palestine.

By the end of 1947, I found myself less and less dedicated to the Habonim mission. I put in my hours and fulfilled whatever assignments were sent my way. What was lacking was any sense of dedication or zeal. My commitment to *Eretz* remained strong, as did my desire to make *aliyah*. What I was losing was my feeling of loyalty to the organization and its ways of conducting business. I was bitter and felt that I had been misled and mistreated. Right or wrong, I knew that once I completed my Dorchester assignment I would be done with the movement. In December of 1947, I informed my immediate overseer and the New York office that I would agree to remain in place until March of the coming year. Following that date, I would no longer be available for assignment. With the exception of Nucky's family, no effort was made to dissuade me. The movement and I had come, without discourse, to a mutual understanding. I felt it best we parted, and apparently so did they.

My plans were to complete the Dorchester work, spend some time in New York with Shoshanah, and then return to Detroit. My return would not be like McArthur's glorious return to the Philippines. This time there would be no heroic welcome or adoring ladies of the Arbiter Ring.

I did, as promised, complete my work commitment, then I expressed my love and gratitude to Nucky and his parents and boarded the train for New York City. Shoshanah's folks came to the city and we discussed the forthcoming engagement party. The event was to be held in mid-May at a very high-end Manhattan hotel. We had decided that we would set aside our own preferences and go along with whatever Millie wished. This would be a party for family and close friends of Leo and Millie, perhaps a hundred or so guests. I knew the question of who was to be invited from my family was bound to be raised. It was an inquiry that I dreaded and was ill-prepared to answer. Nevertheless, when asked, I answered that I did not expect any of my family to attend, as they would then have to make a second trip for the wedding. Our plans were for Shoshanah to visit Detroit, where she would have the opportunity to meet my folks, brothers, and others. The reference to a wedding immediately set Millie off, and in her highest pitched voice she cried, "What wedding? We are not discussing a wedding. There is to be no wedding, at least not for a long, long time. You both promised."

Shoshanah and I exchanged glances, each hoping the other would jump in and save the day. I thought to myself, what the hell, Shoshanah and I had already decided that we would be married in late 1948 and then, a half-year later, go to *Eretz.* It was now public knowledge that on May 14 of 1948, the Jewish government in Palestine would declare the birth of the State of Israel. Our goal was to be among the first of American Jews to immigrate. Between the wedding and our departure, we could live and work in Detroit. We would need to earn money for our passage, study Hebrew, and obtain all the necessary documents and inoculations. Our earlier thinking was that we could get through the engagement gala and then spring the news.

Now I felt there was no alternative but to confess and hope for leniency if not forgiveness.

I tried to make the case that when we first talked about engagement, we were without any precise marriage game plan. We could not have predicted the events that were now occurring in Palestine, or the emergence of a Jewish state. We had never denied our intentions to move and settle in Israel. The only change was that we would now speed up and facilitate the process.

There it was—done—and no matter the parental response, our position had been made clear. Leo said nothing other than, "I see." Millie began to weep and pointed out that things were terrible "over there" and "they would never allow Jews to have their own country." Attempts at comforting words or assurances seemed a fruitless gesture, so we said nothing. Little more was said other than Millie indicating that, given this latest news, she might wish to reconsider the wisdom of having an engagement party. Sure enough, several days later she informed us that there would be no formal engagement party, but a small reception at the home of one of her sisters. All attention would now be given to the planning of a wedding.

I phoned my folks in order to bring them up to date on the new game plan. They had evidently come to the stage where they were no longer surprised by anything that I might propose.

After informing them that I was engaged and would be married within a year, my mother's first question was, "Is she Jewish?"

I answered in the affirmative and Ma said, "Pa wants to know if you can afford a wife".

I came back with, "She comes from a rich family."

I could hear my mother repeating my words to Pa, and his comment, "*Besser, zehr riech* (Better, very wealthy)."

I told them that we would be coming to Detroit in a few weeks. Ma said that she had plenty of room and we could stay with them.

So we came to Detroit in April, and within two weeks we had found jobs and a small apartment. Though I am certain it was a hot topic, Ma and Pa said nothing to me about our living together without rabbinical blessing. No doubt they had concluded that we were already sleeping together, and co-habitation of kibbutz members did not require proof of marriage. This action would just be further evidence of their son's "*mashigas*" (madness).

I went to work as a shoe dog for a low priced, schlock-type national chain. Shoshanah found employment with a branch of the Detroit Public Library. Our goal was to save as much money as possible in the shortest period of time. Our wedding was scheduled for New York in mid-December. We had about six months for earning, going without, and saving. We were also counting on adding to the bottom line through what we hoped would be a surge of cash wedding gifts.

We decided that we would avoid involvement in any Habonim activities. We had both reached the point where we sought to break all ties with the movement. Our thinking was to a find a kibbutz that would have a mix of English speaking members as well as *Sabras*. At NYU, Shoshanah had met several students who were members of a Zionist youth group that had formed an alliance with a like minded group of Israelis. Contact had been made through the helpful offices of the Jewish Agency.

The concept here was to bring together Zionist youth from America, Great Britain, South Africa, and Canada and have them, in partnership with young Israelis, form a new kibbutz. No single political or social ideology would prevail; rather, the goal was to encourage diversity in views and background. The basic and traditional ground rules of a socialistic collective and communal life would be maintained.

A site had already been identified where members would live, work, and prepare themselves for that glorious day ("*Hityashvut*") when we would set out to build our own kibbutz. Life may have been tough at Cream Ridge, but that would seem a piece of cake compared to the real thing. No quick calls home, no quick trips to Trenton or Manhattan, no assurance of water, much less hot water, and always knowing that danger was eminent. No, this was not playing at being a *chalutz*; this was going to be the real thing. We signed on with the understanding that we would be joining the others in April of next year, 1949.

I must admit that I really enjoyed selling shoes, and I was considered one of the top dogs, especially among the old timers. I was highly motivated since I knew that I had a narrow window of earning opportunity. I was particularly successful at pushing hosiery, shoe polish, handbags, bows, and shoe styles now considered to be passe. Sales of these items would bring added stature, plus commissions.

Each of us followed the operation procedures established by management. We were to rotate in approaching new customers; you got one sales crack in each go around. Once having made a shoe sale, you were expected to follow up with the accessories routine: "Wow, these bows would look just great on this lovely suede pump. They are removable, so you would have two different styles of shoes just for the price of one pair."

"How about this genuine alligator handbag? It shows off your new shoes and blends in nicely with whatever you wear."

Credibility and integrity placed a far second behind sincerity. The important thing was to flatter, manipulate, deceive, and of course, sell, sell, sell.

There was only one prohibition, and that was you must never walk a customer. If you could not make the sale, you were required to do a "33"—pass the customer on to another salesman. Timing was critical. Once the customer had put her own shoes back on, she was a lost cause. The ideal transition time was when she was sitting and shoeless. One of my associates, in order to make certain that his customer would not walk, hid customers' shoes behind the cashier's counter.

The "33" process went something like this: "I want to introduce you to Mr. Jones. He is our specialist in wedges (or pumps, mid-heels, ankle wraparound, whatever the customer was looking for), and he knows the fashions and stock far better than me." There were other times when, rather than making a reference to a certain shoe style, you would use the flattery bit: "Mr. Smith attended our Shoe Institute in New York, where his specialty was women with small feet (or narrow feet, or younger women, or older women, or whatever else might help)." On some occasions we practiced our own form of ethnic matching. Assuming you were losing what you thought to be an Irish, Jewish, or, let's say, an Italian customer: "This is Mr. Riley (or Ginsburg, or Tagoni)." We did whatever it would take to keep them in the store. Selling a "33" was an added bonus and gave you ladder rotation priority.

In addition, this experience confirmed some thoughts I had about job related fetishes and behavior. While at Cream Ridge, I became convinced that people who worked with certain animals would eventually take on the charteristrics of those animals. People working in the chicken coops walked and ate like chickens. They would peck at their food and constantly move their heads in a back and forth motion. The same pattern held true for those working with the milking cows. Like cows, they would wobble from side to side as they moved from one place to another. How far I might have carried this analogy remains undiscovered, since we had no pigs, ducks, or donkeys.

With shoe people, it was not so much imitation of the subject as it was foot and leg fascination. I remember one guy would agree to give up his commission if we would "33" him women with very hairy legs. "Gottlieb, I will give you the commission and my next customer for that gorilla-legged lady." For another salesman, it was women with huge, fat, wide feet. A third was into transvestites. It was theater, comedy as well tragedy, and I loved it all.

On the fifth of Iyar, May 14, 1948, an extraordinary event occurred which had great significance for Jews and Arabs. On that day, as expected, the establishment of the State of Israel was proclaimed. In anticipation of that announcement, the Arab armies of Syria, Iraq, Jordan, Lebanon, as well as volunteers from Saudi Arabia and Yemen, were prepared to invade the new State. Military organization, recruitment, and the procurement of arms and equipment were well underway in Israel. The fighting was immediate, widespread, and intense.

The United Nations, as well as individual nations, sought to intervene in order to halt the conflict. The first cease-fire occurred on June 10. The time was used as a breather for both sides to reorganize and redeploy. The conflict was renewed within a month, and a second cease-fire went into effect on July 19. Egypt rejected that cease-fire and the fighting continued.

On the day the State was born, we received phone calls from both sets of parents. My mother's first words were a hearty "Mazel Tov" and "God's blessing of Israel." Her second comment was that perhaps we should consider a brief delay in our travel plans. Shoshanah's mother's words were directed at me as she asked how I could say that I loved her only child and drag her into a place consumed by war. It was a timely and unnerving question, and I had no reasonable answer.

Other than our work, family gatherings, and an occasional movie or concert, we were living a fairly reclusive live. Several times I ran into old Habonim associates, but there was little in the way of in-depth probing or meaningful discussion.

In mid-December we returned to New York to assist in the finalization of wedding plans and preparations for our voyage to Israel. The situation in the Middle East was far from resolved and no armistice was yet in sight. We continued our preparations in hopes that events over which we had no control would not play havoc with our plans.

The wedding took place in December at the Plaza Hotel. Attending in support of the groom were Morris and Sophie Gottlieb, as well as my recently wedded brother Bob and his wife, Teddy. The remaining guests, numbering about 100, were relatives and friends of the bride and her parents. Millie served as producer and director, with Rabbi Herb officiating.

The setting was a large hall, decorated with numerous floral arrangements, including a gardenia bedecked "*chupah*" (traditional Jewish wedding canopy). The ceremony was well balanced in Hebrew and English, thereby holding the interest of most guests. We took our vows. I smashed the glass.

And so, we were married.

Chapter 10

On January 7, 1949, Egypt agreed to a cease-fire and consented to begin armistice negotiations. An agreement with Israel was signed February 24. By July 20 of that year, the final Arab combatant, Syria, came to terms with Israel. The war was over, and Shoshanah and I moved quickly to book our passage to Haifa.

Our sailing date was set for July 26. The ship was an American freighter that accommodated twenty-four passengers. Our sleeping quarters were a small cabin sans shower or bath facilities. It was much more comfortable than the Wedgwood, but similar in being short on amenities. Passengers shared bath facilities and ate in two shifts. The major differences between this voyage and my first were the direct route to Haifa, no concern about the Brits, and freedom from engine room duties.

Most of the other passengers were young people who, like us, intended to remain in Israel. Some would be going to kibbutzim and others had plans to work and live in Tel Aviv or Jerusalem. There was one elderly couple, whose wish it was to be buried in or near Jerusalem.

Since there were no organized ship board activities, most of our time was spent in reading and conversations with others. By day number five, the never changing routine was beginning to take its toll. There were several public disputes between couples, and one incident that called for a stern rebuke from the captain.

The trip itself was uneventful—free of bad weather, equipment failure or any distraction.

On day nine we entered the Straits of Gibraltar, our first sighting of land. Entrance into the Mediterranean appeared to have a positive psychic impact, as passengers were now in a more upbeat mood. By the time we could see the mountains of Haifa, the ship was alive with activity. As in my first voyage, we danced the hora and sang our national anthem, "Hatikvah."

I was amazed at the startling contrasts between my first exposure to Haifa and with this port entry only two years later. When the Wedgwood arrived, the harbor area was filled with thousands of Jews welcoming our ship as well as others of *Aliyah Bet*. That was the time of illegal immigration, and every arriving vessel was considered a symbolic victory. Now, the arrival of boatloads of Jews was nothing unusual. Jews were coming to Israel from many parts of the globe. Most came to explore the new country, some to study, and others to settle.

The English flag, which had flown from the highest point in the harbor, had been replaced with the Star of David. Jews, Hebrew signs, and symbols of the State were everywhere. There were Jewish stevedores, immigration officials, taxi and bus drivers, soldiers, sailors, and, yes, Jewish hookers. The immigration policy of the State was wide open, no matter a person's background, place of origin, or religious preference. If you considered yourself a Jew, "Shalom."

The entry process was completed with minimal bureaucratic hassle. Our passports were stamped and we were granted a one-year, renewable visa. We were classified as newly arriving immigrants. Like all other immigrants who were without a permanent or temporary residence, we were sent to an immigration center. We boarded a bus to a camp some twenty miles from Haifa. The amount of time to be spent at the center was dependent upon the newcomer's physical condition, job skills, Hebrew language proficiency, and housing needs. We anticipated a relatively short stay, since we had confirmation of our membership in a *hachshara* site not far from the city of Netanya.

The camp itself was huge, with dozens of dormitories, numerous dining halls, and instruction buildings. All buildings were one story and constructed of wood. My first reaction was that this place was no different from the displaced persons camps I had seen in Italy. My God, I thought, what would be the reaction of those who had spent the past five years in those places?

There were, however, several important and apparent differences: no fences, no guards, and people could leave if they chose to do so. Effort was made to explain that these were temporary quarters with the goal of facilitating the permanent settlement of each person and family.

Our first stop was a large warehouse where we were provided with bedding, a mess kit, one towel, and a meal ticket. The bedding consisted of a straw mattress, whose cover was of the same texture as a potato sack, and one army surplus blanket, clearly used many times before. No pillow. The very primitive setting and meager amenities certainly sent the message that one would do best to exit this place as quickly as possible.

We were assigned to a non-children dorm, where we selected two canvas-topped cots. The population of residents was as diverse and exotic as I could have possibly imagined. There were Jews from Eastern and Western Europe, Great Britain, South Africa, and the States. Most intriguing were those Jews who had recently migrated from other countries of the Middle East, the Baltic, and Africa. As a result, it was very colorful and lively with the dozens of different languages, customs and clothing.

We were called to dinner by announcements given through a camp-wide public address system. To accommodate the maximum number of newcomers, instructions were given in at least ten different languages.

The dining hall was dimly lit, with most space devoted to long wooden tables, benches, and cafeteria-style serving counters. As you entered the hall, your meal card was punched. Our first dinner was a three-course meal consisting of soup, chicken with a vegetable, and, for desert, halvah. Halvah is a Turkish candy made of honey and sesame seeds. As a child I was given halvah as a special treat. It was a domesticated version of halvah, covered with dark, rich chocolate or laced with almonds—a delicacy that would melt in your mouth. The texture and taste of the halvah served in Israel was quite different. The composition was more like shredded paper, preserved in oil then left to dry in the sun. The stuff was so brittle it would break apart before it could be eaten. All the better, since the taste was not worth the effort. In Israel, halvah was considered a basic food staple, a filling substitute for rice, wheat, and grain. For lunch the next day, halvah was served as sandwich filler with two slices of dark bread smeared with oleo and halvah spread on like peanut butter.

The dining procedure called for finishing the first course, getting in line again for the second course, then once again for the third course. There was no table service and no change of dishes. Each course was placed in your own army-style mess kit bowl. I had assumed that those not wishing to retain the remnants of a prior course would simply dump leftovers in a designated garbage can. I was wrong, and very shortly I would pay for my error.

On each table, spaced some three or four feet from one another, were large metal bowls, called "*kalbonicks*." I do not know the origin of the word *kalbonick* or its precise translation into English. What I do know now, and what I did not know then, is that the purpose of the *kalbonick* is to be the receptacle for discarded food.

Somehow I did not notice people at my table dumping their garbage in to these large, highly visible containers. Perhaps I was lost in thoughts of Ma's kitchen table, where serving bowls were exclusively used for extra helpings.

My tablemates and Shoshanah watched with amazement as I dipped into the *kalbonick* and placed substantial portions of "garbage" into my bowl. I believe some might have thought that this was some kind of joke or perhaps an authorized lesson in the "do's and don'ts" of Israeli culture. They were mistaken, as I eagerly devoured the first mouthful, and then the second and third. Kids at the table laughed, the adults remained stunned, until Shoshanah finally yelled, "David, stop! You are eating garbage!" Once I realized what I had done, I had two immediate reactions: one of humiliation, the other of nausea. I jumped up from the table and ran to the outhouse.

By breakfast the next day, most everyone in the camp had heard about the crazy American who had eaten garbage. By midday the story had taken on a folklore dimension and now it was being said that I had gone from table to table, not missing a single *kalbonick.* Ah yes, *a mensch est un Gottlieb frest* (a man eats and Gottlieb stuffs himself). Shoshanah showed great restraint in not mentioning the unfortunate incident, and at her suggestion we switched dining halls.

A few days later we traveled by bus to Tel Aviv, where we were met and were taken to our new home, Tel Herzel. "*Tel*" is the Hebrew word for light; Theodore Herzel is considered by many to be the father of Zionism, and in 1896 he published the book, The Jewish State.

Tel Herzel was located quite near the coastal city of Natanya. For many years it served as a *Hachshara* facility, preparing pioneers in the skills, organization, governance, and behaviors that would be required by those seeking to establish a new kibbutz. Not unlike Cream Ridge, it had a substantial working farm, dairy herd, and chickens. Unlike Cream Ridge, it also had several ongoing, revenue-generating industries, commercial fishing, and the manufacturing of cement building blocks.

Couples were housed in small, single-bedroom bungalows built with cement blocks produced in Tel Herzel.

Single men and women were housed in dormitory type buildings. Infants and children lived in quarters separate from those of their parents. The greatest care and attention was given to the housing and staffing of the nursery and children's residence.

At the time of our arrival there were some 150 people at Tel Herzel. Most were married couples under the age of thirty-five. The group was pretty evenly divided between English-speaking immigrants and Sabras, the native Israelis named for a cactus-like plant called the sabra. The sabra plant is thorny and prickly on the outside but contains warm milk inside.

It was not difficult to immediately notice the differences between the newcomers and the Sabras. Of course, they knew the language, customs, and land, and we did not. They were tanned and fit; we were not. Many of them, men and women, had fought in the War of Independence; we had not. They all seemed so attractive, with handsome dark men and beautiful, olive-skinned women.

Finally, and most important of all, they knew that we knew that they had the uppper hand, and for at least some period of time they would call the shots. This was their turf and we would be playing by their ground rules.

I was determined to beat them at their own game by becoming a look alike Sabra as quickly as possible. I would talk like them, dress like them, walk like them, and by God, outwork them.

That evening we had our first introduction to collective living and governance as practiced in the big league. The meeting was called to order by the Rosh (leader), followed by an introduction of newcomers, a financial report, and work scheduling announcements.

None of the new English speakers had been at Tel Herzel for more than three weeks. Hence, all of us were considered to still be in the orientation phase of training. Daily work assignments for our group were pretty much limited to light duties—meal servers, kitchen assistants, grounds maintenance, nursery school helpers, and so forth. None of us were considered to be ready for fishing, cement block work, heavy equipment operation, or any of the white collar accounting office and management positions. Nor had any of us yet been approved as voting members of the kibbutz.

The next order of business was dealing with the special requests of individual members. The procedure that was followed went something like this: For whatever reason you need to make a trip to, say, Haifa, you need bus fare and approval to miss two days of work. You submit a written request, which is reviewed by an executive committee, and they decide "yea" or "nay." If you are unhappy with their decision, you may raise the matter at a full meeting of the membership.

That evening there were several such appeals, but I will share only one. A young man, a Sabra of Lebanese descent, had asked for permission to visit his parents in Jerusalem. He was requesting three days and no bus fare. He planned to hitchhike and had volunteered to make up the missed workdays by working a double shift. His stated reason for seeking this visit was to spend time with his ailing grandfather.

The committee spokeswoman explained the reason for denial. The committee members felt that a visit to the grandfather was not really why the *chaver* was seeking a temporary leave. Rather, it was because his offer of marriage to a female member had been rejected. By allowing him to leave, the kibbutz would not be fulfilling its responsibility in seeing to it that all members face up to reality and deal honestly with their personal problems.

I looked over at the guy, as did everyone else in the room. He was slumped over, staring at his feet. What was most disturbing to me was the wave of mocking laughter and giggling coming from the Israeli women. No one asked a question and no one rose to speak on this guy's behalf. The case was closed. As the second case was being reviewed I got up and told Shoshanah that I was going back to our room.

Later that evening we had our first serious disagreement.

Even before the door was closed, I was in her face with, "So how went the inquisition–public whipping or solitary confinement?"

She hesitated in answering since she was not certain as to whether I was serious or just in one of my smart ass moods. Having concluded that I was indeed serious, she went on to point out that she did not understand why I gotten so upset. Her comment only added to my frustration and impatience, and I answered that I was bothered because this was a public act of humiliation directed at a supposed *chaver*.

I went on, "Here is this guy who has been rejected and is seeking some temporary relief. OK, turn down the request, but spare him the ridicule and embarrassment."

"No," said Shoshanah, "It is essential that he deal with the real reason for his seeking a leave and confront his failure."

While I was considering my response, Shoshanah went on to point out that I would have to accept that the values and rules of the kibbutz were unlike those I might have known at Cream Ridge. "This is the hard core world of collective living. No bourgeois values or ground rules here." She concluded with comments to the effect that if we were to make it here, we would need to play by their ground rules. She also reminded me that I had committed myself to outdo and outperform any of the Sabras. Now was my chance.

The very next day I took the first steps in establishing my "I am one of you" status by volunteering to work in the manufacturing of cement blocks. The only component of that tedious and labor-intensive job that represented manufacturing was a two-piece form, which was used to shape the cement blocks. Two guys mixed the cement while two guys made blocks. One filled the form with cement, then leveled off the top with a piece of plywood. The next step was the most difficult: getting the still wet block out of the form and on to a 2 x 4 board without losing the contents. You had to be quick and certain, neither being skills which I possessed. When I did finally manage to get a full block on to the board, the ends or middle portions would sink slowly to the ground.

While I continued to struggle, my Sabra associates were showing their stuff by using fancy one-hand movements in dispensing cement blocks from containers. They continued to remind me by word and deed that cement block making was more a craft than a mechanical task. There was one guy who considered himself the John Wayne of Cement Blocks; he would spin the form with one hand while adding cement with the other hand. They might have made it easier for me with a helpful hint or two, but no one offered any assistance.

There was really nothing malicious here. Rather, it was more like a game or contest between them and us. It was not unlike the situation my father faced when he first came to America. The problems we faced in adjustment were many, since this was a new and different culture for us. We had to learn a new language, a different life style, and adjust to a different kind of climate, food, and social system. Here the immigrant pecking order was a bit more complex, since, unlike most other recent arrivals to Palestine, we were American Jews who had an alternative. We could have stayed home. The sympathy and understanding directed to the survivors were not extended to us. We were certainly not viewed as heroes or saviors. No time was devoted to hand holding, group therapy, or consensus building. From the Sabra perspective, it was "our way or the highway." It was not long before several Americans gave up and left, while others talked about leaving.

In order to facilitate the smooth transition of cement from container to plywood, it is best to hose out each container after each emptying, thus removing any residue that might prevent removal of an intact block. After several weeks of dedicated effort and frustration, I did manage to produce my first successful run of cement blocks. I completed a total of eleven prior to the collapse of block number twelve.

I was rewarded with some helpful advice on block stacking and watering. Leaving just the right amount of space between blocks enabled the proper flow of water among blocks and prevented erosion.

Eventually I was doing 175 blocks per eight-hour shift (still a long way from the 225 produced by my associates). I felt I was getting the hang of things and gaining support from several of my Israeli coworkers. The symbolic gesture of initial acceptance occurred when they referred to me by my Hebrew name, "Dovid," and not "Gottlieb."

I remained the only American in blocks, which, while gaining me more credibility with the Israelis, was costing me with my American friends. In the process of becoming one of them, I was also taking on more and more of the Sabra mentality and style. There was no question that the Sabras saw themselves as superior, and they could be quite arrogant. They were the ones who had fought and won the War of Independence. These impressive and attractive men walked with a stride of self-confidence and determination. There were no fat Sabras; all were lean and trim. No matter their youthfulness, all of them had served in the military, and many of the men had been members of Palmach, a commando special forces group. I sometimes had the impression that the Israeli military was without any enlisted personnel, since everyone I met had at least attained the rank of lieutenant. Both men and women always wore shorts. Khaki was the color of preference. Most of the men had handlebar moustaches, rolled up the sleeves of their shirts, and were well tanned. I thought the moustache was a bit much, but I did go with everything else, including the swagger.

In my wish not be identified as anything but a native, I concentrated on learning Hebrew. When eating I would make it a point of sitting with Israelis so that I would be forced to speak and understand the language.

Several weeks later when I went into to town to get a haircut, I had the opportunity to test out the quality of my Sabra-passing abilities. After getting my regulation native haircut I went next door to a small café serving beer as well as soft drinks. I decided that if I could pull it off there, I could do it anywhere.

A young man behind the counter greeted me with a cordial "Shalom" and asked "*Ma atah rotzeh adon* (What do you wish Sir)?"

I responded quickly and my most self-assured manner, "*Ani rotzeh bakbuk bira, bavakashah* (I would like a bottle of beer, please)."

He smiled and said, "*Tov, azah bakbuk bira atah rozteh* (Good. What kind of beer do you want)?"

What I did not understand was that he was asking me for the brand I wished. Thinking he sought more information about the quantity I desired, I replied, "*Ani rozteh bakbuk gadol* (I want a large bottle)."

He again said, "That's good, but what kind of beer do you wish?"

I was now getting desperate and quickly running out of adjectives. I decided to give it one last shot, "*Ani rotzeh bakbuk bira gadol v kar* (I want a large bottle of cold beer)."

Until that moment he had been more than gracious, but now I could sense that he, too, was running thin on patience.

At that point I was rescued by the intervention of an elderly gentlemen who was sipping a glass of tea while observing my performance. He came over to the counter, raised his hand, silencing all discussion, and asked me if I spoke Yiddish. I answered yes. He asked me what it was that I wanted and I answered, "A bottle of beer." He smiled, turned to the clerk, and berated him for making my life miserable when all I wanted was a bottle of Gold Eagle. The clerk was stunned, attempted to explain his innocence, but was again cut off by my newfound friend. I got my beer, drank it quickly, and with thanks to all departed. I gave myself an "A" for chutzpah and an "F" for Sabra-ness.

While I had managed to make the grade as a regular member of the prestigious cement block-making team, I was having increasing bouts with "*Shil Shul*" (diarrhea). My body seemed unable to retain any food, and the drinking of water only exacerbated the problem. I was sent to the local hospital and given a number of different powders and told to stay on a strict diet. Unfortunately, the foods prescribed were not those regularly served at Tel Herzel. I insisted upon maintaining my usual work schedule, and with the possible exception of Shoshanah, no one argued with me. I knew I was losing weight, since there were two occasions when my work trousers needed to be taken in. I was not aware, however, of the degree of weight loss until one morning when I was putting on my shoes. I was sitting on a cement block, and for the first time in my life I could actually feel the bones of my ass. The fatty flesh that had always been there to protect my tush was suddenly gone. Later in the week, when I once again went to the medical service, I weighed myself and discovered that I had lost more than fifty pounds.

Eventually, my condition improved somewhat, though I continued with the prescribed powders, hoping for a complete cure.

Over the next few months, there was more and more discussion about our group leaving Tel Herzel and establishing our own kibbutz. The rumors were that we would be given a site in the Galilee. Along with the speculation came a growing recognition among the Americans that soon each of us would have to make a "go" or "no go" decision. There had been several meetings of all members where we were given the opportunity to ask questions and express our concerns. It was clear that many of the members of our group had already decided not to participate in the new venture. More than a dozen had arranged to join a group of other Americans in an already established kibbutz. Several others were returning to the States.

My own feelings were mixed and in part influenced by my continued bouts with illness. I saw the decision to stay as a lifetime commitment to collective living. I knew that I did not want to spend the rest of my life on cement blocks, eating with hundreds of people, sharing possessions, living in confined quarters, and sacrificing for the good of the group. Being a pioneer was okay for the short term, but not my idea of a future.

Shoshanah, on the other hand, was adamant in her conviction and dedication. She made it clear that she would stay no matter what I decided. She suggested that perhaps it would be best for me to return to the States for rest and rehabilitation, and then join her later. Her proposal was totally unexpected and, as I made clear, quite unacceptable.

A few days later, the formal announcement was made, and it became public knowledge as to which of us would join in the move to the new settlement. Shoshanah and I were among the handful of Americans who voted yes.

Shoshanah was very much aware that mine was a reluctant affirmation motivated solely by my desire to avoid separation. Our differences in this matter were having an impact on our relationship. We kept conversations to a minimum, and disagreements were becoming more and more a part of our daily lives. We both occupied ourselves with work and making preparations for the move.

One morning, Shoshanah informed me that a group would be making an advanced visit to the site of the proposed kibbutz and that she would be joining them. She did not ask if I cared to participate, only adding that perhaps it would be best if we spent a few days apart. At that point, I could not have cared less, since I was still feeling unwell and generally pissed with the state of our union.

Several days later, Shoshanah returned with a surprising announcement. She had given the matter of our differences a great deal of thought and wished to propose a compromise. Her idea was that we would both return to the States and, following a mutually agreed upon period of time, make a decision with regards to our future. That way, I would have an opportunity to gain back my strength, and we would both have time to assess our options. I was so delighted with her proposal that I did not even bother to ask what brought about this change. For me, it was sufficient that we would be leaving together.

There was some expressed surprise among the Israelis when we announced our decision to return to America. Shoshanah insisted on adding that this was only a temporary move and we would both soon return to our fellow kibbutz members.

Within a month we were aboard a ship bound for New York. We were returning as a couple, but not in any way the intimate, lively, optimistic pair that not so long ago sailed for the Promised Land.

We had decided that we would relocate in Kingston, find jobs, and deal with our issues there. We rented a small apartment, and I found work as a shoe salesman. Shoshanah worked as a clerk in a small gift shop.

In a matter of days I was to have an answer to the question of what had brought about the dramatic turnaround in Shoshanah's change of heart.

The news came from Rabbi Herb, who was once again serving as Shoshanah's confidant and envoy. Herb felt that it would be best to get right to the point. It seems that Shoshanah had fallen in love with one of the Israelis who, being an honorable sort, insisted that she return to the States with me. He insisted that only after she informed me of her change of heart and her wish to live with him would he accept her.

At this point Shoshanah made her entrance and with tears in her eyes said that she regretted that she had hurt me and that had never been her intent. It was just one of those unplanned things that happen, where no one is really at fault

My first and only question was, "Who is it?"

She told me. It was one of the guys that I had worked with on cement blocks—a guy I had liked. "So now what?" I asked.

Shoshanah said that there was really no need to rush into anything; for now, we could maintain the status quo. That was not the response I was looking for.

"What the hell does that mean?" I asked. "You have obviously fallen in love with someone else, and I assume you want to be with him. I have no desire to hang around while you finalize your plans. Let's just end things now."

The firmness of my response seemed to surprise both Herb and Shoshanah. Herb said that perhaps a separation period where we could both think it over would be a wise move. I immediately rejected that idea and said that I was going back to Detroit and that since Shoshanah sought the split, she should go for the divorce. I left and returned to our apartment, where I called my brother Norman. I explained what was happening and packed my stuff.

That afternoon I took the bus to Manhattan, and by that evening I was on a train back to Detroit.

Chapter 11

It was March of 1950, and I was again living with my parents. I had now made up my mind that I would do whatever was necessary to complete my high school diploma and enroll in college.

I was twenty-one years of age and eligible to take the GED, which would gain me a high school diploma. Once again, Norman came to my rescue. While attending the University of Michigan, Norman had a part-time job with an organization offering support and guidance for people seeking high school diplomas. His organization provided study packages and final examinations for a variety of high school courses. Students were encouraged to work at their own pace, but no student could complete more than six hours of credit in any three-month period.

I am not at all clear how he pulled it off, but Norman arranged to have the time restrictions waived and encouraged me to work as fast as possible. Within four months I had completed all of the course requirements. With that done, I took my final exams and was awarded my high school certificate of completion.

Meanwhile, I had found a job, again selling shoes, and a one-room apartment. There had been several phone conversations with Shoshanah, who told me that she would probably not be going back to Israel, at least not for a while. Neither of us mentioned reconciliation. I believe we both understood and accepted that our marriage was over.

A few weeks later, divorce papers arrived. I found a notary, signed them, and sent them back.

My next challenge was enrolling in college. The only viable alternative for me was Wayne State University in Detroit—an urban, public institution catering primarily to older, part-time students and those unable to afford or qualify for one of the state's more prestigious universities.

On a Monday morning, I took the bus down to Wayne University. I knew no one and had no ideas about the working of an academic bureaucracy. My instructions were to go to Old Main and request a meeting with an admissions counselor. I did so and was told to take a seat. Eventually, I was summoned by the receptionist and informed that my appointment with a Mr. Stepworth had been cancelled and that I would need to return the following Monday. I knew then for certain that I was back in school. I said that I could not return in a week, that I had taken time off from work, and that I would be happy to meet with another advisor.

My reaction startled and, I think, frightened the young receptionist. She moved away from me and called over her male supervisor. I told him my tale, adding that I had held up my part of the agreement and now I expected the University to fulfill its obligations. He was one of those smooth, condescending, priggish types that are found in abundance on every American college campus. He informed me that the University had no obligation to me since I was as yet not even enrolled, and that should I persist, I would never be enrolled.

That did it. I grabbed his tie, pulled him toward me, and shouted, "Get out of my face!"

It was at that moment, when I was certain that the jerk was probably right and that they would never have me, that Mrs. Ammerman appeared. She was a woman in her fifties, well groomed, with a warm, authentic smile and firm manner. She inquired as to the reason for all the tumult and was told by the prig that I was causing a disturbance.

I interjected my side of the story and was pleasantly surprised when Mrs. Ammerman said that she would be happy to meet with me, if that would be acceptable. I quickly answered yes and thanked her.

I will never know the chain of events that led me to Mrs. Ammerman, or what force was watching over me on that day. What I do know is that that unscheduled, chance meeting played a most crucial role in my life. What an angel she turned out to be. I was invited to her office, where she asked me to take a few moments and tell her about my background and my aspirations. I did a quick summary, including my erratic school history, being a high school drop out, a sailor, and most recently having lived on a kibbutz in Israel. I closed my review with the fact that I had now earned my high school equivalency certificate and my immediate goal was enrolling at Wayne University.

Mrs. Ammerman was attentive and would from time to time shake her head or smile. When I was finished, she asked me my age. I answered that I was twenty-two. She smiled again and said that I reminded her of her son, who was also twenty-two. The difference, of course, she added, was that while I was traipsing all over the place he was exactly where he was supposed to be. "If you had followed the traditional route," she said, "you would now be in your senior year and not just starting college." Then, almost to herself, she softly said, "I wonder if my son would have survived if he had followed your course?"

There was a brief pause, then she pointed out that we must now get back to the matter of my enrollment. She asked if I had given any thought to an academic major. I said not really, but I would prefer something with limited math and hard sciences. The correspondence courses I had passed did not include any math, no algebra, and certainly no calculus. My last science class had been labeled "General Science," and was taught by Mrs. Green at Winterhalter Elementary. I said that I knew I could do well in the social sciences and humanities.

During our discussion I told her that I would have to work my way through college and perhaps rent a room near the University. Although she was very sympathetic, Mrs. Ammerman was candid in her assessment of my chances. She cautioned me that the transition into college would be difficult, that I was obviously short on study skills and the basic core level academic foundations. Working and trying to take a full schedule would not make sense. What she was able to offer, and what I was happy to accept, was conditional admission. I would be allowed to take a total of three courses (nine credit hours), with the understanding that if I failed to earn a "C" or better in each of these classes, I would be dropped. If on the other hand I did meet that minimum standard, I would be enrolled as a regular student, with the opportunity to carry a larger class load. I was so happy and so grateful that I gave Mrs. Ammerman an unexpected hug. As I left I assured her that I would not let her down and that I would come and visit.

On the home front, things were calm and stable. Pa's store had been expanded and my folks were experiencing their first taste of relative affluence. They had purchased a new home in what was considered to be the suburbs. They were traveling and enjoying life, although Pa never really felt comfortable being away from home or the store for very long.

My brother Bob was employed as the manager of a small, men's clothing store. He and his wife Teddy had a daughter. Harold had completed his high school studies at Northern High School and was turning into an entrepreneur. He was showing skills and drive that none of us knew he possessed. Norman was well on his way to completing his undergraduate degree and was applying for admission to the University of Michigan Law School.

No one in the family seemed either surprised or overly concerned as to the state of my personal life. For my folks, it was enough that I was safe and motivated to take on a college education. My brothers had enough on their own plates, even though they made it clear they would be there for me when their help was requested.

What I soon realized was that in many respects, I had become a stranger in my own land. For long periods of time I had either been out of the country or so consumed with my own insulated world that I had not kept pace with what was happening in America. Certainly much of what would be considered the adolescent stage of my life had been lost. I knew nothing of the current popular culture. Which were the hot bands? Who were the film stars? What movies were big? What were the fashions and fads? On the broader and national scale, what was the political, social, and economic climate? There were many gaps and much catching up to do. Hell, I had even lost track of "Hammering" Hank.

I knew that Harry Truman was still President of the United States, while the country was still enjoying the growth and prosperity that followed the end of World War II. Detroit remained a major automobile-producing city with strong trade unions. But seven years after major race riots tore through the city, there was little evidence of healing. Blacks and whites for the most part continued to live in separate racial ghettos. The black urban population continued to grow as more and more whites moved to newly created suburbs.

Out of nowhere there was something called the "Korean Conflict." In June, North Korea invaded South Korea, and American troops were mobilized. Everything happened so quickly that there was no time for question or dissent. I was intrigued with the terminology being used by the government and the media. In Korea, we had the organized armies of multiple countries, large and small, engaged in a struggle that would take thousands of lives, both civilian and military. But it was not called a "war," but rather a "conflict." More like a "difference of opinion."

We also had a "Cold War" as opposed to, say, a "Hot War." In this case, it was the Soviet Union versus the

United States and the countries of Western Europe. There was no overt conflict here, but rather ideological differences which manifested themselves in rhetoric of threat and suspicion.

On the home front, one of the consequences of the Cold War was a resurgence of concern and fear about the potential threat of Communism. "Red Scares" were not really new and had been rampant following World War II and the late forties. The most recent focus had been on Hollywood and the movie industry. One result was hearings conducted by the HUAC (House Un-American Activities Committee). This Committee, led by Congressman Parnell Thomas, was investigating alleged subversive activities of Hollywood directors, writers, and actors. Since the Committee had little in the way of hard data, it was looking to members of the industry to name names. One very active member of the investigative body was Congressman Richard Nixon, who testified and suggested that there was in fact a small group of "troublemakers" headed by the President of the Screen Actors Guild, Ronald Reagan. Out of all the years of inquiry and intimidation came the dismissal and banishment of ten prominent directors and writers known as the "Hollywood Ten."

Now, three or so years later, the fear of Communism was again upon the land. This time our savior and protector would be the Junior Senator from Wisconsin, Joseph McCarthy. McCarthy's concerns were not with something as frivolous as the entertainment industry. No, his charge was that Communists had infiltrated the very highest offices of our federal government, including the military. Speculation was that McCarthy was having dinner with some friends and shared with them that he was looking for an issue. They kicked a number of ideas around until someone suggested Communism. The timing was excellent. There was Soviet activity in Eastern Europe, the war in Korea, and most recently the trial and execution of Julius and Ethel Rosenberg, who had been accused and found guilty of being Soviet spies.

McCarthy's first public announcement of Communist infiltration of the government took place in Wheeling, West Virginia. Before a meeting of the Republican Woman's Club, he declared, "I have in my hand a list of twenty-five cases of individuals who appear to be either card carrying members or certainly loyal to the Communist Party." His speech brought him immediate media recognition and support from thousands seeking a patriotic cause. Over the next several weeks, McCarthy gave other speeches with a similar format. The only variation was the number of sworn, hard-core Reds. In his next speech, he claimed fifty-seven. Soon the number became eighty-one, in a six-hour speech delivered on the floor of the United States Senate.

In 1950, when I enrolled as a student at Wayne University, McCarthy had mesmerized the land. At that time, however, politics and student engagement were not a serious part of American student culture. Other than studies, students were more concerned with popular music and films, which tended to be on the sweet, sentimental side. There were several good jazz clubs near the University, and some of the best jazz artists played at venues in downtown Detroit. Among the performers I was able to see were Stan Kenton, Benny Goodman, Dizzy Gilespie, Lester Young, and Charlie Parker. Big bands were popular, as was close and intimate dancing. Popular songs were often romantic, simplistic, and schmaltzy. The vocalists and songs most frequently heard on the radio were Johnny Ray ("Cry"), Patti Page ("Tennessee Waltz"), Nat King Cole ("A Blossom Fell"), Pat Boone ("Love Letters in the Sand"), Frankie Lane ("Jezebel"), and Peggy Lee ("You Give Me Fever"). With the exception of the live jazz scene, the other performing arts—be they music, film, or theater—were almost exclusively white in performers and audience.

In the fall of 1950, I moved into a single room, sans toilet and shower facilities, at Webster Hall, a university residential center. Webster was an eight-floor building with rigid gender segregation. Women had floors three through six, and the men were housed on floors seven through nine. Twenty-four hour security personnel were posted at the two exits of each floor.

I reminded myself that a major reason for coming home was to avoid collective living, and yet here it was again. I had to share toilets and showers with about seventy-five guys, and all meals were served in a massive cafeteria. I promised myself that if I got through the first semester I would get a furnished apartment.

I had signed up for three, three credit hour courses. In order to maximize my grade outcomes, I went with content that I was certain I could handle. My choices were "Intro to Sociology," "Intro to Social Psychology," and "Elementary Economics."

The cast of characters teaching these courses was diverse and a bit on the bizarre side. Dr. Butz taught the Sociology course. He was a melancholy-looking guy, about forty, totally disheveled in dress, in need of both a haircut and shave, with a bright red nose that indicated a certain love of booze. In seeking to make his first point—which was that life, while predictable, was nonetheless uncertain—he offered up several verses of the song, "Some Enchanted Evening."

As Dr. Butz was off the screen and a slob, my Social Psychology professor was right out of GQ, dapper and smooth in every way. His name was Dr. Marion, but we were granted permission to call him by his first name, Al. Al explained that he believed in having an informal class with lots of discussion. He was looking for an "intellectual exchange between mentor and learner." Further, he did not believe in taking attendance or examinations. Instead, each of us would undertake a modest research project and submit a paper describing our methodology and findings.

Dr. Sy Sachs was my instructor for Elementary Economics. He was a slight, frail, middle-aged man suffering from a chronic cough. A harsh cough and wrenching clearing of the throat interrupted every second or third sentence when he spoke. It was only after I got into the rhythm of his coughs that I was able to understand how good Sachs was. He knew his field, and despite his affliction was able to hold the interest and attention of his students.

It was my course in Elementary Economics that led to my meeting Charles Samarjian, who would turned out to be my first and best friend at Wayne. Charles was the proprietor of a local bookstore. His inventory was made up primarily of used textbooks and other academic publications. The store was located on the street across from the Old Main Building. The front widows were filthy and the shop was always dark and dingy. Those books that were not thrown onto one of the many bookshelves were piled up on the floor. There was no recognizable logic to the way books were stored. Shelves were unmarked with no reference guide. There was no classification system, either by author, publisher, subject, year of publication, size, or color. There was nothing user friendly about the place and that most surely included the owner. Charles was of Armenian descent and about fifty years of age. He was totally predictable. What you saw was what you got, and that never changed.

In the many years we remained friends, I never saw Charles wear anything other than a wrinkled, long-sleeve white shirt, and a dark blue suit, much in need of cleaning and pressing. He also wore the same blue tie, day after day, but always at half-mast. Charles's face showed five o'clock shadow no matter the time of the day. His presentation of self very much reflected his place of business. As the fit between Frankenstein's monster, and his castle was a perfect match, so it was with Charles and his castle. He never greeted anyone with a smile or a salutation. He never spoke until he was asked a question.

The question he was most frequently asked was, "Do you have (name of book)?" God help the inquirer who did not have the complete and correct title or name of author. I happened to be there one day when a young coed came in and asked for a certain American Literature text. She was not certain of the exact title or author. Charles was furious. " I assume you know your own name and those of your parents, brothers, sisters, the men you sleep with, and no doubt your pet fish!" he said. "Those names are nothing compared to the giants one finds in American literature. You are not a student. You are a sponge, and until you know what you are talking about, go! Go now!" The poor thing just turned and fled the place.

The other thing that would set Charles off was when a student would inquire about a particular book and Charles, without moving from his place, would answer, "No." The customer would invariably ask, "Well, how do you know without looking?" To which Charles would typically respond, "If you go to a grocery store and ask if they have Turner's Pea Soup and they answer no, do you challenge them, do you say go look? Why do you think I am less informed than a simple-minded clerk? Why do you insult me in this way?" The student would try in vain to offer some expression of apology, but it was a wasted effort. Charles had made his point and the humiliated customer was dismissed.

On my first visit, I was intrigued and wanted to wander through the place looking at the thousands of books. Fortunately, I controlled the search impulses and waited for Charles to come to the front of the shop. I said hello and he made no response. Since I was not looking for a specific text, I asked what economics reference book he would suggest for a first year novice. There was still no response as he turned and walked off to the back of the store as I waited. He returned with three well-worn books, placed them on the table, and walked away. I spent the next half-hour looking at the chapter titles and index of each volume before I carefully made my choice. I showed him my selection and he quickly said, "Poor choice. Take this one. It's less money and Sy Sachs quotes from it all of the time."

There were questions that I wanted to ask him but I prudently decided that would be it for this first visit. I paid, thanked Charles, and departed.

Two weeks later I came to the store in the early evening. I did not see Charles, so I decided to wait. Again, I was tempted to browse but confined myself to looking at a dozen or so books on the counter. After about half an hour, Charles appeared and asked me if I played poker. I answered, "Yes, but I am far from being an expert."

"Excellent," he said, "That means you will play and not talk."

I followed him to a room in the back of the store where two other men were sitting at a table. Charles introduced me as an up and coming economist now studying at the University. The other two poker players were detectives of the Detroit Police Department. They were regulars, along with a third officer, who played poker with Charles two evenings each week. I would be sitting in for Ray, who had drawn desk duty. Both of the detectives, Tony and Burt, had guns in their shoulder holsters. They smoked cigars, while Charles preferred his heavily aromatic cigarettes. The game was five-card draw poker, nothing wild. Puts were five cents and dimes, with a quarter limit. Other than the dealer calling out the cards, there was no talking. It was as if a cone of silence had been placed over the small table. The cut off time was set at 10:00 p.m. We played for three hours with each of us rotating as dealer. When the game was over I added up my losses, a total of $2.75.

The stakes were such that it was almost impossible for any player to either win or lose more than a few dollars. As Charles explained to me some weeks later, money was not the motivation for playing. Poker was both a therapy and an opportunity to bond with people who sought several hours of silence and distraction from every day activity.

Dropping in on Charles and his poker buddies was one of the things I most enjoyed. On most occasions, my playing services were not required, so I would sit as a silent observer or study. My relationship with Charles progressed to the point where, given my word that I would always replace a book from the exact spot from which it was taken, I could browse through the huge collection. This was a singular honor, for according to one of the detectives, no one else had ever been granted such license. On other evenings I would sit with Charles and enjoy a glass of sweet Armenian wine or herbal tea. Charles was incredibly well read and spoke authoritatively on almost any subject.

Being with Charles was like having access to my own private research and reference resource. I would share information about material presented in class or something from a reading, and he would provide his analysis and also suggest supplementary readings. There was no question that for the first two years at Wayne University, Charles played a valuable part in my education. Of equal importance was the fact that Charles and his cronies were filling a void in my very restricted social life. When I was not working, in class or the library, I was at the bookstore with Charles and the guys.

Most of the time, I enjoyed my classes. I was not reluctant to either ask or attempt to answer questions. My need for attention and recognition remained great, and I never felt intimidated by other students or my teachers. I was, however, smart enough never to ask a question within three minutes of the end of a class period. I also knew better than tangling with a professor whose ego could not tolerate public challenge. I was, as my brother Norman would say, a "cautious smart ass."

At the end of my first semester, it was with pride and pleasure that I reported to Mrs. Ammerman that I had received "A's" in all three of my classes. She had already seen a copy of my grades, and gave me a letter removing my probationary status. I was now a full-fledged student and could take as many as eighteen academic credit hours. As before, she cautioned me that if I was to take the maximum, I would be doubling my load. She also pointed out that I would now need to take required courses in disciplines other than those for which I seemed to have a flair. What she really meant, but was too polite to say, was that I would now be in courses where bullshit and chutzpah would be of limited value. I heard her, but at that point I was flying so high that I believed I could overcome any barrier.

I ran over to the bookstore in order to share my good news with Charles. Talk about raining on my parade; Charles quickly brought me back to earth. " It is no great accomplishment," he said. "They grade on the curve and your peers are for the most part barbarian illiterates. Further, Wayne is not Harvard, and the faculty here has, and rightly so, very low expectations. When they finally do have a student who is in the least articulate, they lose all sense of objectivity and give away 'A's.' As yet, you have proven nothing."

Well, anyway, my mother and father were impressed.

Prior to the start of my second semester, I made two changes in my life style. I moved out of Webster Hall and into a small apartment with a kitchen and a bath. Secondly, I gave up my job selling shoes and took night shift employment at the local Chrysler Plant. My Monday through Friday work hours were from 10:00 p.m. to 6:00 a.m. I had no car at that time, and so I used public transportation. I figured that time on the bus could be well spent in reading and study. I was wrong, and usually slept going and coming. My reasons for changing jobs were to earn more money and keep my days open for class and study. The new arrangement would also give me some leisure time on weekends.

I signed up for the full eighteen hours, with three courses in the Social Sciences, two in the Humanities, and what I considered to be the least threatening of science courses, Intro to Geology.

Mrs. Ammerman was right. With my night job, travel time, and a full course schedule, it was very tough. I had five of my classes three times a week and the other twice a week. Monday, Wednesday, and Friday my first class was 8:00 in the morning, followed by three other classes, with the last at 4:00 p.m. Tuesdays and Thursdays were a comparative breeze, with classes from 9:30 to 11:00 a.m. I would get back from work at around seven in the morning, shower, dress, and go to class. I would grab something to eat between classes. At 5:00 in the afternoon, I would be back on the bus, en route to work. The majority of my study time occurred in four-hour periods on Tuesday and Thursday, as well as weekends. My visits with Charles were reduced to a Saturday drop in.

My class work was going as well as could be expected. My largest class was Geology. It was a required course, held in a huge auditorium seating over 500 students. With a crowd like that, it had to be show and tell. The majority of our time was spent viewing hundreds of slides and films of rocks and soil formations. The instructor, a young, rural-looking sort, was so consumed with his rock collection that he showed no real interest in whether or not he held the interest of the class. There was constant chatter and movement in the hall. During the first two lectures he passed around rock samples so that we could get a feel for the variations. He asked that we be careful and not drop any of the rocks since they were part of his very rare and valuable collection—a plea that was not only unheeded but taken by some members of the class as a challenge.

As he showed a slide of coprolite, he noted that it was fossilized animal droppings and asked that special care be given as this was a perfect and hard to come by sample. He was already into his next slide when there was tumult in the back of the room. Someone stood up and shouted, “It dropped! It’s broken! It’s broken!”

The instructor stopped, frozen in mid sentence. “Not the coprolite, please not the coprolite!” he pleaded aloud.

The response from the back of the hall was, “Yes, sir, it was the shit rock.”

One week later a sample of cycad, an important fossil floral of the Mesozoic, mysteriously disappeared. We searched the room without success. That was the last time stones, gems, and rocks were distributed. From that time forward it was slides, overheads and films.

Of my other classes, what I enjoyed most was a Sociology course entitled, "Alternative Life Styles," taught by Professor Ward Dunling. Dunling was the senior man (there was female faculty) and enjoyed national academic stature. In addition, he was the most dapper, elegantly dressed, cosmopolitan person I had ever known. He was in his mid-sixties, plump, bald, and married to genuine Russian royalty, descended from the lineage of Tsar Nicholas II of pre-Revolutionary times. As individuals, the Dunlings were most impressive; as a couple, they were an extraordinary presence. At a Detroit Symphony Orchestra concert, when the Dunlings came down the aisle together, the usual pre-concert noise and motion came to an abrupt halt. Silence prevailed as everyone focused their attention on the elegantly attired Dunlings.

On the first day of class Dunling, who had a National Institute of Health grant, informed us that he was undertaking a study of downtown Detroit flop houses. He was seeking to hire three students who would be employed as research assistants. This was a participant observer study, which meant that each researcher would play the role of a homeless person. Without much thought of practical consequences I quickly volunteered.

After class, three of us met with Professor Dunling. He described the purpose and methodology of the study, as well as our role. Each of us would be assigned to a specific flop house location. We would be walk-in clientele, and were expected to negotiate, over a period of three weeks, six overnight stays. His expectations were that we would be in the facility by 9:00 p.m. and not leave until at least 6:00 the next morning. We would be allowed to use regular class time to record our observations and follow up briefings with Dr.Dunling's graduate assistant. We were to be paid expenses as well as a modest hourly fee. An added, particularly attractive feature was that our mid-term and final exams would be waived. Dunling cautioned that we were not to share with anyone at the house that the Department of Sociology or Wayne University employed us. We were not to mention the research project or use our real names. Finally, we needed to recognize that there might be some danger involved, since, as he put it, "Civility is not a common characteristic of flop house inhabitants."

To accommodate my full time job, I decided to fulfill my requirements using three consecutive weekends and staying over on Saturday and Sunday evenings. I was assigned to The Our Lady of the Lake Shelter, operated by the Catholic Diocese of Detroit. Not surprisingly, the shelter was located in a seedy, high crime part of the city. It was a block long, single-floor, old, red brick building. With the exception of a few dingy bars and a beat up burlesque house, there was not much else in the area.

I came to the shelter at about 8:00 p.m. and went directly to the sign up desk. A floor to ceiling cage enclosed the desk as well as the registration clerk. I had not really given any thought to the name I would use. When asked to sign in, the first name that came to mind was Max Weber, a German and one of the founders of Sociology. I was not asked for identification, but I was informed that I would be required to attend an early morning mass. The going rate was fifty cents for a bed and an extra fifteen cents for a shower and towel. I took the total package, paid my sixty-five cents, and was assigned bed #34.

The layout of the place and the condition of the sleeping quarters exceeded my expectations, which were very low to begin with. Few of the beds were occupied yet and most were neat in appearance. The shelter had rigid ground rules prohibiting smoking, alcohol consumption, and loud and vulgar language. As I was to learn much later that evening, many of those coming in were already so drunk that further drinking was probably a physical impossibility.

I checked out the toilet and shower facilities. Bathroom stalls were without doors and commodes without seats. The shower area was one long narrow room with a dozen or so showers. There was one large dining room area, which also served as the venue for morning mass. Breakfast was provided only for those who attended mass. Check out time was 7:30 a.m. There were no long term or permanent residents. Each morning, every man had to pack up his few belongings and leave. Those wishing to spend a second night were required to return later in the day and reapply. This daily clean out process provided employees an opportunity to clean up the place and, most importantly, to prohibit the return of those found in violation of shelter ground rules.

Although I had previously lived in close quarters with men aboard ship and in refugee camps in Europe and Israel, I found that whatever their discomfort and unpleasantness, those experiences could not possibly match my first evening at Our Lady of the Lake.

The sleeping room had beds for 150 "guests," who were admitted up to 2:00 in the morning. After midnight there was only one staff member to register, assign, and escort men to their cots. The closer to the cut off time, the greater the probability of unruly and agitated drunks. Though I was not unacquainted with the occasional passing of wind, coughing, belching, and moaning that comes with sleeping men, I was not prepared for the quantity, volume, and diversity of bodily sounds heard that night. Added to this were the retching sounds of men throwing up, screaming, and cursing.

Sometime during the early morning, I realized that a fat, sweaty, stinking drunk was joining me. This guy had deposited himself on the side of my bed and was trying to get under the blanket. I jumped out of bed, grabbed my shoes, and took off. Fortunately, I had the foresight not to remove my other clothing.

On the first class day after my social research experience, I paid a visit to Dr. Dunling. I told him that I had learned that I was just not cut out for that kind of sociological inquiry and would have to withdraw from the project. He was neither upset nor surprised since, as he informed me, no student assistant had as yet finished a full assignment. I expressed my regrets and added that perhaps in the future there might be some other project. He quietly replied, "Perhaps so."

Though my studies and job occupied much of my time, there was one issue increasingly on my mind. The matter of Israel emerged in a larger context of what was a very popular topic among Jewish College students. The question being asked had to do with our Jewish identity. Were we Jews first and then Americans, or were we Americans who happened to be Jewish? How did Israel fit into the mix and what was the place of a Jewish homeland in our lives? What were the priorities of our loyalty—America, Israel, Judaism, self, or family?

Why this issue seemed unique to young Jews and not others had puzzled me, and I never really gave it much thought. I had never heard anyone speak of the identity search for Catholics, Protestants, or those young people, say, of Irish or Italian descent. Tens of thousands of other peoples, including Irish, Italian, German and Pakistani, had come to America, and each group had to confront the task of integration and acculturation. Yet for some reason it was Jews more so than any other group who wrestled with this question of identity.

Perhaps for my generation it was the combination of three factors: the Holocaust, the creation of the State of Israel, and the current political climate. The Holocaust showed that by the simple fact of being Jews, we were to be despised and slaughtered. Because we had no homeland of origin, we were considered outsiders and not to be trusted. With the establishment of Israel, Jews who so chose could now have a country of their own. Many American Jews, however, were concerned that support of the State and expressions or pride in its accomplishments would bring forth charges of dual loyalty. To further exacerbate this fear of Jews being considered disloyal, there was the arrest of Julius and Ethel Rosenberg in 1950. The Rosenbergs were charged with espionage and accused of providing the Soviet Union with classified information. All of this was taking place at a time when we were being bombarded with frightening tales of Communist infiltration of government, media, and universities. Every time a Jewish sounding name was mentioned, American Jewish anxiety and apprehension increased.

When I participated in one of the "search for identity" meetings, I found it of little intellectual or emotional value. I considered myself an American Jew; however, I was not a religious Jew at all. If anything, I was a Yiddishist, and my connections were strongest with what I considered to be the cultural and ethnic heritage of the Jewish people. I was an unaffiliated Zionist, with no organizational ties. I took great pride in Israel and was hardly objective in my defense of the country, government, and people. At that time, I had no doubt that I would eventually return to Israel, but in what capacity, I did not know.

In 1952, the major issue for Israel was Jerusalem. When the United Nations arranged the truce of 1948, the city was split in two. Israel occupied West Jerusalem and Jordan held East Jerusalem. Both sides had defied the UN ruling, which declared Jerusalem to be an international entity. In further defiance, both Israel and Jordan signed a formal agreement making the armistice lines the boundaries between the two countries. Over the next several years, the Israeli government established West Jerusalem as its capitol. Miles of fortified positions, barbed wire, and huge defensive barricades divided the two sides. Snipers from both sides exchanged gunfire over this no man's land.

By late 1952, the ongoing conflict temporarily ceased as both sides solidified their positions. The Israeli

Parliament moved to West Jerusalem, and the ambassadors of both the United States and Great Britain presented their credentials in the city.*

* In 1974, I made my first return visit to Israel to participate in an international conference dealing with youth. I returned again in 1981, this time as a member of a U.S. Department of Labor team. Our mission was to study the role of the Israeli military in the career training and education of newly arrived young immigrants. Portions of what we learned would later be incorporated into programs offered by the U.S. Army in working with disadvantaged American adolescents. I made a third visit, again as part of a team from the U.S. Department of Labor, in 1991.

Chapter 12

In part because of a wish to comply with a request from one of my Sociology professors, I participated in my first extracurricular activity by agreeing to serve as a co-chair of Wayne Students for Adlai Stevenson.

By 1951, the impact of the unpopular Korean War and accusations that Democrats were "soft on communism" caused delegates at the Democratic convention to abandon Truman and select Adlai E. Stevenson as their presidential candidate. The Republicans nominated Dwight D. Eisenhower as their choice. During World War II, Eisenhower had served as Supreme Commander of the Allied Expeditionary Force. Although a political novice, he was held in high esteem by the American public, and had been credited as the architect of the successful campaign that brought about the defeat of the Axis.

Adlai Stevenson was a liberal and a former Governor of Illinois. I knew little of either candidate and I had little interest in this particular campaign. As long as I could remember, my folks, relatives, neighbors, and parents of my friends were all loyal Democrats. When I was about six or seven years of age, my mother had a job in a factory that manufactured suspenders. FDR was again running for president, and my mother brought each of us boys a pair of suspenders that were colored red, white and blue with the letters "FDR" imposed front and back. I recall wearing them with great pride.

What I did know about Stevenson was that he was a smallish, non-imposing man. He was incredibly smart, articulate, and firm in his denunciations of Joseph McCarthy. Though there was no physical resemblance at all between Stevenson and Abe Lincoln, they were both from Illinois and they were both passionate in their defense of freedom and equality.

There was one more thing about Stevenson that helped to capture my loyalty. It was an accidental event. A photographer had taken a picture of Stevenson while he was sitting on a high stool drinking a cup of coffee. The photo, which was carried by all the wire services, showed a large hole in the sole of one of his shoes. A shoe with a hole in the sole became the symbol of his campaign. Stevenson was clearly the candidate of the common man; however, we were all aware that this would be an uphill battle. All of the polls showed Eisenhower winning in a landslide.

During one of our Stevenson campus rallies I had met the editor of the Wayne University Collegiate, the student-managed newspaper. The Collegiate was published five days a week and had a substantial campus following. The editor asked me if I would be willing to do an editorial piece dealing with why I was supporting Stevenson. I readily agreed, and my first published work appeared a week later. I got some positive feedback from several faculty members and a kind note from Mrs. Ammerman noting that, while she did not agree with my choice of candidates, my arguments were persuasive. The editor invited me to do a weekly column. I was told that I could choose my topics, but he would prefer commentary on contemporary and controversial political and social issues. Again I agreed, and thus began my short journalistic career.

I showed several of my columns to Charles, and as was his custom, he was less than flattering. "Writing is an art form which you have yet to master. I suggest you stay with muckraking, which has greater public appeal and far lower standards."

There was one piece I did of which Charles, while not complimentary, was far less critical. The topic was Charles, his bookstore, and his love of literature and poker. He did offer that I must not have much of a loyal following, since the article did not generate any new customers.

One of my final columns was an open letter to Senator Joseph McCarthy. It was a nasty and sarcastic work in which I thanked the Senator for his great public service in helping all of us learn who among us were true Americans. The column was selected by the Detroit Free Press as the best of the year in political commentary for all statewide campus newspapers. I was awarded a certificate, and the Collegian received a commendation.

In the spring of 1952, Stevenson came to Detroit to deliver a campaign speech. As a co-chair of our student organization, I was invited to present him with a Wayne University warm-up jacket. I was honored and immediately set to work to prepare my comments.

There were several thousand people in attendance, but I felt at ease knowing my four paragraphs of commentary would be well received. A moment prior to my making the presentation, an aide to the candidate took me aside and said, "You have 15 seconds." I was dumbfounded and tried to explain that I had prepared a speech, which I believed would be of great help to the campaign. The aide took my speech out of my hands, saying something about how this happens in every city, and repeated the 15-second limit. I went on to the stage, handed the jacket to Stevenson, and said, "Sir, a gift from all of the students at Wayne University." He thanked me, shook my hand, and I departed the stage. Media coverage of this important moment in American political history was limited to a blurred, 2-inch by 2-inch photo on the third page of the university student newspaper. As an added insult, in place of my name was the name of my co-chair.

Then, of course, Eisenhower won by a landslide.

By the start of the fall 1952 semester, I had completed ninety-nine of the 152 academic credits required for graduation. I had accomplished this by taking course credits by examination, in addition to my regular courses. Students whose GPA's were 3.5 or better could take up to fifteen hours of course work by examination. My GPA at the start of this semester was 3.7. I had received "A's" in every one of my Social Science and Humanities classes, with the exception of Intro to Philosophy where the grade was "A-minus." My one "B" was in Geology.

I had fifty-three credit hours to go and I was determined to finish and earn my B.A. degree by the end of the summer of 1953. To do so I would need to take twenty hours in the fall, twenty in the spring of 1953, as well as ten in the summer and three credits by examination.

Mrs. Ammerman was now a true believer and helped to facilitate my gaining approval for course overloads and credits by examination. Having long been an advocate for flexibility in admission criteria for non-traditional students, she was quick to approve my plans for completing all my degree work within a three-year period. She told me that I had become the model she used in making her case for a more flexible and open admissions policy.

Charles, on the other hand, was far less impressed, and considered my rapid progress as further evidence of minimal academic standards, shoddy teaching, and politics. "You have become an untouchable and none of them dare give you less that an 'A' grade."

He continued, "All must conform or they will be drummed out of the old boys' club. I would wager that were you not to attend another class, no one would give you a failing grade. You are driven by your own compulsive behavior and blessed by being part of a corrupt system."

I knew it was a lost cause to argue with Charles, but I did have to agree with one observation: I was driven and I was compulsive.

As I went through the process of selecting my classes, I also started to give serious thought to what I would do after I had my degree. I had not considered graduate school or what career or employment I would pursue. I knew that business and the world of commerce was not for me. The idea of spending years in graduate school also did not strike me as appealing. I enjoyed the idea of working with people, and felt that teaching or social work might be the route to go. Mrs. Ammerman suggested that I take a course in the School of Social Work, and added that I was too far along to become an Education major.

I followed her advice and signed up for a class in Group Work. The Wayne School of Social Work had a world-class faculty and was especially strong in Group Work. Though the most desirable and senior jobs would go to those with a master's degree, the entry-level opportunities were considered good. I preferred Group Work since I did not see myself as becoming a therapist or a guidance counselor.

My instructor, and my first and only female professor, was Dr. Mary Lee Nicholson. She was dynamic, smart, and attractive. It took no time at all for me to decide that Group Work was my thing. An important course requirement was that each student would serve an internship at some community social service agency. During my interview with Professor Nicholson, I said that I would prefer to work with teenagers. She said that there was an opening in Highland Park, an industrial, working class suburb of Detroit. She went on to say they were looking for someone who would work with a group of young men. "That's the one for me," I said.

An appointment was made with the Center Director. The location was convenient—a straight bus ride from the university. The Center was housed in a large, old, two-story brick house located in a mixed residential and commercial neighborhood. The interior had been rebuilt, with four rooms for individual counseling, a reading room, a small nursery school, plus a kitchen and two offices. There was no gym or swimming pool, nor any room large enough for group gatherings. The one recreational area was a brick garage in the back of the main building. It contained a coal burning stove and a beat up pool table. As I was soon to learn from Mr. Dyer, the Center Director, the recreation facility would be my domain.

Dyer was a big guy, about thirty-five years old, with wavy black hair. He was very upbeat. He took great pride in his Center, noting that although small and without frills it serviced more than 2,500 people. His clients were mostly low income, working people, many who had migrated from the South to work in local automobile plants. He told me that my internship assignment would be serving as a counselor to a group of guys whose ages ranged from seventeen to twenty-one. Most had not completed high school, and about half were unemployed. They met four evenings each week. I told him that I would like to take on the assignment but I was working nights at Dodge Main.

Much to my surprise, Mr. Dyer asked me if I would be interested in a full time job, noting that it would not pay as much was I was now earning. I said that I would consider a shift and asked what he had in mind. He said the Center needed a manager for evenings and weekend activities. The job would include my internship, but my main responsibility would really be custodial and security. I would work 40 hours per week at $4.50 an hour. As an added incentive, Mr. Dyer would allow me to have use of the Center vehicle, a 1949 Dodge truck. The proposed wage was about one third less than my current earnings, but I took the job anyway, figuring I would have plenty of time for studying and some leisure pursuits, as well as my own private transportation.

One week later, I started my new job and met with my young male group for the first time. They were an interesting collection, and certainly unlike any of the young people I had ever known. They were all dressed similarly, manner, each wearing tight, inexpensive trousers, short-sleeved shirts or T-shirts, and black shoes. They were all clean-shaven, but with lengthy side burns. The favored hairstyle was combed back, wavy, and drenched with Vitalis. Most smoked and had their cigarette packs rolled up in their shirtsleeves. They were white and had moved to Michigan from rural areas of the South.

Indifferent to my presence, they promptly grabbed cue sticks and began to play pool. Four guys played at one time, and when they finished a game another four would take the table. Those not playing would watch and place bets—either nickels, dimes, or cigarettes.

Mr. Dyer had not given me any instructions as to whether or not there was an established code of behavior. There was nothing that I could recall from my class lectures or readings which I felt was applicable to this particular situation. What I did remember was Dr. Nicholson saying, "Remember, you are there to do one thing and one thing only. You are there to fulfill not your needs, but the needs of the group." It struck me that they were doing well enough in fulfilling their needs without me.

I finally got the courage to approach several of the guys and introduce myself. No handshakes were forthcoming, so I wandered back to the sidelines and observed them. As the hour for closing approached, I announced that we had another fifteen minutes till closing. There was no response or acknowledgement that I had even spoken.

I tried again in five minutes, noting that they had ten minutes left. This time there was a response of "fuck off." With that, one of the guys came over to me and said that they knew the rules and did not need to be reminded. He added that they did not need a baby sitter and could come and go on their own. His name was Chet, and he was obviously one of the leaders. I said that the arrangement was fine with me and my only concern was getting out of there so I could have some party time of my own. My response did get some attention, and one of the other guys asked me where I partied. I told him I would meet with friends at Wayne and probably have a beer and listen to music. Chet asked if I was another one of those interns and how long did I think I would last on the job. I answered that I was an intern but was also working full time at the Center and expected to be there for at least a year.

Chet laughed and offered his view that my tenure would be determined not by me but by the guys. I concurred and added that if I could not do the job then it would be best for all of us if I left. With that, they put up the cue sticks and departed the building.

The next day I went to visit with Dr. Nicholson in to share my first night experience and get her advice. My first question to her was to explain the difference between a group and a gang. She said there was very little difference with the exception that a gang was eventually destructive to self and others. A group, on the other hand, had the potential to offer all of its members self-confidence and purpose. I followed with the obvious question of how to convert these guys from gang to group. Perhaps I missed the functional wisdom of her words, but her answer offered me little help: "That task is in the hands of the group worker."

My next session with the gang took place two days later. This time several did greet me and asked if I wanted to shoot some pool. I accepted the invitation but did not participate in betting. As did the others, I played one game and then watched. Finally one of the guys asked me about college and what it was like. I answered that it was hard work, but for me it was worth it since I had learned a lot and I believed the education would help me in the future. Chet said something about my having it made since I had a job and my folks had plenty of money.

I responded with a loud and firm, "Bullshit!" I then gave them a brief summary that included my dropping out of high school, going to sea, working the night shift in a factory, and busting my ass in order to graduate. It was an Abe Lincoln-flavored rendition, but I felt it might be the way to build a bridge between us. Following that, I answered questions on how you can get into college without a high school diploma. The second evening ended with a few more of the guys acknowledging my presence; some even adding a passing "goodnight" as they left the Center.

Each of the students in my group work class was required to make a brief weekly report. My reports were usually very succinct, rarely exceeding two sentences. On the occasion of my fifth week report I said, "Same old, same old. There is no progress." Professor Nicholson jumped right in with her opinion, "You are being much too hard on yourself. If you were making no progress the guys would have thrown you out by now." I thanked her for the vote of confidence, which I saw as an expression of coach-like motivational praise. Then I decided that I would change my strategy from passive observer to assertive inquisitor.

I chose Chet as my target since he was a leader and several times had seemed on the verge of talking with me. After he completed his turn at pool I told him that I wanted to ask his advice about something. We walked outside, he lit a cigarette, and I said I needed his help. Before he could answer, I went on to say that my job with the guys was supposed to be more than hanging around while they shot pool. I was supposed to help them start thinking about what they wanted to do with their lives, about education and jobs. I went on to explain that unless the guys talked with me and shared what they were thinking and what they wanted, I could be of no help. I finished with the observation that, since he was the leader of the group, he could help me to help them. Chet stared at me for a moment and in a very soft voice asked, "How are you gonna help me?"

I answered I had no idea and could not even attempt to help unless I knew more about him, his background, schooling, job experience, and most importantly, what he wanted. Chet started by telling me that he and his folks, three sisters, and his grandmother came to Highland

Park four years ago. They had come from Hazard County, Kentucky, and this was the first time any of them had been out of Kentucky. His farther found a job at the GM plant in Highland Park. Two years ago he was laid off and had been unable to find work. Chet's mother worked part time as a sales clerk at Sears. Chet, who was now nineteen, was the eldest of the children. Like his father, he dropped out of school when he was twelve. He worked at a mill until the family left Kentucky. He tried to enlist in the Army but was rejected because of bad teeth and failure to read at the third grade level. Attempts to find anything other than occasional day labor work ended in failure. He had a juvenile record and had served three months in the Detroit House of Corrections. During the past two years his record was clean. I was overwhelmed by his story, and again he asked, "Now, how you gonna help me?"

"I don't know," I answered.

We were about to enter the rec room when there was a loud series of firecracker explosions. Chet grabbed my arm and said, "Don't go in. They're doing buck shot." I waited until the noise stopped and entered the room. All of the guys were huddled together in one corner of the room and laughing hysterically. Alvin, one of the youngest of the group, shouted out, "Bet that scared the shit out of you!"

Chet was right. They had taken a half-dozen shotgun shells and dropped them into the stove. I was furious and shouted for all them to leave and added that they could not return for one week. They were surprised by my reaction. As they were leaving, several of them informed me that they had done the same thing on other occasions and had never been kicked out. I already regretted the course I had taken but the only response I could come up with was, "That was then, this is now."

Chet was the last to leave, and as he went out the door he said, "Now you're going to have to start all over."

In my meeting with Mr. Dyer, I recounted what had taken place and my one-week banishment. He said that my action was appropriate and the boys would have to learn that misbehavior comes at a cost. Though somewhat relieved by his endorsement, I still felt bad.

Dr. Nicholson, as I anticipated, used the old therapist routine, and asked, "Well, if you had to do it all over again, what would you do differently?"

I answered that I was not sure, but I would not have gone the exile route. "Good answer" she said, "You are on the way to having a productive learning experience."

One week later, I arrived at the recreation room earlier than usual. My fear was that none of the guys would show. Again, I was mistaken. I had not recognized how important this place was to them. It was their lifeline, as well as the one place where they could affirm their worth as individuals. Group or gang, the terminology was irrelevant. What was important was the fact that without this place, they were homeless.

As soon as they all had gathered I told them that I had screwed up, that I was angry and wanted to strike back at them. I said that I made a serious error and that I wanted to apologize. Finally, I wanted them to give me another chance, and if they said no, I would quit my job at the Center. Chet answered that they had already talked it over and had agreed that if I was willing to give them another chance, they were willing to do the same. I was so relieved that I almost started to cry. Instead, I shook hands with each of them and said thanks.

The ice was finally broken in week eight of my group work stint. I had checked with several of the counselors at the Center and found the man who was most knowledgeable about help programs for my guys. He was surprised that I felt that some members of the group had reached a point where they would even consider talking to a counselor. When I pointed out that I was not talking plural but thought I had a good chance of getting one member aboard, he answered, "That will be the day."

Needless to say, he was even more impressed and surprised when Chet showed up for his appointed meeting.

I had decided to use a direct approach with Chet. I told him that one of the staff counselors might have some information that he would find useful. I pointed out that it was worth a try, and if he did not like what he heard, he could blow it off.

Not only did he show up for the appointment, but more importantly, he enrolled in an adult literacy program at the local community college. When a couple of the guys made smart-ass comments about his going to school, he answered, "I'm going to college. Where are you guys going?" One month later, three other members were enrolled in some kind of intervention effort.

I was feeling pretty good at the changes that had taken place and felt I was more than deserving of the good words offered to me by Mr. Dyer and Dr. Nicholson. It was two weeks later that I was reminded, on a gut level, the truth of the saying that "no good deed goes unpunished."

I was at home and asleep when I received a call from Mr. Dyer. He told me that I would have to get down to the Highland Park police station as soon as possible. He went on to tell me that some of my guys had been apprehended and were being charged with breaking and entering a neighborhood liquor store. He had no information as to names, numbers, or circumstances. It was 1:30 a.m. I hurriedly dressed and drove down to the station.

As I drove down Woodward Avenue I speculated upon two things: Who were the guys who got busted and why did Dyer tell me to go the station? Soon I had answers to both of my questions.

During the booking process, several of the guys gave my name as the contact person. Because they did not have my phone number, the police called Dyer, who in turn called me. Five group members had been arrested. I was astounded when I looked at the report. The one name I would least expect to see was at the top of the list: Chet.

I was given further details about the break in. They had broken a back window and by doing so had set off a silent alarm. They were not carrying weapons, and it was apparent that some of them had been intoxicated at the time. Three of the five had no prior criminal records. Two did, and one was Chet. They would all be held for a hearing and the judge would determine punishment. The Desk Sergeant was confident that all of them would be given time. He made the point that the two with prior convictions should not expect leniency. I asked if there was anything more he needed of me. He asked if I wanted to speak with any of the guys. I answered no and left.

I did not attend the hearing. I did not want to see Chet or any of the others. By the time I arrived at my apartment, I had decided that I would give up my job at the Center. I had no wish to ever see that place again.

Later in the day, I called Dyer and told him what I had learned at the station and that I was planning on taking a few days off. He asked me if I was okay. I said yes, but I needed some time to think things over.

I had a Group Work class that afternoon, and went over early in hopes that I might see Dr. Nicholson. As I sat down I heaved a big sigh and started my tale of woe. I covered it all, from the first meeting, through weeks of silence, the buck shot incident, and the gradual signs of communication with my wards. I shared with her the wretched events of the past 24 hours. She listened, and when I stopped talking she said, "You shouldn't blame yourself."

I found myself wondering whether it was me or her who didn't get it. There had been at least a half dozen times when Dr. Nicholson's responses were irrelevant and off target. Until that point I had assumed it must be me since she was a distinguished and well-respected therapist. But this time I lost patience. "You don't get it at all," I said, "I don't blame myself. I feel no guilt, and I'm not the one who screwed up."

I tried to explain that I had given a great deal of myself and invested a lot of time in order to help these guys. All that time and effort had gone down the drain, a waste. I went on, "You have told the class so many times that we should always learn from our experience, and I want you to know what I have learned. First, I would bet big dollars that if you ever worked with poor kids, it had to be twenty years ago, because you haven't a clue about them. Next, I have learned that this notion of a person having to place their needs secondary to the needs of others is so much bull. My needs are, and should be, as important as the needs of any other person. Finally, I have learned that social work or group work is not for me."

The meeting was over. Dr. Nicholson stood up and said, "Well, at least we can agree on one thing."

What will always puzzle me is that even though I did not return to class or submit a term paper, she gave me a grade of "A." Perhaps Charles was right—no one wants to rock the boat.

A few days later I informed Mr. Dyer that I had decided to give up the job. He expressed his regrets and asked for the keys to the truck.

In retrospect, I find it ironic that so much of my adult career life has been devoted to research and programs seeking to understand and enhance the status of disadvantaged youth. My doctoral studies included majors in the Sociology of Education and Adolescent Behavior. While a faculty member at Michigan State University, I received commendation from Governor George Romney for having organized the Student Education Corps. The Corps was made up of hundreds of university students who volunteered their time serving as tutors for at risk, low income, and minority public school students. In 1964, I left the university to become an Associate Director of the Job Corps, a major youth program in the Office of Economic Opportunity. The Job Corps is a national residential program providing education, career counseling, and job training for thousands of disadvantaged young men and women. Of all of the many programs that were once part of the Great War on Poverty, the Job Corps is the only one that continues to operate. When I left the Job Corps to take a faculty position at Penn State University, my boss, Sargent Shriver, inscribed a photo of the two of us: "To Dave Gottlieb. Best wishes always from a grateful student of sociology's intricacies explained to the foot soldiers in the war against poverty by a master professor. Sarge."

In the course of my 25-year academic career, I authored numerous texts and journal articles covering a wide variety of youth-related topics. Through grants provided by the U.S. Departments of Education, Labor, and Army, I directed studies of youth in the military, labor force, and educational institutions. I also served as a consultant to federal and state agencies, as well as Robert Kennedy's Task Force on Juvenile Delinquency. My first assignment in the Job Corps was to interview the first thirty young men enrolled in the program—fifteen were white and fifteen were black. As fate would have it, all of the white kids were from Hazard County, Kentucky. It was Chet and the guys revisited. Through my academic training and work experience, I managed to navigate an interdisciplinary path that combined the empiricism of Sociology with the applied applications of Group Work.

* * * * *

But in 1953, I still had the spring and summer semesters to go.

I took a job as a research assistant with a faculty member who was conducting a major demographic study of the changing Detroit population. The work paid enough to cover my expenses, and was of some interest to me until, in the late summer of 1953, I received my B.A. degree.

I knew that a professional career in Sociology, be it academia, government, or the private sector, would require a doctorate degree. I knew that I would be accepted for graduate work at Wayne, but Mrs. Ammerman, as well as members of the Department, advised me that it would be best for me to go elsewhere. Dr. Dunling was emphatic and noted that there was little for me to gain by hanging around with the same faculty. "Whatever we had to say of any value, you have already heard and hopefully digested," he declared. He also made the point that my currency in the academic marketplace would be improved by having exposure to others' viewpoints.

Mrs. Ammerman concurred and proposed that being in a different environment and meeting new people would be beneficial. The question was where to go and who would have me.

Both the University of Michigan and Michigan State offered the doctorate in Sociology, but I preferred an urban setting. There were two universities which were of excellent quality, and both were located in major metropolitan areas: the University of California at Berkley and the University of Chicago. Of the two, I leaned toward Chicago, since it had both the more liberal admissions policy and more scholarship opportunities. My preference for Chicago was also influenced by the fact that the Department had a strong commitment to Applied Sociology and Urban Studies. Unlike Berkley, which was heavily oriented to quantitative research and mathematical modeling, Chicago appeared to embrace both qualitative and quantitative inquiry.

The Chicago school was renowned for linking empirical inquiry to social change. In addition, because of my weakness and dislike for all things mathematical and a fear of statistics, Chicago seemed the obvious choice. So I submitted my application along with the required GPA documentation and letters of recommendation.

As I anticipated, my lack of math was the barrier to unconditional acceptance. The Department would admit me on a trial basis, with the understanding that I would need to pass a remedial statistics course. Upon fulfilling this requirement, I would be granted full admission and financial aid. It was with trepidation that I accepted the offer and the challenge.

I was fortunate in finding a fellow student who was a statistics wizard, a man of infinite patience who agreed to be my tutor. He had little to work with, as I was not only averse to things mathematical, I was also math dumb. For example, a basic concept of statistics is the law of probabilities. If you continue to flip a coin, let's say a penny, eventually the number of times the penny will come up either heads or tails will be equal. That is a fairly simple minded concept, one that is accepted by college students throughout the world. I, however, not only questioned but also insisted upon empirical evidence. It was only after hours of endlessly flipping pennies that I was willing to accept the proposition as indeed valid.

My struggle with statistics was endless, and on more than one occasion I was prepared to call it quits. My tutor, however, was a product of the Old Testament and firmly believed that if a student fails, look to the teacher. My eventual failure or success would also be his failure or success. Ultimately, his perseverance and dedication paid off and I passed the course with a C.

I was in and life was good.

I had about six weeks to close up shop in Detroit and relocate to Chicago. I bid farewell to my few friends and some of the faculty. I invited Mrs. Ammerman to a farewell lunch and presented her with a dozen roses. I promised her that I would write.

Charles surprised me with a dinner served in his store, with two of the police poker players attending. It was an extraordinary feast—and a culinary accomplishment, given that his cooking apparatus consisted of a double electric hotplate. The card table had been converted into a dinner table, complete with a white linen cover, linen napkins, wineglasses, pewter candlestick holders, plastic spoons, knives, and forks. Charles was most apologetic, but in his haste he had forgotten silverware. Even so, it was quite elegant, and we all enjoyed the Middle Eastern and Armenian delicacies he prepared, along with a few bottles of wine.

With dinner finished, Charles passed out cigars, small cups of sweet, thick Turkish coffee, and brandy. Each of the guests was invited to say a few words in honor of this event, which Charles referred to as "Gottlieb's Last Supper." The detectives raised their glasses and gave slight praise to my academic achievements, but were lavish in extolling my accomplishment in being the first student Charles had ever invited to the poker game.

I had already steeled myself in preparation for the toast to be offered by Charles. He stood, raised his glass, and said, "Gentlemen, it is clear that I have succeeded. Recall that I began with little more than an empty vessel, and through my wisdom and guidance I have created a new and better Gottlieb. I will also say that he is the first person to accept me fully and without condition."

As a farewell gift, he gave me a much used, tattered text entitled, "Introductory Statistics."

It was my turn, and I could think of nothing to say other than to thank each of them for their friendship and kind words. I walked over to Charles, hugged him, and said that I would never forget him, his shop, or the dinner.

Some fifteen months later when I returned to Detroit, I went to see Charles. His bookshop was gone, replaced by a diner and a new parking lot. I inquired but no one knew or seemed to care about what had happened to Charles.

My last farewell dinner was with my folks. Ma had gone out of her way to prepare a special dinner, which included what she considered to be my favorites. Her frame of reference was a time when I was thirteen years old and weighed 180 pounds. I was now nine years older and in the 150-pound range. When Ma served food, it was like a love offering; refusal would be taken as a rejection of her love. I ate much and well—matzoh ball soup, chopped liver, kischke, kugel, and for dessert, her dynamite fladel. I explained to them about my acceptance and scholarship and that I would be in graduate school working on my doctorate degree. Ma quickly asked what kind of doctor would I become. I explained that it was not like being a medical doctor; it was a different kind of doctor. She was still confused and wanted me to be more specific.

As soon as I responded, "a doctor of philosophy," I knew I had made a mistake. I quickly added that no matter if you are a lawyer, dentist, engineer, or professor, the highest honor is being a doctor. This seemed to satisfy her.

Ma began to sob, and Pa came over and placed his hand on my shoulder. With that simple gesture I could feel his love and his pride.

This was, as in the past, yet another of the many times that I would say goodbye to my folks. There had been so many times in my earlier years where my behavior had both puzzled and worried them. There were so many instances when they were anxious about where I was and what I was doing. I could only guess how often they would ask each other, "What will become of him?"

Now, however, I was doing something that, although they might not have fully understood, they knew had to be good, because I was going to a university and I would become a doctor.

As soon as my mother was able to compose herself, she took my hand and whispered, "Finally a *mensch.*"

I knew her pronouncement was premature and silently to said to myself, " Perhaps almost a *mensch*, but not quite."

Afterword

When Bob, my oldest brother, died, my other two brothers and I began to talk about a subject which apparently had been on all our minds—namely, who would be the next to go. Did Bob's demise establish a chronological pattern with the next oldest brother, Norman, being next, followed by me and then Harold? This was one of those rare instances when Harold failed to complain about being the kid brother. Norman, in a desire to dispel the inevitability of falling dominoes, offered that since only the good die young, there was no need for immediate concern. Given the fact that we were each in our seventies, it was not surprising that the conversation turned to reflection and self-assessment of our lives.

Harold wished to point out that although Bob's accumulation of wealth was modest, he was perhaps the most successful of all the brothers. Everyone loved Bob; his children and grandchildren had remained close; his wife, brothers, and friends all found him to be a kind-hearted, gentle soul. No one could recall a bad word ever being said about Bob. Of no less importance, none of us could recall Bob ever having uttered a bad word about anyone else.

While I agreed that kindness and altruism were indeed worthy traits, I felt they fell short as a true measure of a successful life. Maybe wealth alone was not the sole criteria, but there had to be more than just being a nice guy. I said that I thought each of the brothers had achieved success in careers and led good, productive lives. I asked them to give me their own assessments.

Harold jumped right in and said that he could characterize each of us with no more than a few words. “We are now as we always have been,” he said, “Bob the ‘*gutter*’ (good), Norman the ‘*kluger*’ (smart), David the ‘*mashigner*’ (crazy), and Harold the ‘*schlecter*’ (bad).”

There were many times when I disagreed with Harold, but I had to admit he was right on target with me. I was indeed the crazy one.

Whereas my three brothers lived their early youth and adult lives in the Detroit area not far from where we were all born, my homes changed every few years from places like Israel to Boston to New York before I ended up in Texas, where I now live.

Each of my brothers married once and found fulfillment with their first choice. My course to marital happiness did not come easily or early in my life. It was not until my mid-sixties that I found my ideal partner.

My career path also diverged greatly from my brothers’. For most of his life, Bob was in sales. Norman earned his law degree and Harold embarked upon a career as an accomplished business entrepreneur. My adult work life has included employment as a professor and dean in academia, executive positions in the federal government, a vice president in a major land development and energy company, and most recently as a CEO of a regional performing arts organization.

Oddly, I do not recall ever asking myself such questions as “What do I want to be at age X?” or “When and where do I wish to retire?” I never really thought about a career ladder or what position or how much money I might ultimately wish to achieve. But I can honestly say my life has always been interesting and fulfilling. All I know is that at this point in my life, I still look forward to every day and, to paraphrase a popular Paul Simon song, “still *mashigah* after all these years.”